COMMUNICATION AND CULTURE IN WAR AND PEACE

D1556986

COMMUNICATION AND HUMAN VALUES

SERIES EDITORS

COMMUNICATION AND CULTURE IN WAR AND PEACE

edited by Colleen Roach

preface by Johan Galtung

SAGE Publications
International Educational and Professional Publisher
Newbury Park   London   New Delhi

For information address:

SAGE Publications, Inc.
2455 Teller Road
Newbury Park, California 91320

SAGE Publications Ltd.
6 Bonhill Street
London EC2A 4PU
United Kingdom

SAGE Publications India Pvt. Ltd.
M-32 Market
Greater Kailash I
New Delhi 110 048 India

Printed in the United States of America

Library of Congress Cataloging-in-Publication Data

Main entry under title:
Communication and culture in war and peace / edited by Colleen Roach.
    p. cm.—(Communication and human values)
  Includes bibliographical references and index.
  ISBN 0-8039-5062-4 (cloth).—ISBN 0-8039-5063-2 (pbk.)
  1. Communication and culture. 2. Mass media—Social aspects.
3. Peace. I. Roach, Colleen A. II. Series: Communication and
human values (Newbury Park, Calif.)
P91.C539 1993
302.2—dc20   92-35951

93 94 95 96 10 9 8 7 6 5 4 3 2 1

Sage Production Editor: Astrid Virding

To the memory of Archie Singham (1932-1991):
ardent, impassioned, much missed struggler for Peace.

Contents

Acknowledgments

There are many different people who contributed in one way or another to making this book possible. Ping Ferry and Carol Bernstein provided several kinds of sustenance, including research and travel funds and their own clipping service, tailored to my needs. Other forms of material assistance came from the Exploratory Project on the Conditions of Peace (EXPRO). The following individuals read sections of or the entire manuscript and offered invaluable suggestions: Laurien Alexandre, Grace Boggs, Elise Boulding, Andrew Calabrese, Donna Demac, Johan Galtung, Liane Norman, Dallas Smythe, Mike Traber, and Bob White. Rick Vincent facilitated communications at the University of Hawaii, which was a great help. Various other people whom I met through the EXPRO project offered insights, camaraderie, and most of all, the inspiration of their lives as peace activists: Dietrich Fischer, Robert Irwin, Randy Kehler, Arjun Makhijani, and Mark Sommer. During the early stages of this project, I was fortunate enough to have as a research assistant Benny Jose, from Fordham University's sociology department. The Research Foundation, City University of New York, also made available to me certain monies necessary for the final stages of manuscript preparation.

Several women I would like to thank helped me out with the literature of feminism, to which I was a relative newcomer before work on this book began: Elise Boulding, Sheila Collins, Riane Eisler, Beth Jacklin, and Liane Norman. My many long conversations with Melanie Welch, in Ann Arbor, also helped to sharpen my thinking on feminist theory. May every writer have the same good fortune as to work with someone like Ann West, Sage's former communication editor, who offered myriad forms of backing for this book. Sophy Craze, Mary Curtis, and Astrid Virding at Sage continued as essential midwives in its birth.

Last, but certainly not least, I would like to thank the two editors of this series: Mike Traber and Bob White. They believed in this book project from the very beginning and offered continuing help of many kinds. That is, they did everything conscientious editors are supposed to do (e.g., reading and commenting on the entire manuscript in its various stages) but, in my opinion, went beyond the call of duty: They showed constant concern for the integrity of the book as both a scholarly and political statement.

Preface

JOHAN GALTUNG

This is an important book. In no way shall I try to conduct a guided tour through the chapters written by so many specialists in the field; the reader will be perfectly capable of that. Rather, I would like to say something about how the four heavy words strung together in the title resonate with me.

I will begin by referring to the media, one of the most important elements of communication/information this book deals with. As I am writing this, a desperate fax came in from the Helsinki Citizens' Assembly Secretariat in Prague, collecting signatures for an appeal to the European Community (EC), the United Nations (UN), and the United States about the situation in Yugoslavia. The plea is urgent: "Consult those ordinary people who long for peace and democracy in the region." It ends, "Will the West take the historic responsibility for the devastation of the Balkans?" And then a telling indictment: "The international media, too (in addition to the EC, the UN, and the United States) have failed to recognize the many democratic anti-war movements in different regions of former Yugoslavia . . . receiving almost no coverage in the Western media at all."

Not only do the media have this perverse fascination with war and violence; they also neglect the peace forces at work. Of course, some of this is the result of governmentalism, the fascination with power in addition to violence. How about some fascination with peace? And with people? How about giving them more voice?

As the media work, they amplify the sound of the guns rather than muting them. Is this because we have the media we deserve? Hardly. It is more because the people who run them are badly trained, looking only upward in society, registering the sudden and the negative, not the patient, long-term work of thousands, millions of citizens.

This is the major reason why so many people were so surprised at what happened in Europe in the fall of 1989. It looked as if the regimes were suddenly imploding, merely from inner fatigue. "Nobody could have predicted this" was the conventional wisdom from all over, from the media and the people in high places. Of course, when the work of some million ordinary Europeans all through the 1980s—greatly stimulated by NATO's decision to deploy missiles and the first Reagan administration's talk about "limited nuclear war"—goes unrecorded by the media, then it *will* come as a major surprise that the regimes have been weakened through the cumulative impact of nonviolence, citizens' diplomacy, and visions well propagated through society by the dissidents and the peace movement (and one statesman: Gorbachev). But for those who had their ears to the ground and participated in all of this there was no surprise, only the feeling that it could all have happened much earlier if the West had not reinforced the Eastern regimes with nuclear threats.

But it is the media that are certainly to blame for the lack of a peace perspective. The same thing was repeated in the Gulf War, when all the propaganda about no alternative (at least four solid negotiation offers) and "surgical war" (250,000 killed?) was widely accepted.

Peace is the usual condition of *Homo sapiens,* in spite of the bad record for violence in general and the collective violence of centrally organized groups, in particular wars. But why say *Homo sapiens* when in reality almost all of this is done by males? How about changing the terminology, from *war* to *male-war* or something like that? Of course, women sometimes play a supportive role, and not only because they are soldiers and not only in a reproductive role. But it is such a modest role, relative to the male branch of the species!

In addition, the very word *war* suffers from another anomaly. We have used that word and its equivalent throughout centuries in spite of the tremendous transformations of war as a social institution. Primitive, traditional, modern, and postmodern collective violence are all referred to as *wars,* which would be much like referring to industrial and postindustrial societies as *hunter-gatherers.* Needless to say, in a certain sense we still hunt and gather, but something would have been lost had we kept the old terms.

This semantic inertia makes it so easy to talk about war glibly, not reflecting on what it means. How about calling the present variety *megawar*? The impact of this little semantic improvement, which would mean talking about "the doctrine of just megawar," might be considerable. An even better improvement might be "the doctrine of just male megawar." That doctrine also becomes more true the moment we start experimenting in our minds with doctrines of just slavery and just colonialism as cost-benefit rationale, supported by pure minds with no ulterior ends, and so on. But we never learn to think in these terms, because the information we receive from the media is biased precisely by trying not to be, by keeping the war variable constant.

Why is the relation between information, war, and peace like this? Because of the fourth factor in the title: culture. The dominant world culture right now is Western culture—a mix of hard and gentle Judeo-Christianity, the roots of which are not too different from Islam—which is centralistic in its image of space; highly dramatic with cathartic and apocalyptic understanding of time; inconsiderate to nature, nonhuman life, and human life that stands in its way; highly individualistic and competitive; and given to monotheistic dedication, hard work, a certain puritanism and greed. In the crevices of this culture beautiful plants are nevertheless emerging: the rule of law and human rights, privacy and private property, arts and science. The fragility of the construction is seen very clearly in the atrocities committed by the colonial powers from 1492 onward, followed by the Nazis doing the same in Europe and the savage brutality of the West when its grip on countries in the third world is loosening.

What one would expect from that kind of culture is, of course, little ability to reflect on itself; the media then become the masters in nonreflection. One would also expect general applause when the West wins and despair when the West loses. What one would not be entitled to expect would be "objectivity" or anything like that. The all-Western nationalism is too well internalized for that to happen, with steep Self-Other gradients from us to them, the Muslims, the colored people, the third circle. Rather, we would expect the media, by and large, to be as eloquently silent on bad aspects of Self as on good aspects of Other. And they are.

In other words, there is a limit to how much we should criticize the media. Not that we have the media we deserve, but we have the media one would expect in a culture of that kind. Or, to be more precise and more just, we would expect mainstream media to reflect mainstream Western culture and should not be surprised when this near-tautological hypothesis is confirmed. It would be far more surprising were it falsified.

What this means is, in my view, that culture is where we have to direct most of our attention. We can do some cosmetic surgery on the media, write some dozens of norms and rules and do's and don'ts. But the chances are that bad habits will be reproduced as long as we have not had some kind of cultural transformation. We might, for instance, learn from the softer voices in Western culture, like the Catholic bishops and the Methodists who wrote their famous antinuclear treatises in a dramatic period in the early 1980s. Or we could turn to non-Occidental religions like Buddhism, Taoism, and Bahá'í. There is much to learn; many sources, many women.

This book is dedicated to the late Archie Singham, also a very dear friend of mine. Archie was so wonderfully filled with contradictions, having lived many cultures in his life. His speech had a Western leftist tinge. Underneath was a deep compassion with common people all over, with the victims of all this madness around us. Many people are more motivated by hatred of those high up than compassion for those lower down. There are reasons for the former; it is not irrational. But the latter will probably bring us much further in the struggle for peace. Archie showed the way. We miss him deeply.

Introduction

COLLEEN ROACH

Peace Studies: A Missing Perspective?

The first program on peace studies in the United States was founded in 1948-1949 at Manchester College, in northern Indiana. Four decades later, there were some 180 universities or colleges with an undergraduate major or minor in peace studies, and another 150 institutions offering courses in the area (Thomas & Klare, 1989). At the international level, there are dozens of other institutes of higher learning that now include aspects of peace studies in their curricula. In September 1988, academic leaders from nearly two dozen countries met at Tufts University's European Center to discuss how their commitment to peace education could be expanded around the globe.

The reasons for the continuing growth of peace research and teaching are self-evident. Although there was a short interlude in the late 1980s when it seemed that the era of glasnost and the end of the Cold War would diminish the need for the study of peace, this hope vanished as quickly as the promised "peace dividend."

The brief history of peace studies in the United States has always been marked by its antithesis: war. Some writers even go so far as to state that peace research has focused much more on war than on peace (Dugan, 1989, p. 78). In any case, it is certain that the first American program was developed shortly after the ravages of World War II and that the heightened interest in peace studies on campuses around the country in the 1970s was a direct response to the highly divisive war in Vietnam.

Given that the context of war has marked the field, will the war in the Persian gulf of 1990-1991 signal another "new era" in the study of peace? Even a preliminary answer to this question should begin by stating the obvious. First of all, peace researchers, activists, and ordinary peace-minded people must go back to the drawing board. The war, among other things, was a profound statement that past strategies have not worked.

Some of the most fundamental premises of peace studies are now up in the air. Who could have predicted that the United Nations (UN), dedicated to building world peace, would have offered its mandate for such a war? When Mayor, director-general of UNESCO, came to New York in January 1991, I publicly asked him how it felt during a UN-mandated war to be the head of a UN agency whose constitution begins with an invocation of the need for peace. He stated that UNESCO still worked for peace, but really had no answer. What could he say?

In addition to the changing role of the United Nations, other questions need to be asked. What can one say about the well-known world order studies of the 1970s and 1980s, that were one of peace studies' major components? Can the term *world order*, and its five values—peace, social justice, economic equity, ecological balance, and political par-ticipation—ever be connected to peace again, now that the West's world order is being established around the globe?[1]

An essential premise of this book is as follows: As peace researchers and activists ponder how the new world order of the West may impact their work, it is essential that the field integrates more fully issues relating to culture and communication. Indeed, one aspect of the recent debacle in the Persian Gulf is the price to be paid for ignoring the myriad ways culture and communication contribute to war. Several examples from the literature of peace and international conflict research will illustrate my point.[2] In July 1989, the *Annals of the American Academy of Political and Social Sciences* published a special issue devoted to the theme "Peace Studies: Past and Future" (Lopez, 1989). The twelve articles, written by noted specialists in the field, offer an essential perspective on the current state of peace research. However, there is not a single article dealing with the relationship between the mass media, communication or culture, and war and peace. The only author to deal with communication, even briefly, makes passing reference to concerns in the south about information inequality embodied in the movement for a "new world information order" (Alger, 1989). While the overall work of Galtung (one of the "fathers" of peace research) is cited by several authors, there is no mention made of Galtung's essential writ-ings relating communication, culture, and language to peace and war.[3]

Similar omissions are noteworthy in the February 1991 issue of UNESCO's *International Social Science Journal* devoted to the topic "International Conflict Research." Of the eleven thematic contribu-

tions, only one deals with a topic even remotely connected to communication and culture: the role of enemy images in conflict escalation
(Spillmann & Spillmann, 1991). Although an excellent study, this
article concentrates not on the media's use of enemy images but rather
on the cognitive and psychological dimensions operative in the reception
of these images. The other articles follow the thematic trend signaled in
the issue's editorial, which notes that the goal of international conflict
research is "to contribute to conflict resolution, through the elucidation of
political, military, economical, social, ethnic, cognitive, and psychological
factors which condition conflicts" (Kazancigil, 1991, p. 4). That is to say,
there is virtually no connection whatsoever established between communication and culture and international conflict research.

   Three 1991 issues of the *Journal of Peace Research* (one of the main
academic publications in the field) offer only a slightly better record.
The February 1991 issue devoted to "international mediation," has nine
articles, none of which deal with the media, culture, or communication.
The May 1991 issue has one out of six articles that deals with communication: "Improving Communications Links between Moscow and Washington" (Ball, 1991). In the August 1991 issue, an anthropological case
study of the role of culture in conflict is the subject of one of the five
articles: "Cultural Style and Solutions to Conflict" (Billings, 1991).

   This literature's lacunae are all the more curious, given that researchers
have been connecting communication and culture to peace for many years.
The International Peace Research Association (IPRA), one of the main
professional groups in the field, has had a study group on communication
since 1977.[4] Varis, a Finnish communication researcher, integrated communication into peace research as former head of the Tampere Peace
Research Institute and subsequently at the UN Peace University (Varis,
1986). *Media Development,* a leading journal in international communication, published a special issue called "Communication and Peace"
(1983) a decade ago. International communication research organizations, such as the International Association for Mass Communication
Research (IAMCR) and the International Communication Association
(ICA) have also promoted, for years, work that examines the many
ways that the mass media and culture are bound up with peace. The
ICA's 1988 annual conference was devoted to the theme of communication and peace. Members of the Union for Democratic Communication
(UDC), including five of the authors in this book, have been publishing
research on communication and peace for a long time. Other national-
based research organizations, such as the Speech Communication

Association (SCA) have also set up special commissions and study groups on peace and communication.[5]

Therefore, if peace research finds itself at a new "crossroads," occasioned by the war in the Persian Gulf, any new path that is charted must take into account research that has a long and respectable tradition. Communication and culture must finally be given their due.

The Origins of the Book

The origins of this book testify to the fact that what follows is by no means a *culturalist* or reductionist approach to the study of war and peace, as it originated out of a wide-ranging, multidisciplinary attempt to understand and act for peace.

In 1984, a group of activists, writers, and academics concerned about world peace came together to pool their resources. Known as the Exploratory Project on the Conditions of Peace (EXPRO), the group's philosophy was based on several key ideas. First of all, what united the various people working on the project, all of whom had a long history of involvement with actions for peace and social justice, was a definite disillusionment with the traditional peace movement in the United States. It was believed that peace was almost exclusively defined in terms of war, that is to say, nuclear weapons, military equipment, and atomic arsenals. The EXPRO people were convinced that the nature of the beast was much more than just bombs and battles. They were, in fact, confronting an entire *war system,* with deep political, economic, and cultural roots. Hence, to change this system, something equally comprehensive must be built: *a peace system.*

The second idea was that their work should not be just an intellectual exercise. It was thought that one of the long-standing problems with American social movements was an unbridgeable gap between activists and intellectuals (the doers and the thinkers, to put it crudely). Hence attempts were made to involve community organizers in the work of EXPRO. It was also hoped that policymakers might eventually be reached.

Over and above organizers and policymakers, however, EXPRO set itself a very ambitious goal: to involve "the people." Ferry, one of the principal backers of EXPRO, was straightforward: Ordinary people are much more likely to make peace than policymakers.

From 1984 to 1988, EXPRO functioned as a think tank, with its members gathering several times a year to discuss how to replace the present war system with a peace system. In 1987, EXPRO moved beyond this stage and created different "tracks" to deal with the following dimensions of war and peace: economics and social justice, political participation and conflict resolution, information and culture, individual and collective defense, and ecology and technology.[6]

In June 1988, Singham asked if I would be interested in directing the information and culture track. I was asked, first of all, to examine how information and culture buttressed the war system and how, alternatively, they might be turned around to help build a peace system. In addition, I was asked to integrate into my work two issues believed to have a singular importance for peace and justice: feminism and racism.

Needless to say, this mandate was very wide-ranging. But I knew from my years at UNESCO, the UN agency specifically dedicated to peace, that EXPRO was on the right track: Building peace *is* an enormous undertaking that goes well beyond the battlefields. What are the principal connections between communication and culture, and war and peace? In attempting to answer this question, I sought the collaboration of a number of authors, all of whom already had been working for many years in relating their area(s) of specialization to issues of war and peace: Peter Bruck, Sheila Collins, Riane Eisler, Howard Frederick, Vincent Mosco, Herbert Schiller, and Majid Tehranian.

In addition to these individual contributions, many other people helped shape this book. The working style of EXPRO was, during my involvement, that of a collective whose members got together several times a year to talk in the tranquil surroundings of the Stony Point, New York, Peace Center. Those quiet brainstorming sessions—a welcome relief from the rough-and-tumble world of academia—yielded much insight that I have tried to incorporate into my own work. Through EXPRO I also made many contacts with people and groups working in various areas such as racism, sexism, and cultural democracy. Many of their thoughts also found their way into this book. The grandfather of critical communication, Dallas Smythe, even served as a sort of informal consultant to the track, giving me the opportunity to correspond and talk with someone whose work I had long admired.

The Themes of the Book

All of the authors whose specialty is communication—Mosco, Schiller, Tehranian, Frederick, Bruck, and me—draw on a very wide body of literature that connects the media and information technology to war and peace. People who are unfamiliar with *critical* communication research may, in fact, be surprised to find that some of the pioneer figures in this school—such as Smythe, Schiller, and Mattelart—have been connecting communication to war and peace for well over 15 years.

In the first chapter I conceptualize and provide an overview of the various ways communication and culture are related to war and peace. The reader will note that *communication* has been primarily defined here in terms of the communication that takes place through information products, mainly the mass media. The reader will, therefore, not find a discussion here (or in the other chapters) of the war and peace dimensions of what American academics refer to as a distinct area of communication called *human* or *interpersonal* communication. This area is certainly important for war and peace (and, of course, is not unrelated to mass communication) but was simply beyond the scope of this book.

Some of the common themes that are touched on by Mosco and Schiller include the military-industrial-communication complex, cultural imperialism, and transnational control of communication. Schiller argues forcefully against the idea that the age of imperialism is over, and draws a stark parallel between the U.S. troops stationed in the Persian Gulf and the continued control of global culture by the transnational corporations. Mosco's chapter, analyzing the role of communication technology in the war of the north against the south, could hardly be more timely. Mosco reminds us of the historical validity of seeing the war in the Gulf as a direct outcome of the military-industrial-communication complex.

Bruck's work on the media's role in war and peace summarizes both the structural and ideological connections between communication and the machines of war. By anchoring his argument against the idea of a dominant ideology in the waters of media concentration and interlocks, he succeeds in not throwing the baby out with the bath water, as many postmodernists are wont to do. Tehranian's chapter dissects the West's new world order, referring to it as a *dysorder* that has fanned the political and cultural flames of ethnic conflict. And yet, he argues that a renewed vision of culture based on spirituality and community is probably the only defense against the "onslaught of modernity."

Frederick's chapter on international communication law reminds us that there has been a consistent attempt to deal with all of the ways the media and culture contribute to war, sexism, and racism for well over a century. His emphasis on the emerging notion of *people's rights* is particularly appropriate for the direction of this project.

The chapters by Eisler and Collins complement some of the hard connections between communication and war made by the other authors. Thus Collins offers a precise treatment of exactly which values in capitalist culture promote the war system. Eisler offers particularly arresting insights from anthropology and archaeology on how the *dominator* cultures symbolized by the blade have, since prehistoric times, repeatedly overtaken the partnership cultures embodied in the symbol of the chalice. She offers both present and future strategies for creating a partnership world aimed at peace and survival, such as the feminization of power based on humanistic goals and the reintegration of the "personal and political" in a restructured society. As feminists, both authors are also concerned with some of the "soft" issues relating to war and peace. Eisler, for example, focuses on the worship of nature and the absence of war in goddess societies and the need for a *remything* process in our present war system. In a similar vein, Collins talks about how our concepts of earth and life have been lost in commodity fetishism and how our myths of scientific knowledge invalidate insights based on intuition, dreams, and the creative imagination. My chapter on feminist peace researchers shows that this generally unacknowledged body of literature can help us to understand how the war in the Persian Gulf was related to militarism, sexism, and our pervasive war culture.

The various chapters, however, are not really disparate in tone or substance. They share common concerns and perspectives, such as their notable aversion to the awesome role of the media in molding our war culture. Other common themes include gender, language, bureaucratization, and concern for the countries of the south.

Reflecting the action-oriented philosophy of EXPRO, the authors are also united in asking the perennial question, What Is to Be Done? In addition to responding to the goals of this particular project, however, the pragmatic prescriptions offered by many of the authors embody an essential aspect of peace research. Although many social scientists strive for relevance to the real world, peace research, as defined by many of its practitioners, has a virtual mandate to aim at action. One writer, summarizing the development of peace studies, noted, "Apart from being interdisciplinary and international in its organization, peace research aspired to be relevant and applicable; its findings had to be applicable to the most pressing problem of the day, viz. the prevention of war" (van den Dungen, 1983, p. 135). Another researcher says something very similar, but places it within a policy context: "Peace studies is explicitly a policy science, policy-oriented in the sense that it aspires to describe, explain, and

recommend policy relating to the conditions of peace to both governments and social movements" (Stephenson, 1990, p. 4).

The writings of Freire (1974) are often cited by writers on peace to
illustrate the necessary balance between research and praxis:

> Liberation is a praxis: the action and reflection of men upon their world in
> order to transform. . . . When a word is deprived of its dimension of action,
> reflection automatically suffers as well; and the word is changed into idle
> chatter, into *verbalism;* into an alienated and alienating "blah." It becomes
> an empty word, one which cannot denounce the world, for denunciation is
> impossible without a commitment to transform, and there is no transforma-
> tion without action. On the other hand, if action is emphasized exclusively,
> to the detriment of reflection, the word is converted into *activism.* (pp. 66,
> 75-76)

Peace action is thus a fairly common term used in establishing curricula
based not only on research and education but also on fieldwork. Going
out into the world to work for peace, armed with research findings, also
translates an essential goal in building a broad-based peace movement:
uniting intellectuals and activists or, to use Freire's terms, ensuring that
researchers and the people become coinvestigators (noted in Alger,
1989). In an era when the increasing political role played by grass-roots
groups around the world is becoming more and more evident, bridging
the gap between the doers and thinkers is essential. Although written
from an Indian perspective, the following description of this challenge
is highly relevant to the peace movement in North America:

> It is the dialectic between micro-practice and macro-thinking that will
> actualize a new politics of the future: In brief, a macro vision is the prime
> need of these groups and movements, and this can be satisfied only by a
> growing partnership between activists and intellectuals in the process of
> social transformation. (Sheth quoted in Alger, 1991, p. 256)

The Context of War

A new term being used by researchers challenging the dominant
production of ideas is *situated knowledge*. Situated knowledge, as
defined by another Indian writer, Parajuli, is neither objective nor
relativistic. It is built on the struggle of people's everyday lives. "Situated knowledge is a knowledge that is accountable to the knower. It is

a knowledge that acknowledges being located in time and space; it is always a marked knowledge" (Parajuli, 1991, pp. 183, 195).

The "time and space" that have marked the knowledge produced in this book are defined by the war in the Persian Gulf. For anyone not having lived in the United States in 1990 and 1991, it is almost impossible to convey the wholesale contribution of the mass media and mass culture to the country's war frenzy. The mass media's complicity in the war effort was so total that by the time the thousands of Iraqi soldiers departing Kuwait were being incinerated, many of us were so sickened by the spectacle that we could no longer even look at television.

But "situated knowledge" is also a knowledge born of resistance. In dialectical fashion, the media's promotion of the war prompted new forms of media activism, with several thousand people taking to the streets of New York to protest network coverage of the Persian Gulf. As anyone attending the much larger antiwar marches on Washington can attest, many of the placards and posters targeted the mass media. Activist collectives monitoring the war coverage of local media sprang up around the country.

As time passes, it has also become apparent that, paradoxically, the short-term collective memory created by television has helped undo its effects: the American "victory" in the Persian Gulf War is fast fading in the minds of many people, now preoccupied by the increasingly difficult daily struggle for economic survival.

Speaking of struggle reminds me of Archie Singham, who first introduced me to this project. Six weeks before he died Sheila Collins and I paid a final visit to him. Here was a man who knew he was dying and who in his last days, was seeing his worst fears come to pass. His life's work had been dedicated to the struggle of the south against racism and neoimperialism.

He was still lucid enough to have realized the meaning of the war. And yet, incredibly, Archie was optimistic. I asked him what he thought about things, and he said that when he looked around at the number of people struggling for change here in the United States, he had never seen more reason for hope. This book shares in the same hopeful struggle.

Notes

1. A French journalist, writing on American foreign policy in Africa, cited the U.S. view of the UN's role in the new world order, given by the assistant secretary of state for

Africa at a press conference: "America does not want to maintain order or exercise any kind of military domination in Africa or anywhere else. We want the United Nations to do this" (Leymarie, 1992, p. 13).

2. Most writers amalgamate peace research and international conflict research. Others, such as Kazancigil (1991) and Katz (1989), see the two fields as complementary.

3. In 1971, Galtung published his classic study titled "A Structural Theory of Imperialism." Using *center-periphery* and *dominance-dependence* constructs, Galtung outlined how distinct patterns of international news flow follow the structures of imperialism, and offered strategies for breaking up the dominance-dependency cycle. For other examples of his research relating the media and language to peace, see Galtung (1986, 1987).

4. The main themes of the 12th General Assembly of IPRA, held in Rio de Janeiro in 1988, were culture and communication. For a collection of papers given at this conference, see Boulding, Brigagao, and Clements (1991).

5. For two recent SCA publications, see Korzenny and Ting-Toomey (1990) and Troester and Kelley (1991).

6. The collected work of several of these tracks has been published in Shuman and Sweig (1991). Makhijani's (1992) work has also been published. Another EXPRO member, Irwin (1989), has published a manual for building a peace system.

References

Alger, C. F. (1989, July). Peace studies at the crossroads: Where else? *The Annals of the American Academy of Political and Social Science, 504,* 117-127.

Alger, C. F. (1991). Creating global visions for peace movements. In E. Boulding, C. Brigagao, & K. Clements (Eds.), *Peace, culture & society: Transnational research and dialogue* (pp. 241-260). Boulder, CO: Westview Press.

Ball, D. (1991, May). Improving communications links between Moscow and Washington. *Journal of Peace Research, 28*(2), 135-159.

Billings, D. K. (1991, August). Cultural style and solutions to conflict. *Journal of Peace Research, 28*(3), 241-262.

Boulding, E., Brigagao, C. & Clements, K. (Eds.). (1991). *Peace, culture, & society: Transnational research and dialogue.* Boulder, CO: Westview Press.

Communications and peace [Special issue]. (1983). *Media Development, 30*(2).

Dugan, M. A. (1989, July). Peace studies at the graduate level. *The Annals of the American Academy of Political and Social Science, 504,* 72-79.

Freire, P. (1974). *Pedagogy of the oppressed.* New York: Seabury Press.

Galtung, J. (1971). A structural theory of imperialism. *Journal of Peace Research, 8*(2), 81-117.

Galtung, J. (1986). On the role of the media for world-wide security and peace. In T. Varis (Ed.), *Peace and communication* (pp. 249-266). San Jose, Costa Rica: Editorial Universidad para la Paz.

Galtung, J. (1987). Language and war: Is there a connection? *Current Research on Peace and Violence, 9*(1), 2-6.

Irwin, R. A. (1989). *Building a peace system.* Washington, DC: EXPRO Press.

Katz, N. H. (1989, July). Conflict resolution and peace studies. *The Annals of the American Academy of Political and Social Science, 504,* 14-21.

Kazancigil, A. (1991, February). [Editorial]. *International Social Science Journal, XLIII*(127), 3-4.

Korzenny, F., & Ting-Toomey, S. (Eds.). (1990). *Communication for peace: Diplomacy and negotiation.* Newbury Park, CA: Sage.

Leymarie, P. (1992, April). Les États-Unis, Nouveaux parrains du continent Africain. *Le Monde Diplomatique, 457,* 12-13.

Lopez, G. A. (Ed.). (1989, July). Peace studies: Past and future [Special issue]. *The Annals of the American Academy of Political and Social Science, 504.*

Makhijani, A. (1992). *From global capitalism to economic justice.* Croton-on-Hudson, NY: Apex Press.

Parajuli, P. (1991, February). Power and knowledge in development discourse: New social movements and the state in India. *International Social Science Journal, XLIII*(127), 173-190.

Shuman, M., & Sweig, J. (Eds.). (1991). *Conditions of peace: An inquiry.* Washington, DC: EXPRO Press.

Spillmann, K. R., & Spillmann, K. (1991, February). On enemy images and conflict escalation. *International Social Science Journal, XLIII*(127), 57-76.

Stephenson, C. M. (1990). *Peace studies: The evolution of peace research and peace education* [monograph]. Honolulu: University of Hawaii Institute for Peace.

Thomas, D. C., & Klare, M. (Eds.). (1989). *Peace and world order studies: A curriculum guide.* Boulder, CO: Westview Press.

Troester, R., & Kelley, C. (Eds.). (1991). *Peacemaking through communications.* Annandale, VA: Speech Communication Association.

Van den Dungen, P. (1983). International initiatives in peace research. *Media Development, 30*(2), 34-37.

Varis, T. (Ed.). (1986). *Peace and communication.* San Jose, Costa Rica: Editorial Universidad para la Paz.

1

Information and Culture in War and Peace: Overview

COLLEEN ROACH

War and Peace

War and peace, as Tolstoy might argue, are two of the most timeless and touching themes in the history of humanity. The widespread organized death and destruction of war have, for centuries, inspired poets, philosophers, and politicians to ponder its origins. In the last century, with the rise of the social sciences and, particularly, since the explosion of the atom bomb, academics and researchers have also turned their attention to what lies behind war and peace. But just as all poets have not condemned war (think of the opening lines of Virgil's *Aeniad: Arma virumque cano,* "I sing of arms and the man") so it is with social scientists, all of whom have by no means turned their skills to the search for peace.

The following overview of the connections between war and peace, and information and culture will not, however, orient the reader to the literature in communication and culture that supports the war system. Like many of the pieces in this book, it implicitly casts doubt on the hallowed Western doctrines of objectivity and rationality, which have done so much to exclude normative and value considerations from the social sciences and which are increasingly felt to be one of the deepest bedrocks of the war system. Indeed, as we shall note, *objectivity* has

AUTHOR'S NOTE: The author would like to acknowledge the assistance for this chapter provided by EXPRO. She would like, in particular, to thank the following individuals: Ping Ferry (a bountiful source of information); Arjun Mahkijani, Liane Norman, Robert Irwin, Dietrich Fischer, and Randy Kehler (for their helpful comments and moral support). Benny Jose, a doctoral candidate in sociology at Fordham University, provided invaluable research assistance.

also served as one of the major professional justifications for the mass media's contribution to war.

The chapter proceeds in the following directions. First of all, because many of the key concepts used, such as *peace, information,* and *culture,* have a wide range of definitions, their particular usage here will be explained. The next section deals with the way culture is connected to war. Here, this relationship will be examined not so much in terms of our *war culture*—including war toys, video games, and *Rambo* movies—since this terrain has been fairly well explored over the last decade. Rather, it will deal with some subjects not commonly connected to war, such as mythology and the debate on multiculturalism. The contribution of information to war, specifically the mass media, is next presented. Because television has so profoundly modified our communication and cultural landscape since the 1950s, special attention is given to its role in the war system. A section is also devoted to some of the international ramifications of cultural domination and resistance, especially in the countries of the south. Readers are also briefly introduced to ways in which the war system impacts women and minorities, topics that are more fully explored in later chapters by Eisler and Collins. Following the peace movement's philosophy of "aiming at action," this chapter closes with some suggestions for change.

Defining the Terms

Peace

Many peace researchers distinguish between a "negative" and a "positive" definition of peace. Thus, writing in 1968, Galtung states,

> Two concepts of peace should be distinguished: *negative peace,* defined as the absence of organized violence between such major groups as nations, but also between racial and ethnic groups because of the magnitude that can be reached by internal wars; and *positive peace,* defined as patterns of cooperation and integration between major human groups. (p. 487)

Structural violence, a concept initiated by Galtung, is used by many peace researchers to refer to the types of injustice not strictly covered by negative peace. Not unlike liberation theology's *structural sin,* it may be defined as follows:

a political economic system in which the chances for participation in power are extremely unequal, a system in which (using the center-periphery model) the peripheries are subject to directives by the center—in the interest of the latter, of course. (Becker, 1982, p. 233)

In a more recent article, Alger summarizes the thinking of many peace and justice groups around the world, incorporating the ideas of structural violence into the definitions of negative and positive peace. Alger's remarks emphasize that peace must be seen not just as the absence of war, but as the prevention of all structural and social inequalities.

A second crossroads that peace studies must encompass is the intersection between negative and positive peace, that is, between peace in the sense of stopping the killing that results from direct violence—bombs and guns—and peace that prevents the loss of life and human capacity that occurs through structural violence, that is, through social structures that are responsible for death and incapacity. . . . I believe that there is now broad agreement in peace studies that the opposite of peace is not war but peacelessness, that war is but one kind of peacelessness. (Alger, 1989, pp. 118-119)

Many feminist researchers, because of their concern with a holistic approach to violence, war, patriarchy, domination, and inequality, have validated the wide-ranging positive definition of peace. Bruck-Utne (1985), a Norwegian researcher, writes that "when the concept of peace implies that every human being regardless of sex has the right to a life in peace and peace is defined as justice, the right to fulfillment of basic needs, to self-determination, most feminist research can be called research on women and peace" (p. 3). Reardon (1985), another feminist peace researcher, is of the same opinion: "Positive peace, the conditions of justice and equity necessary to achieve the absence of war, is a concept profoundly infused with feminist values" (p. 63).

Both the positive and negative definitions of peace have been used in this introductory chapter. Information and culture will thus not only be related to questions directly connected to war, such as organized violence and militarism, but also to the structural violence of the mass media, which fosters injustice and inequality.

Culture and Information

One of the difficulties of defining culture is that it is used in many different contexts. The following references give some idea of how newspapers such as the *New York Times* employ the term: "electronic culture," "the cultural incompatibility of different corporations," "the culture of poverty," "the political culture of a newspaper," and the "cultural rape of a nation."

These references, although indicating the many meanings of the word *culture,* do not offer a definition. A Canadian author, addressing the problem in the UNESCO journal *Cultures,* stated that "the trouble with culture is that there are too many definitions of it. As such, culture is an extremely ambiguous and elusive term. It is a fluid struggling to survive in an age of solids" (Schafer, 1980, p. 36). And yet, culture is increasingly felt to be the center of modern life, as stated in an editorial on culture and contemporary society, also from *Cultures:*

> For centuries, religion, politics, economics were held to be the forces that shaped the destiny of nations; in the last third of the twentieth, we have gradually come to recognize that human and social behaviour are deeply rooted in culture. Economic problems, social problems, personal problems, even religious attitudes are often treated as cultural by assumption, and solutions are accordingly sought in cultural terms. (UNESCO, 1975, p. 1)

More than a century ago, Tylor (1874) offered what is now considered a classic definition of culture: "Culture . . . is that complex whole which includes knowledge, beliefs, art, morals, custom and any other capabilities and habits acquired by man as a member of society" (Tylor, 1924, p. 1). Although I would change "man" to "men and women," Tylor's words seem to have stood the test of time: anthropologists now generally acknowledge that culture is a way of life, ranging from what we eat to how we dress to what we think and how we act. In short, the very air we breathe.

In thinking about culture, I have also drawn on the work of Galtung and Holt. Galtung (1986) has used the term *cosmology* to refer to culture and makes the essential connection with ideology:

> Cosmology is here used as a concept covering "deep culture" (with "deep ideologies" as an important special case) and "deep structure"—the unquestioned aspects of culture and structure found in a civilization, both of them taken to define what is normal and natural. (p. 255)

Galtung's work is also of special interest because it is linked to our related area of exploration: the mass media. In his view, the dichotomous good/evil Western approach to covering international affairs, for example, does not reflect just the ideology of capitalist media owners but also their cosmology (Galtung, 1989a). Thus seeing reality as black and white, whether it be George Bush versus Saddam Hussein or the Contras versus the Sandinistas, reflects at least thousands of years of Western civilization and not just the current dictates of capitalism. Holt (1987) emphasizes that in relating culture to peace, one must prioritize culture as an agency establishing value systems. Thus if a country's values promote militarism, one must look to culture.

Compared with culture, information is a relatively easy concept to define because it will be used in this chapter primarily to refer to the products of the mass media. Two points, nonetheless, should be stressed: (1) the mass media, while important in virtually all areas of modern life, have a particular role to play in times of war and (2) the mass media intersect with culture.

Since the 1970s, we have been told by establishment academics, policymakers, and corporate hucksters, that we are living in an information age or information society. Much of this rhetoric has been dressed up in the finery of terms such as *information abundance* and greater *information-age democracy.*[1] Critical researchers (Mosco & Wasko, 1988; Slack & Fejes, 1986; Schiller, 1986; Webster & Robbins, 1986), however, have pointed out the built-in contradictions of the information society: Among other things, not everyone has equal access to the fruits of the information age, and in the United States, an information society par excellence, usually less than 50% of the citizens vote in presidential elections.

Nonetheless, it is essential to acknowledge the "surface truth" behind the ideology of the information age: In advanced industrial societies, information *is* increasingly important. For questions of war and peace, what this means, in the simplest terms, is that most of the time most people get most of their information from the mass media. Whereas the media's coverage of domestic and local news can be somewhat mediated by personal experience or interpersonal communication, the same does not usually apply to coverage of international events. Because war and peace issues usually belong to the latter category of news, the media's power is all the more invasive. To take the recent example of the Gulf War, television was the main source of information for 89% of Americans, one of the highest figures ever reported in public opinion polls (Dennis, Stebbene, Pavlik, et al., 1991, p. 90).

In focusing on this very high figure, one might ask, As Americans sat, glued to their television sets, to use the proverbial phrase, was this a mass media or mass culture event? Although the means of transmission was clearly a mass medium, there is much to suggest that the millions of Americans engaged in the same activity were also partaking in a shared cultural experience, evidence of what Carey (1989) refers to as a cultural or "ritual view of communications." The fact that television was complemented by the mobilization of a vast mass culture complex, which included not only radio and the print media but also movies and even T-shirts and yellow ribbons, suggests the deeper resonances of a cultural phenomenon. In short, it is no longer possible to speak of the power of the media without also referring to the power of culture.

Culture in War and Peace

The Primal Questions

To begin at the beginning of the relationship between culture and peace, one must examine certain primal questions, such as, Are men and women innately aggressive? and Is there a biological instinct of violence? The answers to such questions should help one to examine an issue of direct relevance to this chapter: Is war a phenomenon of instinct or culture?

Although there is no overall consensus in the literature of anthropology, psychology, and sociology, certain remarks can nonetheless be made. First of all, the Freudian view of the nature of man has had an enormous—but not unchallenged—influence on thinking on violence and aggression. Freud's thinking could be summarized as follows: (1) aggression is a response to frustration of impulse, and (2) there is an innate, independent instinct of man toward aggression. Culture (or civilization) in Freud's mind, was society's way of instituting "high demands" on mankind to curb his aggressive instincts. Biological determinists reach a conclusion not unlike that of Freud by holding to the assumption that the roots of war and collective violence lie somewhere in the biological mechanisms that animals and man have in common (Eskola, 1987).

Nonetheless, although Freudian adepts and biological determinists undoubtedly still populate many institutions of higher learning,[2] there has also been a consistent challenging of the idea that our darker instincts propel us to war. Although some authors believe that in the final analysis the debate comes down to personal beliefs about human nature, there is an impressive body of research indicating that we are not simply traveling through a gray area. Writing in 1957, Pear summarized one of the most oft-cited refutations of Freudian theses:

> Firstly, comparative ethnological evidence, e.g. by Margaret Mead and others, indicates that aggression and competition are not found as predominant or approved modes of response in some cultures. This evidence would tend to indicate that competitiveness, aggressiveness, rivalry, sadism are not the basic instincts Freud assumed. If they were and had simply been successfully repressed by the societies in question, Freudian theory would anticipate a host of unbalances and complexes as a consequence. Such complexes due to thwarting of aggressive impulses are not found in a consistent way. (pp. 132-133)

Pear (1957) also reviews an impressive body of developmental material (for example, indicating that competitiveness with other children is seldom found among 2- and 3½-year-olds, and commonly found among 5- and 6½-year-olds) and concludes that "certainly the bulk of evidence in child psychology indicates no need for positing an innate human tendency towards aggression as a basic instinct" (p. 133).

The argument that people are biologically or genetically programmed for war was soundly rejected by a group of prominent biologists and social scientists participating in a meeting of the International Society for Research on Aggression in 1986. The meeting adopted a widely circulated document on the question, known as the Seville Statement on Violence.[3] Among its conclusions:

> It is scientifically incorrect to say that we have inherited a tendency to make war from our animal ancestors. . . . Warfare is a peculiarly human phenomenon and does not occur in other animals.
>
> The fact that warfare has changed so radically over time indicates that it is a product of culture. . . . War is biologically possible, but it is not inevitable. . . .
>
> It is scientifically incorrect to say that war or any other violent behavior is genetically programmed into our human nature. . . .
>
> It is scientifically incorrect to say that in the course of human evolution there has been a selection for aggressive behavior more than for other kinds of behavior. . . . Violence is neither in our evolutionary legacy nor in our genes. (The Seville Statement on Violence, 1991, pp. 169-170)

Moreover, a growing number of anthropologists and psychologists interested in peace research are essentially concluding that war is above all a *cultural* phenomenon. The anthropologist Greenhouse argues that while one may draw up explanations of war as competition or war as politics, it is pointless to attempt to define causality, because causality itself is a culture-bound category of analysis. Second, she joins with those authors cited above in stating that there is no evidence that "warfare among human populations is due to innate aggression" (Greenhouse, 1987, p. 37). While acknowledging that armed conflict goes back to the Paleolithic era, she traces its roots back to culture, defined as "the realm of preferences, values and understandings" (Greenhouse, 1987, p. 43).

Holt, a psychologist by training, also argues forcefully against the Freudian-derived idea of an instinctual basis for war. Noting the existence of many peaceful societies in history and modern times, Holt (1987) even posits that a case can be made for "an innate biological basis for peace," because "it is much more nearly universal than war, and has obvious survival value" (p. 8). Holt's central argument, like that of Greenhouse, is that war is primarily part of a vast cultural complex.

Ideology Versus Mythology

Two essential components in this vast cultural complex are ideology and mythology.[4] Although most writers do not define their usage of these terms, they would seem to originate in, politically speaking, different analyses of society. In general, it has been the Marxist school of social scientists who privilege *ideology*. Marxist writers who refer to ideology usually view it as an all-pervasive set of ideas, norms, and values transmitted through the institutions of education, mass culture, religion, and the mass media. Marxist notions of ideology are based on several assumptions. First of all, although there has been a fairly widespread challenge of the notion that ideology is solely determined by economics, most coherent Marxists still see a clear connection between the economic system of a country and its ideology (i.e., capitalism produces a capitalist ideology; socialism produces a socialist ideology) and between economic and ideological domination (of special importance for neoimperialist strategies in the third world). Second, dominant ideology (often referred to just as *ideology*) is very much related to what Gramsci referred to as the *hegemony* of the ruling class. Third, Marxists view the secret of ideology's success to be its "disappearing act": it is always there, it is our everyday common sense, and yet most people neither see it nor realize that it works to the benefit of the ruling class. In sum, ideology is firmly rooted in a *political* analysis of society.

I would be remiss if I did not briefly refer to the lively—although largely academic—debates of the last decade on the nature of ideology. By the early 1980s, writers who privileged concepts such as dominant ideology and hegemony came under increasing attack from those who held that such notions were too mechanistic and that the dominant ideology of an era did not dominate the "dominated" nearly as effectively as claimed. Some writers argued that audiences of television, for example, were actually active and not passive receivers (hence the term *active audience*). Certain writers who disputed the dominant ideology school seem to have genuinely believed it was too simplistic and attempted to make its theoretical underpinnings more sophisticated by asking how variables such as gender, race, and class influence message reception (i.e., a poor, black, Latina woman may have a different reaction to *Dallas* than a white, middle-class man). Others, however, seem to have been motivated solely by a reactionary political project: to undermine the important influence on American campuses in the 1960s and 1970s of professors whose teaching and writings were based on dominant ideology (Gramsci, Althusser, and the Frankfurt School). Critics of the latter, many of whom were anti-Marxists parading in the clothes of neo-Marxism, clearly threw the baby of ideology out with the bath water. Riding on the crest of the postmodern wave of the 1980s and abstruse French writers, they went so far as to state that it was pointless to speak of the Meaning of mass media products, because everyone processed messages *à sa façon*.

Although this debate on ideology has for the most part not made inroads into peace literature, it is certainly worthy of note, as shown in the chapters by Schiller and Bruck, both of whom spend some time addressing the question from different perspectives. To summarize the implications of this controversy for peace research, most peace researchers critical of the mass media's role in promoting war assume that the latter are indeed powerful shapers of consciousness, but there has been not inconsiderable questioning of this premise among certain communication scholars in the 1980s. Although the most judicious view would probably lie somewhere in the middle (i.e., different meanings for different audiences can coexist with a dominant ideology), the debate has been highly politicized, with the detractors of the dominant ideology school implicitly or explicitly attacking the political-economy, structuralist analysis of the media that underlies the dominant ideology position. In short, the debate on ideology has itself become very ideological, reflecting the climate of the 1980s, surely one of the most ideologically controversial eras of the postwar period. Similarly politicized polemics have surfaced in other social sciences in American universities, and like them, the debate on ideology has not reached closure.

Although Barthes's (1972) classic *Mythologies* analyzed myths from a very political perspective, that is, within the context of dominant ideology, there are many other writers particularly influential in the United States who have emphasized other factors. In sum, there is a substantial literature of mythology that has less politicized hues than those of ideology, being anchored much more deeply in the waters of the unconscious, religion, and spirituality. People who reject an analysis based on the ruling class's control of ideas may readily accept the premise that myths tap into the essence of a country's culture.

Mythologist Keen (1988) defined *myth* as "referring to interlocking stories, rituals, rites, customs, and beliefs that give a pivotal sense of meaning and direction to a person, a family, a community or a culture. The dominant myth that informs a person or a culture is like the 'information' contained in the DNA of a cell. . . . Myth is the cultural DNA" (p. 44). Although myths can change over time, they are thought to be much closer to some profound idea of a culture's "truth," not unlike Galtung's idea of cosmology. And although there are as many different myths as there are cultures, mythologists such as Campbell also point to a certain universality in myths: all cultures, for example, seem to have myths of the battle between good and evil, the journeys of a hero, and so on.

When one looks more closely at some of the modern-day cultural icons of the war system, such as the Ramboesque myth of he-man white superiority and the *Star Wars* personification of American technological supremacy, one can appreciate the overlap between mythology and ideology. While the two concepts are clearly not synonymous, both have an important role to play in understanding how and why people accept war.

The Myths of War and Peace

What exactly are the myths that sustain war? In an article written shortly after the end of the Vietnam debacle, Norman (1975) drew extensive parallels between Captain Ahab's obsession with the white whale in *Moby Dick* and the mythological obsessions put forward to the American public by U.S. leaders. In addition to the "cosmic battle between good and evil," she found a host of other images and mythologies that have sustained American imperialism: the belief in justified revenge for an imagined wrong, tyrannical centralization of power, the belief that the United States stands as God's trustee of civilization, an obsession with technology, and the fear of losing. Essentiaᴸ mythology of war making is, of course, the need to view the "Othↄ ᴀs an enemy: "It felt good to eradicate people who, when left to themselves, expressed a preference for peasant agriculture, ancestor worship and cooperative effort" (Norman, 1975, p. 18).

In a recent interview, Keen (1991) elaborated on some of the myths and images of the Gulf War:

> We first kill people with our minds, before we kill them with weapons. Whatever the conflict, the enemy is always the destroyer. We're on God's side; they're barbaric. We're good; they're evil. Its [television's] rapid-fire images help to create a Superbowl atmosphere that puts viewers into a high alpha, dreamlike state that blocks out almost all thought. In the Gulf War this provoked the Nintendo-game atmosphere that made the ultimate dehumanization possible—turning the enemy into a number, a blip on the radar screen. Instead of a bloody conflict, we have a triumph of American technology. (p. 18)

Nonetheless, many writers who have examined how war relies on a culture's mythology also point out that the story is not entirely bleak, for all cultures also have in their "cells," to use Keen's metaphor, a store of peaceful, loving myths. Eisler (this volume), for example, points out that throughout time and across cultures there have been legends and stories of a more peaceful age where not coincidentally men and women lived in harmony. Boulding's (1988) research has also shown that peaceful imagery is by no means absent from the annals of history, although there is currently "a lack of general awareness of this imagery" that "compounds the feeling that war is inevitable" (p. 17). She cites the "Greek celebrations of Elysian fields where former warriors laid weapons aside and walked arm in arm through green meadows discoursing on philosophy and declaiming poetry," the Norse warriors "who feasted and shared like brothers on the mythological plains of Ida," and the ancient Hebrew prophecy that "swords shall be beaten into plowshares, and nation shall not lift up sword against nation" (Boulding, 1988, pp. 17-18).

Multiculturalism Versus Eurocentrism and Cultural Literacy

Although mythology can undoubtedly be harnessed to contribute to peace, a much more significant arena of cultural transmission that touches virtually everyone, is the educational system. If war thrives on the creation of an enemy Other in our minds and myths, then it stands to reason that learning more about other peoples and cultures will diminish the likelihood of organized aggression or, at the very least, public support for such actions. In the recent Persian Gulf War, for instance, one wonders if the media's demonization of Saddam Hussein and degradation of Islamic/Arab culture would have been so effective if the American public knew more about the history of Middle-Eastern civilizations. As Galtung (1989b) notes, "peaceful education, including socialization, would probably imply exposure to multiple cultures and then a dialogue" (p. 32).

The dialogue between cultures Galtung speaks of would have been very difficult for American journalists covering the Gulf War, since few if any spoke Arabic. According to a Freedom Forum survey of these journalists, designed to be "representative of the diverse media organizations and individuals who covered the war," none of them were fluent in Arabic or even able to conduct an interview in the language. Moreover, many of the journalists interviewed stated that being fluent in the language would have been "an enormous advantage" (Dennis et al., 1991, pp. 26, 33).

The failure of the American educational system in educating people about other cultures has been, since the late 1980s, the subject of a very contentious debate in the United States. To simplify, those defending ideas based on Eurocentrism and cultural literacy have been pitted against the proponents of multiculturalism. In 1988 the publication of two books, in particular, set the terms of the debate: Hirsch's *Cultural Literacy* and Bloom's *The Closing of the American Mind.* Hirsch's work, subtitled "What Every American Needs to Know" argues that at the root of U.S. educational problems lies a lack of shared knowledge and information, possession of which would give people cultural literacy. His solution is preservation of mainstream culture through a nationally established core curriculum. An idea of what this curriculum would emphasize can be gleaned from the appendix to his book, which contains a list of nearly 4,000 facts, concepts, and sayings that every culturally literate American should know. The blatantly Eurocentric bias of this list, as well as Hirsch's palpable distrust of multilingual and multicultural education reveal the true objective of his argument: to restore respect for Western civilization within American education. One of the strongest critiques of Hirsch's work is its implication "that blacks and other minorities will continue to suffer social and economic disabilities as long as they fail to obtain 'cultural literacy' " (Clark, 1988, p. 147).

Bloom's theses present a much more sweeping indictment of the American educational system, particularly insofar as its "purity" has been tainted by what he perceives to be the after-effects of the 1960s. He is against feminism and affirmative action for minorities and in favor of the restoration of Western philosophy as the core principle of American education. His ideas have been mainly targeted for their elitism and his deification of Western-based education.

Multiculturalism, which has been a direct response to the increasing demands of minorities and women in academic institutions for more cross-cultural and gender-sensitive curricula, implies a very different educational agenda. Although the term *multicultural* has been in use in educational circles since the late 1960s, the writings of Hirsch and Bloom upped the ante, so to speak, and brought the debate into national prominence. Multiculturalists argue that the traditional teaching of history, philosophy, the social sciences (and even the exact sciences) has privileged perspectives and contributions from white men of European origin. Two components of this chapter figure prominently in the debate: racism and sexism. The initial call for a multicultural curriculum in the late 1980s was closely linked to the movement for a more Afrocentric view of history that did not neglect past contributions (e.g., reclaiming of Egyptian civilization by African scholars) or the more recent work of African-American writers, scientists, and statesmen (Asante, 1988; Bernal, 1987, 1991). Opponents of sexism have similar grievances against the educational system, noting that women's lives and work, both past and present, are denigrated if not denied in the traditional Eurocentric approach to history and the sciences (Weiler, 1988).[5]

Arguments for and against multiculturalism have not been confined to the higher ranks of the educational system. In June 1991, a New York State panel of experts produced a report on how to revamp the public schools' teaching of social studies to give greater recognition to the role of nonwhite cultures in American society. The report, titled "One Nation, Many Peoples: A Declaration of Cultural Interdependence," advocated, for example, teaching American schoolchildren why their traditional Thanksgiving holiday, celebrating the "discovery" of America is a day of mourning for native Americans. The celebration, in 1992, of the quincentennary of Columbus's landing in the Americas, in fact, served as a sort of rallying cry for multiculturalists in both educational and art circles. Many "counterquincentennary" activities were organized around the country.

Some of the most intense controversy about multiculturalism has, however, focused on institutions of higher learning. Since 1988, several of the country's elite universities, including Stanford, the University of Michigan, and the University of Texas, have revamped their curricula to include more courses sensitive to issues of race, ethnicity, and gender. The dialectics of struggle have brought into the fray well-known intellectuals such as the historian Schlesinger, who argues against the so-called politicization of history and the "reduction of history to ethnic cheerleading." In a coauthored letter, Schlesinger writes that

> the Western tradition is the source of ideas of individual freedom and political democracy to which most of the world now aspires. The West has committed its share of crimes against humanity, but the Western democratic philosophy also contains in its essence the means of exposing crimes and producing reforms. (Ravitch & Schlesinger, 1990, p. E7; see also Schlesinger, 1991)

Former Reagan administration heavyweights such as William Bennett, ex-secretary of education, and Lynn Cheney, head of the National Endowment for the Humanities,[6] have also been outspoken. Both Bennett and Cheney have been telling anyone who will listen that the current crisis of American education can best be met by a Western-based core curriculum.

Others, however, have argued much more convincingly that people in the United States need to know more—and not less—about other cultures. In 1988, Simonson and Walker edited an eloquent response to Hirsch and Bloom called *Graywolf Annual Five: Multi-Cultural Literacy.* In the introduction to this anthology of writings by African-Americans, native Americans, women, and Hispanics, the editors state their case:

> We do take issue with Hirsch's and Bloom's definition of what (or whose) culture should be taught. We are alarmed by the number of people who are so enthusiastically in agreement with the Hirsch/Bloom argument that they fail to discern its overridingly static, and so shallow, definition of culture. Both writers seem to think that most of what constitutes contemporary American and world culture was immaculately conceived by a few men in Greece, around 900 BC, came to its full expression in Europe a few centuries later, and began to decline around the middle of the nineteenth century. (Simonson & Walker, 1988, p. x)

From the above examples, it should be evident why the idea of cultural equality for all races and both genders is a central aspect of a vision of a peaceful world.

But there is a more explicit connection between the debate on Western civilization and war. Veeser, of Columbia University, researched the origin of Western civilization courses in this country and found that they were a direct outcome of preparation for war. In 1918, during World War I, the U.S. War Department drew up a plan for subsidizing male undergraduate education and guaranteeing a pool of officer recruits. Under this plan, known as the Students Army Training Corps (SATC), recruits were subsidized to attend colleges and universities. The schools, in return for a much-needed boost in enrollments, helped establish an SATC curriculum, of which one war issues course came to be a key component. This course was designed to provide students with a cross-disciplinary approach to "the historical and economic causes of war . . . and the national ideals of the various countries engaged in the struggle" (Veeser, 1989, pp. 18-19).

After the war, Columbia University was so taken with its war issues course that it decided to incorporate it into a peace-time curriculum, but under a new name: "Introduction to Contemporary Civilization." It was first brought out during the Red Scare of 1919, for as Veeser notes "Dean Hawkes [actual name] clearly considered Bolshevism a greater threat than Kaiserism." This quickly evolved into a Western civilization course that became the model for similar offerings at other universities around the country.

Cultural Democracy

One of the most powerful antidotes to the current attempts to establish Western civilization as *Civilization* is to promote the concept of cultural democracy. Cultural democracy has acquired greater importance in recent years because of the multiethnic composition of many societies and the need to protect the rights of all groups: minorities as well as disfavored people such as women and the poverty-stricken. One researcher even refers to cultural democracy as "the lab of peace" wherein "consensus and separation coexist" (Vitanyi, 1986, pp. 217-219).

In the United States, the Alliance for Cultural Democracy (ACD) actively promotes the idea that all social groups should be able to participate in the country's culture. Begun in 1976 as the Neighborhood Arts Program National Organizing Committee (NAPNOC), its founding purpose was to give community artists a voice in cultural politics. Since this beginning, it has expanded its concerns to include progressive cultural workers in all locations and occupations of culture. In 1983, the organization's name was changed to reflect its present organizing principle: cultural democracy.[7]

The ACD defines this principle in the following terms:

> Cultural democracy means that culture is an essential human need and that each person and community has the right to a culture or cultures of their choice; that all communities should have equitable access to the material resources of the commonwealth for their cultural expression; that cultural values and policies should be decided in public debate with the guaranteed participation of all communities. (Cultural Democracy, 1988, p. 2)

One of ACD's projects is the promotion of a new form of cultural policy. The ACD is now circulating a "Draft Declaration of Cultural Human Rights." The opening "foundations" of this declaration clearly place cultural human rights within the context of peace and justice:

> In order to advance the struggle for those political and economic rights recognized by all people in pursuit of a democratic, just and peaceful world . . . in order to supplant passivity with creative action, desecration with beauty, waste with husbandry, alienation with community, exploitation with cooperative harmony, and cultural chauvinism with appreciation and respect for diversity. . . . We declare and now act to guarantee the cultural rights of all peoples. (Draft Declaration of Cultural Human Rights, 1988, p. 1)

On the practical level, one of the most important aspects of the ACD declaration is its emphasis on the need to promote popular participation in cultural policymaking. Reflecting the long experience of American cultural activists, it acknowledges the following reality: Cultural policymaking is dominated by corporate and government elites who use public monies to buttress the dominant culture. Against this reality, the ACD proposes a genuine *public* policy that does not exclude the people:

> We believe that written and unwritten public policy must acknowledge that all people are entitled to their rights: to choose to participate in public debate, regardless of gender, sexual preference, income, class, ethnicity, geography or culture. (Draft Declaration of Cultural Human Rights, 1988, p. 4)

Finally, the ACD declaration does not ignore the important role of the media in its concept of cultural democracy. Thus *people's policymaking* (my term) must replace the notion of "mass communication" (which only involves the masses as receivers) with public communication. Reform of the mass media would mean not only structural changes in their ownership and operation but also increased access of all social groups to the production and circulation of media messages[8] (Draft Declaration of Cultural Human Rights, 1988, pp. 2-3).

Information in War and Peace

It is not by accident that the concept of cultural democracy invokes the mass media, because, as already stated, both forces are clearly linked. There is a very substantial body of literature, much of which will be reviewed in subsequent chapters, examining the mass media's role in the war system. An overview of this role can be broken down into three aspects: (1) the military-industrial-communication complex; (2) structural-operational aspects of the mass media; and (3) news values, sources, and censorship.

The Military-Industrial-Communication Complex

Writers who have tried to establish why the mass media generally support war much more than peace have come up with a number of different reasons. The first point of reference is what is commonly referred to as the military-industrial-communications complex. First mention of the military-industrial complex (without the communication component) was made by President Eisenhower (1982) in his farewell address in January 1961:

> In the councils of government, we must guard against the acquisition of unwarranted influence, whether sought or unsought, by the military-industrial complex. The potential for the disastrous rise of misplaced power exists and will persist. (pp. 543-545)

Since Eisenhower's prescient speech in 1961, a new component has been added to the military-industrial complex: communication. By the mid-1970s critical communication writers had coined a new term: *the military-industrial-communication complex.* In 1986, the intersection between communication, industry, and the military became most apparent when General Electric (GE), one of the world's major defense contractors, bought RCA and with it NBC. Like many multinationals, GE is not above corporate chicanery: In 1983 it was indicted in a court of law for defrauding the government and had to pay several million dollars in fines. In July 1992,

GE was again found guilty of defrauding the government in a scandal involving the sale of military jet engines to Israel, and had to play close to $10 million in fines (Stevenson, 1992, p. D1).

In their examination of GE's role in the military-industrial-communication complex, Lee and Solomon (1990) are forthright: "GE and other military contractors made out like bandits during the Reagan administration, which presided over the largest peacetime military buildup in U.S. history. And bandits is exactly what they are, as the Pentagon procurement scandal . . . amply demonstrates" (p. 80).

Other major media also participate body and soul in this complex. Again, Lee and Solomon (1990):

> Cap Cities/ABC and CBS are interlinked with other huge conglomerates that are part of the military-industrial complex. The boards of directors of the Big Three are composed of executives, lawyers, financiers and former government officials who represent the biggest banks and corporations in the U.S., including military and nuclear contractors. . . . There are numerous interlocks between the board of directors of the *New York Times* and the nuclear industry, which partially explains why it has been a fanatical supporter of nuclear weapons. (p. 81)

Theologian Fore (1991) notes that the interests of the military-industrial-communication complex played a direct role in television's coverage of the Gulf War:

> Sponsors also greatly influence the kind of entertainment and the way news and information is portrayed. Dupont, IBM, AT&T and IT&T, for example, are all major sponsors on TV and all have major stakes in the public support for the development of high-tech armaments. Who benefits from coverage which celebrates smart bombs and surgical strikes? (p. 52)

Structural-Operational Aspects of the Mass Media

The media component of the power complex described above is built on a very specific structure of ownership and financing. This structure is based on four interrelated foundations. First, American media are almost exclusively financed by the private sector. Although many other industrialized countries, driven by the privatization imperatives of late-20th-century monopoly capitalism, are now turning over public broadcasting to the private sector (especially in Western Europe), it is nonetheless an historical fact that there is virtually no other country in the world that has had such an exclusive control of its media by private-sector interests.

Second, the mass news media in the United States depend on the advertising industry for the majority of their revenue. The corresponding figures are as follows: broadcasting, almost 100% dependence on advertising; newspapers, 75%; and general-circulation magazines, 50% (Bagdikian, 1987). Third, the mass media in the United States are not just purveyors of news and entertainment but are all large *corporations*. As Bagdikian (1987) emphasized, more than one half of the dominant media firms are *Fortune* 500 companies. Thus it is much more appropriate to think in terms of *"New York Times,* Inc."; *"Washington Post,* Inc."; and "CBS, Inc." than to think simply of newspapers and networks. Gerbner, dean emeritus of the Annenberg School of Communications has used the term *private ministry of culture* to refer to corporate domination of American media. What this means to Gerbner (1987) bears repeating:

> The mechanisms that govern the mass media marketplace are those of property and money. Such mechanisms include technology, capital investment needed to enter the communications marketplace, reliance on corporate sponsors, and relative insulation from democratic (public) participation in policy-making. (p. 15)

The fourth and final point in this structural survey of mass media monopolization is as follows: The number of major news media is steadily declining. Bagdikian (1987) detailed this phenomenon: "Despite 25,000 media outlets in the United States, 29 corporations control most of the business in daily newspapers, magazines, television, books and motion pictures" (p. 7). The Time-Warner merger in 1989, creating the biggest megamedia conglomerate in the world, not only reduced this number to 28 but offered ominous support for those who project a near future when only a handful of massive firms will control all major media outlets.

What does the above analysis of the mass media have to do with war and peace? In the 20th century, decisions to engage in organized violence against another country (war) have been made by governments, corporations, and elite policymakers. If it is true that the mass media are intimately tied into this process, then it is essential to understand how the media function; that is, their basic structures as outlined above. To take the example of the Gulf War, public opinion polls indicated that before the onset of hostilities in January 1991, the

American public was split 50-50 about whether or not the country should go to war or continue economic sanctions (Osborn & Davis, 1991, p. 15). During this crucial period, when public opinion was being formed, if antiwar voices had been heard in the mass media, the outcome could have been drastically different.

Although the *reasons* why these voices were denied access to the media would involve a complex discussion of the American political process and social history, it is clear that this denial of access was implemented through the structures of the mass media. To put it baldly, ordinary peace-minded citizens and the peace movement could not be heard in the mass media because in the United States they are controlled by a diminishing number of large, private corporations that depend on advertising and not the public for their survival. A structural overview of the media also helps us to understand what changes are necessary if a peace system is to be built.

Our definition of *peace* in this peace system has, however, not been limited to war. The concept of positive peace implies that structural situations of injustice and inequality are also part of peacelessness. In this connection, several of the operational aspects of the mass media should be mentioned here, particularly because they impact both minorities and women.

Prevailing employment structures in the mass media definitely discriminate against both minorities and women. In 1984, presidential candidate Jesse Jackson denounced the racial discrimination of our major media: "92% of all US newspapers have no black editors, and 61% have no blacks in their news rooms. After 61 years of weekly publication, *Time* still refuses to license a black person to obtain a senior executive position at the magazine" (Cockburn, 1984, p. 6).

Since 1984, the situation has not improved as shown in statistics from 1988 cited in *The Minority Trendsletter* (1989):

Estimates are that people of color will comprise 25 to 30% of the population by the year 2000; last year, only 7% of newsroom employees were Black, Latino, Asian and Native American, up just half a percent from the year before. Fifty-five percent of the dailies still have no minority newsroom staff. (Bad news: Minorities and the media 20 years after Kerner, 1989, p. 7)

The same survey also reported that in 1985 the Institute for Journalism Education at the University of California, Berkeley, found that 40% of minority journalists planned to leave the field because of dissatisfaction with their prospects of advancement (*The Minority Trendsletter,* 1989, p. 7).

The entertainment industry also discriminates against both minorities and women in its employment patterns. According to a 1989 report by the Writer's Guild titled "Unequal Access, Unequal Pay," the major television companies and movie studios have a "bleak record" in hiring practices of screen writers (cited in Harmetz, 1989, p. C25). Black writers, of whom there are only 101 among 6,396 members, were hired only to write for series featuring black families. In 1987, only 15.5% of the screenwriters at major studios were women. Their median income was $30,000 compared with $47,125 for their male counterparts.

Another report, done by the University of Missouri in 1989 (cited in Rasky, 1989, p. C22) also detailed the sex bias in news companies. Statistics were compiled indicating that although women make up 52% of the U.S. population, they hold only 6% of the top management jobs in the news media, and earn only 92 cents for each dollar earned by men in the profession. The study also showed that in February 1989, women reported 22.2% of the stories on CBS that month, 14.4% of the stories on NBC, and 10.5% of the stories on ABC. The percentage of stories in which women were the subject or the focus of interviews was 13.7% on ABC, 10.2% on CBS, and 8.9% on NBC. Commenting on another study of the front page of 10 major American newspapers, showing that only 11% of the individuals quoted were women and that very few news items even mentioned women, Friedan remarked: "The fact that 52% of the population does not exist on the front page of the newspapers is a symbolic annihilation of women" (quoted in Rasky, 1989, p. C22).

News Values, Sources, and Censorship

Sociologists of the news media often speak of the dominant news values that determine what and how stories are covered. At least two of these dominant values help to understand the media's role in the war system: conflict and objectivity.

The news value of conflict is singled out by many writers as one of the most important, if not the most important, criteria for determining what is newsworthy (Bennet, 1988; Gans, 1980). Since the early 19th century development of a mass, commercial press in the United States, both local and large-scale violence have fed into the news media's thirst for the kind of sensationalism that would increase sales. Although the days of the yellow press and circulation wars are over, the print and broadcast media continue with only somewhat mitigated news criteria. Gerbner (1988) noted: "Violence and crime are the staple diet of commercial news reporting . . . their legitimacy is so well established that their social and political functions are rarely noted" (p. 11).

The conflict criterion of newsworthiness has also been targeted by critics from the south, who, as we shall note in the following section, complain bitterly that their countries are only covered when disaster strikes or there is armed upheaval. Hackett (1989) adds another dimension, noting that "the news value of conflict renders peace groups' efforts at consensus-building non-newsworthy" (p. 14).

The news value of objectivity has a less obvious but no less vital connection to the media's role in the war system. Hackett notes that objectivity is used to justify journalists' aloofness from peace advocates, who are viewed as having an ax to grind. He also states that "objective journalism's respect for 'prevailing social standards of decency and good taste' likely mutes reportage of the brutality of war, and the suffering of victims, helping to turn war into a watchable spectacle rather than an insufferable obsenity" (Hackett, 1989, pp. 10-11, 13; see also, Hackett, 1991).

Bagdikian (1987) traces the origins of objectivity back to the 19th century, emphasizing that it was developed when newspapers became a mass medium, subject to the laws of the marketplace. American newspapers thus became less and less journals of opinion and increasingly came to respond to the commercial logic of offending as few people as possible and playing to the least common denominator, much as television would do in the 20th century.

The intuition that objectivity has kept out of the news coverage of peace issues within a framework of values and morality is supported by authors who emphasize the doctrine's close links to Enlightenment notions of scientific rationality. Schudson (1978), for example, sees objectivity as part of an overall movement toward scientific detachment and the culturewide separation of facts from value. D. Schiller (1979) takes a similar view, noting that in the 19th century, " 'the facts' in turn were equated for the first time with the total mission and ideal content of the newspaper. . . . Beginning in the penny press, news was gathered and written by journalists who now were to become ideally neutral or even invisible" (p. 49). Objectivity thus reflected scientific deference to facts and the idea of science, serving an ultimate public good. Again, D. Schiller (1979): "Objective news accounts thus supported the major intention of the commercial press: to become a chief social agency for the organization of public enlightenment" (p. 49).

Hallin's (1986) study of the media's role in the Vietnam War showed that the ethic of objectivity was used to rationalize the media's commitment to what he calls the national security consensus of the state. Hallin (1986) notes that the *departisanship* of the press "grants to political authorities certain positive rights of access to the news" and acceptance, for the most part, of "the language, agenda, and perspectives of the political 'establishment' " (p. 8).

The selective use of information sources, alluded to by Hallin, is also part of the daily operations of the news media. Although the canon of American journalism whereby officials and experts are always in the know (which most often means "on the Rolodex") supposedly ensures knowledgeable news reporting, in point of fact it excludes women, minorities, dissenting voices, and often, the truth.

There is a very substantial literature on what Gitlin (1980) refers to as the *framing* of news through the use of official information sources (see also Gans, 1980). Schudson (1989) summarizes this literature by concluding, "One study after another comes up with essentially the same observation, and it matters not whether the study is at the national, state or local level—the story of journalism, on a day-to-day basis, is the story of the interaction of reporters and officials" (p. 271).

Bruck (this volume) provides details on one of the most widely circulated recent studies on news sources, which was published by Fairness and Accuracy in Reporting (FAIR) (Hoynes & Croteau, 1989). This report, an extensive study of ABC's *Nightline* news program, shows that the overwhelming majority of guests were white men of the establishment; women, minorities, and representatives of labor and public interest groups were scarcely represented at all.

Both objectivity and reliance on official information sources were operative during the Gulf War. A FAIR study of the media coverage of the war noted: "Usually missing from the news was analysis from a perspective critical of U.S. policy. The media's rule of thumb seemed to be that to support the war was to be objective, while to be anti-war was to carry a bias" (Naureckas, 1991, p. 5). The network's reliance on official sources resulted in "a one-sided procession of retired military brass, ex-government hawks, right-wing pundits and politicians, scholars from think-tanks with generally conservative bents" (Naureckus, 1991, p. 4) The Freedom Forum's extensive study of the most quoted experts in the print and broadcast media from August 1, 1990, through February 28, 1991, also showed that the number one spot was held by Admiral William Cross, former chair, Joint Chiefs of Staff (Dennis et al., 1991, p. 43). The nonstop parade of military analysts on the news was so widespread that it even resulted in some media self-mockery, with a comedian on the popular *Saturday Night Live* show quipping, "You know who I feel sorry for? It's the one retired army colonel who didn't get a job as TV analyst" (Naureckas, 1991, p. 4).

Not surprisingly, what this reliance on official news sources meant was that voices of dissent were shut out of the media. A FAIR survey examining 878 on-air sources during the war used by ABC, CBS, and NBC showed that only one was a representative of a national peace organization; in contrast, seven players from the Super Bowl were asked to comment on the war (Naureckus, 1991, p. 5).

The self-censorship of the news media during the Gulf War should not, however, obscure the very real censorship imposed by the Pentagon. Honed during the invasions of Grenada in 1983 and Panama in 1989, the allied forces engaged in unprecedented wartime censorship, made operative through the use of news pools, official scrutiny of dispatches, and the assignment of military escorts to reporters.[9] The question that begs to be answered is, Why?

The common view, as propounded publicly by pundits and generals, is that the *media* lost the war in Vietnam. Consequently, so the argument goes, the government wanted to ensure that, this time around, public opinion would not be turned against the war in the Gulf by media coverage. But this theory does not hold water. Hallin (1986), whose study of the media's coverage of Vietnam is regarded as one of the definitive works, argues convincingly that this is one of the "most persistent myths" about Vietnam.[10] He states that the media (television in particular) did not present a sober view of the war "until the public, Washington, and the soldiers in the field had already lost confidence that the war could be won. Television, in other words, was more a follower than a leader of public opinion" (Hallin, 1991, p. 21).

A much more persuasive answer than the Vietnam myth to the "Why censorship?" query can be deduced from the work of social critic Chomsky. In a talk delivered at the University of Wisconsin in 1989, Chomsky provided an essential historical review of the manipulation of public opinion by the power elites. According to Chomsky, since at least the early part of the 20th century, there have been consistent efforts at manufacturing consent.[11] These efforts reach their prime precisely during periods of war because, he argues, the American public is basically pacifist and has to be cajoled, duped, and manipulated into going to war (Chomsky, 1989, 1991). In light of the by-no-means-bellicose public opinion polls before the war in the Gulf, this thinking offers a logical explanation for both the war frenzy and censorship of the mass media during this most recent military exploit of the United States.

Television and War

The Bomb and Technopatriotism

It is not surprising that television—the most powerful mass medium—has a clear connection to war. Canadian author Nelson's (1987) study of television and war begins with the premise asserted by radical filmmaker Watkins: "The escalation of the nuclear arms race almost year by year parallels the development of television. There has been a very strange synchronism or timing there, actually" (Nelson, 1987, p. 29). Nelson's book, titled *The Perfect Machine: TV in the Nuclear Age,* makes a compelling case for the argument that television and the bomb, "crawled from the same fruitful womb," to paraphrase a line from Brecht.[12] Nelson points out that in the late 1940s and early 1950s, many of the major corporations that were involved in the manufacture of television sets and sponsorship of early television shows, such as GE, Westinghouse, and Du Pont, were simultaneously working on atomic weaponry.

Nelson's critique of television technology's relationship to war is anchored in a feminist and ethical perspective. Television is thus viewed as a perfect example of an antipeople technology that reifies patriarchal values such as hierarchy, efficiency, and rationality at the expense of the more feminine side of the human psyche; "the part in all of us that is deeply rooted in human feelings, bodily instincts, the rhythms of nature, and sense of containment within the larger forces of earthly life" (Nelson, 1987, p. 21). Her ethical appraisal of television technology comes out of a long tradition of writers such as Ellul, who view the development of technology as stimulating what Kroker refers to as a "hyper-atrophied moral sense" (Kroker, 1984, p. 127). After the bombings of Hiroshima and Nagasaki, censored footage of irradiated Japanese was not made available to the American public until 1980. Instead, television—still in its experimental stage—participated in a carefully orchestrated government strategy of presenting this catastrophe not in terms of the horrendous damage to human beings, but as a feat of technical prowess, what President Truman referred to as "the greatest achievement in organized science in human history." Nelson recalls that once television sets were in most American homes, atomic blasts were never presented in terms of their real-life dangers to human life but rather as picturesque mushroom clouds.

In more recent times, the participation of American television in war has continued along lines very similar to those traced by Nelson. During the 1980s, American television during the Reagan reign fostered *technopatriotism:* government-sponsored television commercials used sophisticated technological gadgetry to sell the administration's "Star Wars." The most awesome conversion of war into technological spectacle was during the Gulf War of 1990-1991. From the earliest weeks in January 1991, when the bombs began to drop on Baghdad, television commentators giddily compared what they saw to Fourth of July fireworks. Because the military censorship of the news media prevented the gathering of hard news, many of the networks entertained viewers with footage from Pentagon files, detailing the sophisticated weaponry being used by the allies. Had this been counterbalanced by real-life scenes of death and destruction, its effect might not have been so mesmerizing. To quote Fore (1991):

> And what did the Gulf War sell? We were inundated with images of *technology:* powerful and exotic aircraft taking to the sky night after night; tanks speeding across the desert, stopping only to shoot at (and always hit) a distant target. In case we missed the point, narrators assured us that the bombs were 'smart' and the strikes 'surgical.' . . . The meaning? That this war was distant, remote and quite separate from our daily lives—which may have been why some people tried so hard to 'sell' the war to others, through yellow ribbons, bumper stickers, and even paid outdoor advertising. (p. 51; emphasis in the original)

Television and Violence

The "primal" connection between television and war, however, is undoubtedly the relationship of the "perfect machine" to individual and group violence in society.

Does research support the popular perception that mass media violence leads to real-life violence? What are the larger societal implications of violence in the media? What policy implications can be drawn? Gerbner (1988), an American researcher who over the last two decades has carried out the most extensive studies on mass media violence, summarized the enormous body of literature on this question for a UNESCO publication (excerpts are reprinted here by permission of UNESCO).

One can begin by stating the obvious: American television is saturated with violence.[13] Moreover, Gerbner's (1988) Cultural Indicators Project, an ongoing analysis of violence on dramatic television begun in 1967, indicates that the 1980s were particularly bad years:

> The index of violence reached its highest level since 1967 . . . in the 1984-85 television season. Eight out of every 10 prime time programs contained violence. The rate of violent incidents was nearly 8 per hour. The 19 year average was 6 per hour. . . . Children in 1984-85 were entertained with 27 violent incidents per hour (the third highest on record). The 19-year average for children's programs was 21 violent acts per hour. (Gerbner, 1988, p. 17)

Another evident but significant observation: American television has been much more violent than that of other countries. As early as 1953, one researcher found that BBC television programming broadcast during a 2-week period had about half as much violence as a sample of television programs broadcast in New York City. A study done in 1987 concluded that imported U.S. programs were about three times as violent as British-made shows (Gerbner, 1988, pp. 17-18).

Women do not fare well in the media's panorama of violence. Gerbner (1988) is one of the few male researchers to focus on women's portrayal on television:

> Males outnumber females by at least 3 to 1 in all major media presentations. Male domination and the related conflict and power-orientation of mainstream media news and fiction provide the social context in which violent representation seems natural and realistic. (p. 15)

Moreover, the Cultural Indicators Project indicated in 1986 that women were much more likely to be presented as victims than men. This gender-bound pattern of violence, as Gerbner (1988) notes, seems "to cultivate a differential sense of vulnerability" (pp. 17, 26) placing a heavier burden of dependence on women.

Needless to say, the most vital question about television's violence is whether or not it is related to real-life acts of aggression. On the one hand, there is an overwhelming body of research indicating that there *is* a relationship between violence on television and real life aggression.

In 1980, an advisory committee from the Surgeon General's Office examined ten years of research and confirmed "the consensus among most of the research community . . . that violence on television does lead to aggressive behavior by children and teenagers who watch the programs" (Gerbner, 1988, pp. 23-25).

Of special relevance to issues of peace were several studies indicating that dramatic violence tended to cultivate "a sense of hierarchical values and forces," (Gerbner, 1988, p. 25) was related to "feelings of apprehension, insecurity and the necessity of war," (Gerbner, 1988, p. 25) and was found to lead to "mistrust . . . a desire to have protective weapons and alienation" (Gerbner, 1988, p. 25).

Nonetheless, like most social scientists, Gerbner is reluctant to infer causality from research on human behavior, that is, to establish a direct relationship between television violence and actual aggression. What Gerbner thinks is the far more significant result of what he calls the "mean and dangerous" world of television is that *all* people—not just those who commit acts of violence—develop a sense of fear, victimization, mistrust, and insecurity, in short a feeling of alienation and gloom. The most radical aspect of Gerbner's analysis is of far-reaching significance: Television's cult of violence keeps intact the social order. Television's effects on individual behavior (e.g., aggression) are thus overshadowed by "the more pervasive functions of demonstrating power and cultivating acceptance of one's 'place' in society's power structure" (Gerbner, 1988, p. 27).

Gerbner also reflected on the role of television in promoting the war in the Gulf. At a conference in Rome in June 1991, he cited television as an obstacle to a truly new order, stating that it was controlled by a "handful of global conglomerates with something to sell and its daily content left the world drenched . . . in expertly choreographed brutality" (cited in Wicker, 1991, p. A29). Gerbner also noted that the worldwide "tidal wave of television" produced support for political decisions leading to wars, from populations conditioned to believe that violence could improve their security (cited in Wicker, 1991, p. A29).

Finally, Gerbner's (1992) prognosis on television's role in the new world order of the West merits close attention:

> An overkill of violent imagery helps to train the military mind and to mobilize support for taking charge of the unruly at home and abroad. Bombarding viewers by violent images of a mean and dangerous world, without illuminating the real costs of violence and war, is, in the last analysis, an instrument of intimidation and terror. It was indispensable to the triumph

of instant history in the Persian Gulf. It *is* a preview of the shape of things to come in a unipolar world with no effective democratic opposition or geopolitical counter-force. (pp. 257-258) (emphasis in the original)

Cultural Domination and Resistance in the South

The contribution of information and culture to perpetuating peaceless-ness has had enormous effects on the countries of the south. Some of the most important actors in the cultural domination of the south have been transnational corporations (TNCs). It was in the 1960s that the TNCs, whose power often rivals that of small nation-states, emerged most forcefully on the world scene. These corporations, by definition, must rely on the use of advanced communication technology—satellites, computers, fiber optics—to ensure the smooth functioning of their far-flung operations. Moreover, communication TNCs (which include not only such media behemoths as Time-Warner but also electronic manufacturers such as GE, IBM, and AT&T) play a special role in the political economy of U.S. foreign relations: They sell American media and culture around the world as well as the electronic hardware for the other TNCs' operations. Because of the symbiotic relationship between the U.S. government and the TNCs, defense of the TNCs has historically been an essential component of U.S. foreign policy.[14]

However, since the end of World War II, the TNCs have not been the only new global actors on the world scene. National liberation move-ments, from Vietnam to South Africa to El Salvador, have contested Western hegemony, including the power of the TNCs. An important part of this struggle against Western hegemony has taken place precisely in the arena of culture and communication. More than a decade before the West popularized the term *new world order,* the countries of the south had used precisely this phrase to call for global changes in international communication. In effect, since 1976, the south has called for nothing short of a New World Information and Communication Order (NWICO).

The demand for a NWICO, although officially launched in 1976, was the result of a long-standing concern with cultural and information sovereignty that had been on the agenda of the Non-Aligned Movement since its founding in 1955 (Singham & Hune, 1986). By the mid-1970s, leaders of former colonies in Africa, Asia, and Latin America were con-scious of the fact that formal political independence did not necessarily prevent the continuation of cultural colonization, which, in turn, dove-tailed with ties forged by economic dependence. Although the Non-Aligned Movement was the originator of the call for a NWICO, it was taken up most forcefully at the main UN agency responsible for international communication: UNESCO. Beginning in 1976, under the tutelage of Director-General Amadou Mahtar-M'Bow, of Senegal, UNESCO lent its considerable backing to this movement.[15]

The NWICO debate at first centered on what came to be known as the *news flow* question. The major Western international news services—AP and UPI of the United States, Agence France Presse of France, and Reuters of the United Kingdom—were criticized for their monopoly control over the flow of news to and from developing countries and exercising it from a limited perspective reflecting the economic and cultural interests of the industrialized nations. The Western press was repeatedly attacked for creating negative stereotypes of the third world that did very little to promote peace and understanding among peoples. Expressions such as "coups and earthquakes" were frequently used to describe the crisis reporting of third world events.

The flow of television programming was soon incorporated into the debate, in large measure owing to a study by two Finnish researchers, Nordenstreng and Varis (1974). Published by UNESCO in 1974, their study demonstrated that a few Western nations, with the United States topping the list, dominated the flow of television programs around the world.

Gradually, other concerns about unbalanced communication flows were integrated into the NWICO debate. Imbalances in the assignment of spectrum frequencies and orbital slots for future satellites were taken up not only at UNESCO but at the International Telecommunications Union (ITU), which also became a forum for third world concerns in the 1970s and 1980s. The international flow of advertising and information technology, also controlled by the West, became increasingly important issues.

In 1978, UNESCO's member states adopted an historic declaration on the mass media, which embodied many of the concerns cited above. The declaration clearly established a connection between the movement for world peace and the NWICO movement, as shown by its title: *The Declaration of Fundamental Principles Concerning the Contribution of the Mass Media to Strengthening Peace and International Understanding, to the Promotion of Human Rights and to Countering Racialism, Apartheid and Incitement to War.*

Article III of the Declaration specified the role of the media in peace:

The mass media have an important contribution to make to the strengthening of peace and international understanding . . . in countering . . . incitement to war. . . . The mass media, by disseminating information on the
aims, aspirations, cultures and needs of all peoples, contribute to eliminate
ignorance and misunderstanding between peoples. (UNESCO, 1979, p. 13)

Becker (1982) and Varis (1981), whose writings played an important
role in the NWICO debate, explicitly connected their work to issues of
international peace. Becker (1982) extended the concept of structural
violence to unequal information relations between the core and periphery
countries and concluded, "Only when the mass media open up to a process
of democratization on all levels—to the so-called New International Information Order—will the mass media fulfill their functions as contributors
to a peaceful society" (p. 227). Varis, who was director of the Tampere
Peace Research Institute in Finland during his involvement in the NWICO
movement, also connected media flow studies to world peace. His study,
"Peace and Communication in the Light of the Flow Studies," starts from
the premise that "very much depends on the mass media and international
communications what will be the international climate accelerating or retard-
ing such processes as detente, disarmament, and peace" (Varis, 1981, p. 1).

The most concrete treatment of the NWICO issues was what became
known as the MacBride Report, produced by an international commission
of researchers and media professionals from around the world (UNESCO,
1980). The MacBride commission, chaired by the late Sean MacBride,
winner of both the Nobel and Lenin peace prizes, was set up by UNESCO
toward the end of the 1970s to define the deficiencies of the old order. Its
findings zeroed in on the global information imbalances that have made
many countries of the south dependent on the north. Particular attention
was paid to the control exercised by communication transnationals. Although the work of the commission became embroiled in north-south and
east-west controversies, its report still stands as a major historical document on the NWICO movement.

Demands of the south for a new information order embodied in the
MacBride Report were met by consistent hostility from the Western
world, with the United States leading the attack. The NWICO movement, which had been supported by the then-Socialist bloc well into the
1980s, was systematically portrayed as a Communist plot to shackle the
free press throughout the world (Roach, 1987a, 1987b).

After a massive press campaign against UNESCO, linked to congressional and private sector lobbying against the organization, the United

States withdrew in 1985; a year later the United Kingdom followed suit.[16] In 1987, a Spanish pro-Westerner, Mayor, was elected Director-General of UNESCO. Since that time, UNESCO has jettisoned the concept of a NWICO, with Mayor openly disavowing it as a violation of human rights (Roach, 1990). Although the organization now adheres to the free flow of information—the cornerstone of U.S. international communication policy—there is still significant support for the movement. In the United States, the Union for Democratic Communication (UDC) has been one of the most steadfast supporters of the NWICO. Internationally, the World Association for Christian Communication (WACC) has played a very important role, particularly in backing the grass-roots stage of the movement. The International Organization of Journalists (IOJ), one of the original backers of the NWICO, has also continued to offer its vital support.

One of the most significant developments in the evolution of the NWICO movement is directly linked to the people's power orientation that informs this chapter. Many advocates of the NWICO are now calling for a genuine grass-roots movement that can overcome the elitist contradictions of the past. It is increasingly believed that the power structures of nation states (including governments of the south and the United Nations) may preclude genuine democratization of communication (Sparks & Roach, 1990).

At a MacBride round table[17] on the NWICO, held in Istanbul in June 1991, a declaration was adopted that connected the movement to many of the concerns of this book. One passage, in particular, reads,

> Great efforts must now be made to develop a culture of non-violence, of dialogue and negotiations, practicing the art of democracy, and promoting a culture of peace. This effectively means to demilitarize cultural products and processes. Politically, alternative systems of peace and security need to be established, both on the global and regional levels. The United Nations, and especially, UNESCO, should play a central role in this, thus becoming what they were always meant to be, peace-making and peace-keeping bodies. (The Istanbul Statement of the MacBride Round Table on Communications, 1992, p. 32)

What Is to Be Done?

In thinking of the query "What is to be done?" I am reminded of what Gertrude Stein is reported to have said on her deathbed. When asked

"What is the answer?" she replied "What is the question?" Although this overview has addressed the peace question at several levels, including both peace in the positive and peace in the negative sense as well as both culture and the mass media, I have no certitude that the right question has been posed. Nor do I know if I have been radical enough, in the sense of really going to the roots of the problem. Although referring specifically to the "woman question," the words of feminist legal scholar Mackinnon (1987) come to mind:

> Think the determinism of structural force and the possibility of freedom at the same time. Look for the deepest meanings in the least elevated places. Be more radical than anyone has ever been about the unknown, because what has never has been asked is probably what we most need to know. Take the unknowable more seriously than anyone ever has. (p. 9)

Before looking at a possible path to the unknowable, let us briefly resume some of the knowns. As Galtung rightly states in the preface to this volume, many people are presently engaged in peacemaking activities around the world. Therefore any attempt at answering the question "What is to be done?" must begin by acknowledging that much is already being done. Popular culture, for example, often derided for contributing to sexism and racism, can also be a conveyor of peace. Peace researchers have even found messages of hope in somewhat unlikely places, such as rock lyrics (see McClearey, 1991). There are many other less spontaneous, organized efforts to direct the media and communication systems toward peace. Of the many activities that are too numerous to list here, Peacenet and Paper Tiger Television come immediately to mind. Peacenet, a computer-based communication system that allows peace activists to communicate globally via a phone call, was widely used during the Persian Gulf War. Activists and researchers used Peacenet to exchange information not available in the mass media, to organize protests, and to send messages of solidarity. Paper Tiger Television, which was founded to counter the myths of the information society, presents a weekly call-in program with a critical reading of the mass media. During the Gulf War, an affiliated organization, Deep Dish network, aired a 10-part Gulf Project series. It also transmitted countercelebratory programs on Columbus's conquest of the New World throughout 1992. Outside of the United States, in late 1991, a group of journalists associated with the UN Peace University in Costa Rica, constituted the International Journalists Association for Peace (AIPP), whose objective is to promote a culture of peace.

In addition to organizations such as the UDC, there are a number of other institutes set up to create a more democratic media system within the United States and to offer solidarity on international media issues: FAIR; the Institute for Media Analysis (IMA); the Alternative Media Information Center; the Center for War, Peace, and the News Media; and the National Alliance of Third World Journalists (see the Appendix).

Another organizational effort to change the communication landscape in the United States has been launched by Gerbner and a group of like-minded researchers and activists. Some of the aims of the Cultural Environment Movement are as follows: to abolish existing concentration of ownership, to extend cultural liberation to other countries, to promote media literacy, and to place cultural policymaking issues on the sociopolitical agenda.[18]

It is quite clear, nonetheless, that the peace question goes well beyond the scope of the media, communication, or even the more wide-ranging concept of culture. It is here that one can return to the idea of "looking for the deepest meanings in the least elevated places," of taking the unknowable more seriously than ever before.

The best—perhaps the only—hope for creating a different, more peaceful world lies with the excluded, the marginalized, the victims, the grassroots movements, which have their own "situated knowledge" to communicate to us. A thinker of the 1960s, Marcuse (1964), explains why:

> Underneath the conservative popular base is the substratum of the outcasts and outsiders, the exploited and persecuted of other races and other colors, the unemployed and the unemployable. They exist outside the democratic process; their life is the most immediate and the most real need for ending intolerable conditions and institutions. Thus their opposition is revolutionary even if their consciousness is not. Their opposition hits the system from without and is therefore not deflected by the system; it is an elementary force which violates the rules of the game and, in doing so, reveals it as a rigged game. . . . The fact that they start refusing to play the game may be the fact which marks the beginning of the end of a period. (pp. 256-257)

The difficult task before us, therefore, is to learn to listen to what this substratum is saying. The path to peace most surely lies in their direction.

Notes

1. For example, at a conference on popular culture, sponsored by the American Enterprise Institute, in Washington D.C., conservative critic Wattenberg stated that the

remote-control zapper was "one of the great democratic instruments in history" (quoted in Grimes, 1992, p. C17).

2. In an article titled "Why We Fight," on the work of a University of Michigan professor, a typical view of the biological determinists is presented: "But why does humankind fight in general? To answer, 'It's human nature,' is a simplistic response—except when it's the preliminary answer of an evolutionary biologist like Bobbi S. Low. Habits of thought and behavior have evolved over the course of millions of years, Low says, giving primates a taste for fighting that is just as natural as our preference for candy bars over rhubarb leaves" (Why we fight, 1991, p. 1).

3. After its adoption in 1986, the Seville Statement was subsequently endorsed by many organizations including the following: Psychologists for Social Responsibility, the American Psychological Association, the American Anthropological Association, the International Society for Research on Aggression, the Society for the Psychological Study of Social Issues, the American Association of Counseling and Development, and Movimiento por la Vida y la Paz (Argentina).

4. I would like to thank Andrew Calabrese for his helpful comments on this section.

5. For an excellent analysis of Eurocentrism, see Amin (1989).

6. The husband of Lynne Cheney was the Bush administration's Secretary of Defense, Richard Cheney.

7. Information on the ACD may be obtained by writing to the following address: Alliance for Cultural Democracy / P. O. Box 7591 / Minneapolis, MN 55407. Information on the ACD's Draft Declaration may be obtained by writing Judy Branfman / 27 Parkton Road / No. 2 / Jamaica Plains, MA 02130 or Lisa Knauer / 234 E. 5th St. Apt. D / New York, NY 10003.

8. For another treatment of the concept of cultural democracy, see Adams and Goldbard (1988).

9. For overall analysis of the media coverage of the war, including details on the use of pools, see Dennis et al. (1991), Mowlana, Gerbner, and Schiller (1992), MacArthur (1992), and Fialka (1992). The following journals and magazines have also brought out issues on the media and the Gulf War: Media & Values (Fall 1991, no. 56), Media Development (October 1991, special issue), Propaganda Review (Fall, 1991, no. 8), and Columbia Journalism Review (March/April 1991). For an excellent "manual," useful for both researchers and activists deciphering primarily the French-language media coverage of the war, see Collon (1992). For an analysis of how the war represents the apotheosis of the military-industrial-communication complex, see Mattelart (1992).

10. Other writers, such as MacDonald (1985, pp. 176-178), concur with Hallin.

11. The phrase manufacturing consent is also used in a book on the political economy of the media (Herman & Chomsky, 1988).

12. "Arturo Ui," referring to Adolf Hitler: "Let none of us exalt too soon, the womb is fruitful from which this one crawled"; from Brecht, The Resistable Rise of Arturo Ui.

13. Violence is defined as hurting and killing, or threatening to do so, in any way and in any context.

14. It can be argued that the TNCs are no longer so exclusively associated with American hegemony. There are many more players in the field, and joint ventures among American, European, Japanese corporations are now common. This is one aspect of what is often referred to as the globalization trend (Roach, 1992a).

15. For a full summary of this debate, see MacBride and Roach (1989). A very important literature on the NWICO has been produced, particularly from writers in the

south. Most of the following are in this category: Arrieta, 1980; Gonzales Manet, 1979; Gunaratne, 1988; Ibrahim, 1981; Mankekar, 1981; Masmoudi, 1986; Nordenstreng, 1984; Reyes Matta, 1977; Somavia, 1979. *Development Dialogue* (Uppsala) published several issued on the NWICO in 1976 (nos. 1 & 2) and 1981 (no. 2). For two bibliographies on the NWICO, see: Roach, 1985, and Roach, 1992b.

16. Several books have been published dealing with the U.S. press campaign against UNESCO and the NWICO (e.g., Giffard, 1989; Preston, Herman, & Schiller, 1989).

17. For the texts of the statements adopted at the MacBride round table, see Traber and Nordenstreng (1992). For an overview of recent events related to the NWICO, see Mowlana and Roach (1992).

18. Information on the Cultural Environment Movement can be obtained by writing George Gerbner, The Annenberg School for Communication, University of Pennsylvania, 3620 Walnut Street, Philadelphia, PA 19104.

References

Adams, D., & Goldbard, A. (1988). Cultural democracy: A new cultural policy for the United States. In M. Raskin & C. Hartman (Eds.), *Winning America: Ideas and leadership for the 1990s*. Boston: South End Press.

Alger, C. F. (1989, July). Peace studies at the crossroads: Where else? *The Annals of the American Academy of Political and Social Science, 504,* 117-127.

Amin, S. (1989). *Eurocentrism*. New York: Monthly Review Press.

Arrieta, M. (1980). *Obstáculos para un nuevo orden informativo internacional*. Mexico City: Editorial Nueva Imagen.

Asante, M. K. (1988). *Afrocentricity*. Trenton, NJ: Africa World Press.

Bad news: Minorites and the media 20 years after Kerner. (1989, Spring). *The Minority Trendsetter, 2*(1), 6-8.

Bagdikian, B. (1987). *The media monopoly*. Boston: Beacon Press.

Barthes, R. (1972). *Mythologies*. New York: Noonday Press.

Becker, J. (1982). Communication and peace. The empirical and theoretical relations between two categories in social sciences. *Journal of Peace Research, 19*(3), 227-240.

Bennet, W. L. (1988). *News: The politics of illusion*. New York: Longman.

Bernal, M. (1987). *Black Athena. Vol. I: The Afroasiatic roots of classical civilization: The fabrication of ancient Greece, 1785-1985*. New Brunswick, NJ: Rutgers University Press.

Bernal, M. (1991). *Black Athena. Vol. II: The archaeological and documentary evidence*. New Brunswick, NJ: Rutgers University Press.

Bloom, A. (1988). *The closing of the American mind*. New York: Simon & Schuster.

Boulding, E. (1988). Image and action in peace building. *Journal of Social Issues, 44*(2), 17-37.

Brock-Utne, B. (1985). *Educating for peace*. New York: Pergamon Press.

Carey, J. W. (1989). *Communication as culture: Essays on media and society*. Boston: Unwin Hyman.

Chomsky, N. (1989, March 15). Manufacturing consent: The political economy of the mass media. Talk delivered at the University of Wisconsin, Madison. (Videotape available from The Madison Media Collective / Worthwhile Films / 104 King Street / Madison, WI 53703.)

Chomsky, N. (1991, Fall). Twentieth century American propaganda. *The Propaganda Review* (8), 8-11, 37-44.

Clark, C. (1988). Ideas, history and the crisis in education. *Radical History Review, 42,* 144-154.

Cockburn, A. (1984, July 7-14). Old world information order. *The Nation.* pp. 6-7.

Collon, M. (1992). *Attention médias! Les médiamensonges du Golfe. Manuel anti-manipulation.* Brussels: Editions EPO.

Cultural Democracy. (1988, Summer). *Cultural democracy.* Newsletter of the Alliance for Cultural Democracy, *36,* 2.

Dennis, E. E., Stebenne, D., Pavlik, J., Thalimer, M., LaMay, C., Smillie, D., FitsSimon, M., Gazsi, S., & Rachlin, S. (1991). *The media at war: The press and the Persian Gulf conflict.* New York: Gannett Foundation Media Center.

Draft declaration of cultural human rights, A. (1988). (mimeograph). Minneapolis: Alliance for Cultural Democracy.

Eisenhower, D. D. (1982). Farewell address, January 17, 1961. In R. Hofstadter & B. Hofstadter (Eds.), *Great issues in American history.* New York: Vintage Books.

Eskola, C. F. (1987). Human consciousness and violence. In R. Varynynen (Ed.), *The quest for peace: Transcending collective violence and war among societies, cultures and states* (pp. 19-31). London: Sage.

Fialka, J. J. (1992). *Hotel warriors: Covering the Gulf War.* Baltimore: Johns Hopkins University Press.

Fore, W. F. (1991, October). The shadow war in the Gulf. *Media Development.* (Special Issue: *Reporting the Gulf War*), pp. 51-52.

Galtung, J. (1968). Peace. In D. Sills (Ed.), *International encyclopedia of social sciences* (pp. 487-496). New York: Macmillan.

Galtung, J. (1986). Peace theory: An introduction. In E. Laszlo & J. Y. Yoo (Eds.), *World encyclopedia of peace* (pp. 251-260). New York: Pergamon Press.

Galtung, J. (1989a, May). Plenary address presented to the Annual Conference of the International Communications Association, San Francisco.

Galtung, J. (1989b). Cultural violence. Unpublished manuscript, University of Hawaii, Manoa.

Gans, H. J. (1980). *Deciding what's news.* New York: Vintage Books.

Gerbner, G. (1987, Fall). Minority culture, the USA, and the "free marketplace of ideas." *The National Forum,* 15-17.

Gerbner, G. (1988). *Violence and terror in the mass media* (Reports and Papers on Mass Communication, No. 101). Paris: UNESCO.

Gerbner, G. (1992). Persian Gulf war: The movie. In H. Mowlana, G. Gerbner, & H. Schiller (Eds.), *Triumph of the image: The media's war in the Persian Gulf—a global perspective.* (pp. 243-265). Boulder, CO: Westview Press.

Giffard, A. (1989). *UNESCO and the media.* New York: Longman.

Gitlin, T. (1980). *The whole world is watching: Mass media in the making and the unmaking of the new left.* Berkeley: University of California Press.

Gonzalez Manet, E. (1979). *Descolonización de la información.* Prague: International Organization of Journalists.

Greenhouse, C. (1987). Cultural perspectives on war. In R. Varynynen (Ed.), *The quest for peace: Transcending collective violence and war among societies, cultures and states* (pp. 32-47). London: Sage.

Grimes, W. (1992, March 11). American culture examined as a force that grips the world. *New York Times,* p. C17.

Gunaratne, S. (1988). *Global communication and dependency: Links between the NIEO and NWICO demands and the withdrawal from UNESCO.* Moorhead, MN: Moorhead State University.

Hackett, R.A. (1989, May). Spaces for dissent? The press and the politics of peace in Canada. Paper presented at the Annual Conference of the International Communications Association, San Francisco.

Hackett, R. A. (1991). *News and dissent: The press and the politics of peace in Canada.* Norwood, NJ: Ablex.

Hallin, D. (1986). *The uncensored war: The media and Vietnam.* New York: Oxford University Press.

Hallin, D. (1991, May). Living room war: Then and now. *EXTRA, 4*(3), 21.

Harmetz, A. (1989, May 25). Report cites unequal pay for female film writers. *New York Times,* p. C25.

Herman, E. S., & Chomsky, N. (1988). *Manufacturing consent: The political economy of the mass media.* New York: Pantheon.

Hirsch, E. D. (1988). *Cultural literacy: What every American needs to know.* New York: Vintage Press.

Holt, R. (1987, May). Converting the war system to a peace system: Some contributions from psychology and other social sciences. Paper presented at EXPRO Conference, Cohasset, ME.

Hoynes, W., & Croteau, D. (1989). *Are you on the* Nightline *guest list*? New York: FAIR.

Hunter, A. E. (Ed.). (1991). *Genes and gender VI: On peace, war and gender.* New York: The Feminist Press of the City University of New York.

Ibrahim, S. M. (1981). *The flow of international news into Sudan, the Middle East and Africa.* Khartoum: Al Sahafa Press.

Keen, S. (1988, December). The stories we live by. *Psychology Today,* pp. 44-47.

Keen, S. (1991, Fall). Why peace isn't covered. *Media & Values* (56), 18.

Kroker, A. (1984). *Technology and the Canadian mind: Innis/McLuhan/Grant.* Montreal: New World Press. (Quoted in J. Nelson (1987). *The perfect machine: TV in the nuclear age.* p. 21.) Toronto: Between the Lines Press.

Lee, M., & Solomon, N. (1990). *Unreliable sources.* Secaucus, NJ: Lyle Stuart.

MacArthur, J. R. (1992). *Second front: Censorship and propaganda in the Gulf War.* New York: Hill & Wang.

MacBride, S., & Roach, C. (1989). New international information order. In E. Barnouw (Ed.), *International encyclopedia of communications* (Vol. 3, pp. 168-174). New York: Oxford University Press.

MacDonald, J. F. (1985). *Television and the red menace: The video road to Vietnam.* New York: Praeger.

Mackinnon, C.A. (1987). *Feminism unmodified: Discourses on life and law.* Cambridge, MA: Harvard University Press.

Mankekar, D. R. (1981). *Whose freedom? Whose order?* New Delhi: Clarion Books.

Marcuse, H. (1964). *One-dimensional man.* Boston: Beacon Press.

Masmoudi, M. (1986). *Voie libre pour monde multiple.* Paris: Economica.

Mattelart, A. (1992). *La communication-monde. Histoire des idées et stratégies.* Paris: La Découverte.

McClearey, K. E. (1991). To redeem the work of fools: Peace communication and rock-'n-roll. In R. Troester & C. Kelley (Eds.), *Peacemaking through communication* (pp. 103-109). Annandale, VA: Speech Communication Association.

Mosco, V., & Wasko, J. (Eds.). (1988). *The political economy of information.* Madison: The University of Wisconsin Press.

Mowlana, H., & Roach, C. (1992). New world information and communication order: Overview of recent developments and activities. In M. Traber & K. Nordenstreng (Eds.), *Few voices, many worlds* (pp. 4-17). London: World Association for Christian Communication.

Mowlana, H., Gerbner, G., & Schiller, H. (Eds.) (1992). *Triumph of image: The media's war in the Persian Gulf—A global perspective.* Boulder, CO: Westview Press.

Naureckus, J. (1991, May). Gulf War coverage. *EXTRA, 4*(3), 3-10.

Nelson, J. (1987). *The perfect machine: TV in the nuclear age.* Toronto: Between the Lines.

Nordenstreng, K. (1984). *The mass media declaration of UNESCO.* Norwood, NJ: Ablex.

Nordenstreng, K., & Varis, T. (1974). *Television traffic—A one-way street?* Paris: UNESCO.

Norman, L. (1975, October-December). The whale in the rice paddy. *Bulletin of Concerned Asian Scholars,* 17-27.

Osborn, B., & Davis, J. F. (1991). Images of conflict (Learning from media coverage of the Gulf War: A media literacy workshop kit). Los Angeles: Center for Media and Values.

Pear, T. H. (1957). The psychological study of tensions and conflict. In J. Bernard, T. H. Pear, R. Aron, & R. C. Angell (Eds.), *The nature of conflict: Studies on the sociological aspects of international tension.* (pp. 118-176). Paris: UNESCO.

Preston, W., Herman, E. S., &. Schiller, H. (1989). *Hope and folly: The United States and UNESCO, 1945-1985.* Minneapolis: University of Minnesota Press.

Rasky, S. F. (1989, April 11). Study finds sex bias in news companies. *New York Times.* p. C22.

Ravitch, D., & Schlesinger, A., Jr. (1990, August 12). Remaking New York's history curriculum. *New York Times, p.* E7. (In "Where We Stand," column of Albert Schanker, President, American Federation of Teachers.)

Reardon, B. (1985). *Sexism and the war system.* New York: Columbia University Teachers College Press.

Reyes Matta, F. (Ed.). (1977). *La información en el nuevo orden internacional.* Mexico City: Instituto Latinoamericano de Estudios Transnacionales.

Roach, C. (1985). Selected annotated bibliography on a New World Information and Communication Order (NWICO). In P. Lee (Ed.), *Communication for all: New World Information and Communication Order* (pp. 131-155). Maryknoll, NY: Orbis.

Roach, C. (1987a, Autumn). The U.S. position on the new world information and communication order. *Journal of Communications, 37*(4), 36-51.

Roach, C. (1987b). The position of the Reagan administration on the NWICO. *Media Development, 34*(4), 32-37.

Roach, C. (1990, July). The movement for a new world information and communication order: A second wave? *Media, Culture and Society, 12*(3), 283-307.

Roach, C. (1992a, January 11). Global communication: Concentration, control and deregulation. Paper presented at the Interregional Consultation on International Communications, National Council of Churches, Manila.

Roach, C. (1992b). Bibliography on the New World Information and Communication Order. In M. Traber & K. Nordenstreng (Eds.), *Few voices, many worlds: Towards a media reform movement* (pp. 75-78). London: World Association for Christian Communication.

Schafer, D. P. (1980). Cosmos, religion, culture. *Cultures, 7*(2), 35-58.

Schiller, D. (1979). An historical approach to objectivity and professionalism in American news reporting. *Journal of Communication, 29*(4), 46-57.

Schiller, H. (1986). *Information and the crisis economy.* New York: Oxford University Press.

Schlesinger, A., Jr. (1991). *The disuniting of America.* New York: Norton.

Schudson, M. (1978). *Discovering the news.* New York: Basic Books.

Schudson, M. (1989, July). The sociology of news production. *Media, Culture and Society, 11*(3), 263-282.

Simonson, R., & Walker, S. (Eds.), (1988), *The Graywolf Annual Five: Multi-cultural literacy.* St. Paul, MN: Graywolf Press.

Singham, A., & Hune, S. (1986). *Non-alignment in an age of alignment.* New York: Lawrence Hill.

Slack, J., & Fejes, F. (Eds.). (1986) *The ideology of the information age.* Norwood, NJ: Ablex.

Somvavía, J. (1979). *Democratización de las communicaciones: Una perspectiva latino-americana.* Mexico City: Instituto Latinoamericano de Estudios Transnacionales.

Sparks, C., & Roach, C. (1990, July). Farewell to NWICO [Editorial]. *Media, Culture and Society, 12*(3), 275-281.

Stevenson, R. W. (1992, July 23). G. E. guilty plea in U. S. aid to Israel. *New York Times.* p. D1.

The Istanbul statement of the MacBride round table on communications. (1992). In M. Traber & K. Nordenstreng (Eds.), *Few voices, many worlds* (p. 31-32). London: World Association for Christian Communication.

The Seville Statement on Violence. (1991). In A. E. Hunter (Ed.), *Genes and gender VI: On peace, war, and gender* (Appendix, pp. 168-171). New York: The Feminist Press at the City University of New York.

Tylor, E. B. (1924). *Primitive culture.* New York: Brentano's.

Traber, M., & Nordenstreng, K. (Eds.). (1992) *Few voices, many worlds.* London: World Association for Christian Communication.

Troester, R., & Kelley, C. (Eds.). (1991). *Peacemaking through communication.* Annandale, VA: Speech Communication Association.

UNESCO. (1975). Culture and contemporary society [Editorial]. *Cultures, 2*(2), 9-10.

UNESCO. (1979). Declaration on fundamental principles concerning the contribution of the mass media to strengthening peace and international understanding, to the promotion of human rights and to countering racialism, apartheid and incitement to war. (Adopted at the 20th session of UNESCO's General Conference, November 22, 1978). Paris: UNESCO.

UNESCO. (1980). *Many voices, one world* [MacBride report]. Paris: UNESCO.

Varis, T. (1981). Peace and communication in the light of the flow studies (Occasional Paper No. 20). Tampere: Tampere Peace Research Institute.

Veeser, C. (1989). War, propaganda, and civilized values. *Peace Review, 1*(1), 17-20.

Vitanyi, I. (1986). Cultural Democracy. In E. Laszlo & J. Y. Yoo (Eds.), *World encyclopedia of peace* (pp. 217-219). New York: Pergamon Press.

Webster, F., & Robbins, K. (1986). *Information technology: A Luddite analysis.* Norwood, NJ: Ablex.

Weiler, K. (1988). *Women teaching for change: Gender, class and power.* South Hadley, MA: Bergin & Garvey.

Why we fight. (1991, December). *Michigan Today, 23*(4), 1-3.

Wicker, T. (1991, June 5). A not-so-new order. *New York Times,* p. A29.

2

Communication and Information Technology for War and Peace

VINCENT MOSCO

One of the most important communication components of the war system is information technology. As pointed out in Chapter 1, by the 1970s this component was so noteworthy that communication writers had updated Eisenhower's original terminology to refer to the military-industrial-*communication* complex. Mosco's chapter reminds us that the alliance between the government, business, and the military is nothing new: it was already forged in the 19th century when the telecommunications industry was first developed. Since that time, we have witnessed the gradual emergence of global information technology systems dominated by the transnational corporations (TNCs) and market mechanisms.

Mosco's treatment of the increasing privatization of information technology brought about by these forces is a concrete example of the positive peace perspective outlined in Chapter 1. Meaningful peace will not be possible unless the structural inequalities of the information age are remedied, that is to say, the poor, minorities, women, and children must be given more access to communication technology.

Unfortunately, however, negative peace (the prevention of war) has special relevance for information technology, which, as this chapter shows, has played a pivotal role in the war system. As demonstrated in the Persian Gulf War, advanced communication technology, buttressed by the Star Wars initiative, has played a significant part in the West's new world order. Mosco's analysis of Star Wars is particularly significant, because it shows that even though it may not be working militarily, on the ideological level it has been a success.

In spite of the chapter's strong critique of information technology, Mosco is not a modern-day Luddite. On the contrary, he informs us of some of the ways information technology can be part of a peace system: making technological literacy available for all sectors of the population, using information technology in peace curricula, extending the work of electronic networks such as Peacenet, and making use of information technology in an economy committed to peace.

The Potential, the Threat, Fundamental Principles

Introduction

We are experiencing a communication revolution of vast proportions. Powerful technologies such as computers that process information, communication satellites and sophisticated cable systems that move signals at the speed of light, and high-definition screens for display create the potential to bring people and ideas together as never before.

But this potential has been noted frequently in the course of techno-logical development. Just 150 years ago, Samuel Morse and Stephen Vail exchanged the first telegraph message and pundits hailed it as a major step on the way to a democratic communication system. In reality, however, the telegraph established a pattern of development, generally reflected in subsequent technologies including the telephone, radio, and television, that actually increased the power and control of business and government, particularly the military. Specifically, the pattern encom-passed furious early competition among inventors; rapid growth of monopolized corporate control; and considerable government, espe-cially military, assistance to strengthen monopoly control. A public interest movement that forced government and business to pay some attention to fairness and equity, in the face of the drive for profit and control, was also a part of this pattern.

Now, as we enter the age of computers linked to satellites, of com-munication systems that can literally overcome the boundaries of space and time, we have to ask: Will history repeat itself? This is not an easy question to answer. What we do know is that technology alone does not guarantee democratic control.

Communication Technology: Capital and Control

As Smythe (1981) observed in *Dependency Road,* technologies are shaped in a particular global matrix. Today that matrix is characterized by an international market system that uses profit as its yardstick to determine "the kind, purpose and amount of productive activity," thereby shaping "the nature, extent, and location of invention and innovation." Nation states under the control of a dominant class, but divided by contradiction and conflict, join transnational businesses to direct the flow of resources from the less developed and dependent part of the world to the wealthy core of Western societies. States and corporations propagate ideologies that, disguised as axiomatic propositions, defend the system as the "one best way" to steer the world. These include notions such as modernity, which "requires uncritical acceptance of technology." In this way of seeing, it is crucial that people accept the view that technology is politically neutral and socially inevitable. This ideology and the states and businesses that promote it are challenged by the struggles of those who understand and experience the oppressive characteristics of technology and work to use technology to build a global system that overcomes class, gender, and racial boundaries (Smythe, 1981, pp. 92-93). In essence, for us to make the computer revolution a revolution for everyone, we need to work for the fullest possible democratic control over the production, distribution, and use of information technology.

Business and government are deeply involved in the development of new communication and information technologies for fundamentally important reasons. Simply put, the new technology makes it possible to *measure* and to *monitor* electronic communication and information transactions and to *package* and *repackage* information and entertainment in a profitable form. For business and government, these developments are the keys to profit and social control in the coming decades. They are striving to build what D. Schiller (1985) calls the *global grid,* a set of communication highways that would provide transnational companies and major governments with the means to tighten, in the frequently used lingo of the Pentagon, international command and control capabilities.

It is no wonder that commentators now refer to information as a strategic form of capital *and* a strategic means of control. For business, this means that information technology has opened the way to a truly international division of labor, because it enables companies to take advantage of the lowest cost and most easily managed sources of raw materials, capital, and workers with fewer and fewer space and time constraints. Boeing can link military aircraft engineers in Seattle and Tokyo for real-time aircraft design work. American Airlines can hire data-entry workers for $1 an hour at satellite-linked remote processing centers in Barbados. In essence, as Bell (1973) and Schiller (1973) began to show years ago, the global economy is increasingly becoming an information economy.

The U.S. communication and information system has historically steered an uneasy course among the principles of profit, control, and public access. Profit and social control take precedence, but over the years, organized labor, educators, and other supporters of widespread access have occasionally won some measure of protection by fighting for the laws, regulations, and institutions that provide for some measure of citizen access to information, notwithstanding one's ability to pay. As a result of this public pressure, the mainly private for-profit communication industry also includes public education, public libraries, a public mail service, near universal telephone service, public broadcasting, and a system of broadcast regulation that provides support for fairness and access. Now, even this system of public safeguards is threatened.

The technological ability to measure and to monitor information products, users, and transactions undermines earlier protections based on the difficulty or costliness of subjecting every information transaction to market criteria. Now, however, technology makes it possible for telephone companies to charge by the second of phone use and measure in seconds how quickly telephone operators complete their work. Television companies can determine the demographic composition of their audience with exact precision and by cross-tabulating these data with marketing and attitudinal profiles, promote pay-per-view programs to precisely targeted audiences. Information services companies can measure the amount of usage in precise time intervals and charge accordingly. The end of unlimited local telephone dialing and the movement from free television to pay per month, pay per channel, and now pay per view are steps on the way to making every electronic communication a market transaction (Mosco, 1992).

The Haves Versus the Have-Nots

The likely result of this is to deepen class and race divisions in America, creating the specter of a society that pits information rich against poor. Even under traditional policies that promoted universal access to the telephone, major gaps in access persist for the very people who need service the most. According to a 1987 government study, 25% of Americans subsisting below the poverty line did not have telephone service. This was also the case for 31% of food stamp households and 24% of homes in which children participate in subsidized lunch programs (General Accounting Office [GAO], 1987). A 1991 federal government report put subscribership among all blacks at 83.5% and among all Hispanics at 82.7% (Federal Communications Commission [FCC],

1991, p. 27). Universal telephone service is simply not a reality for America's poor and for its racial minorities. The 1980s brought no improvement in the situation. In fact, that decade marked the first in this century when telephone penetration rates did not rise to fill these persistent and significant gaps in service. This is likely to get worse under pay per call. Moreover, in the absence of a government program to assist in the equitable distribution of computers, access again divides along class and race lines. According to a 1988 report, 37% of children in families earning over $50,000 a year had access to computers in their homes. The figure for children in homes with incomes below $10,000 dropped to 3.4%. In this case, social class mattered by a factor of 10. The implications for racial division are also quite significant. Of all white children 17% made use of a computer at home; the figure dropped to 6% for black and 5% for Hispanic children (*The Economist,* April 23, 1988, p. 31; cf. Office of Technology Assessment [OTA], 1990).

The technology is, however, only partly responsible for increasing the division between the information haves and have-nots. Information technology does not have to be used in this way. A more democratic response would include a strong political commitment to redressing these technologically induced inequities and to using the technologies to strengthen widespread access. But the political response has moved in the opposite direction. Deregulation, privatization, and funding cutbacks for public education, public broadcasting, public libraries, and the public mail system are making it more likely that the potential for the technology to deepen divisions will be realized. Pressure from the United States and shifting internal political forces have led to acceptance of deregulatory and privatizing policies in Europe, Canada, and Japan.

Essentially, these policies advance the interests of transnational businesses in two key ways. First, they benefit the producers of communication and information who are freer to make the most profitable use of the technology. Broadcasters can sell as much commercial air time as they choose, telephone companies can raise local telephone rates, private mail carriers and cable television companies can service only the most profitable routes, and electronic information companies can package data for upscale clients. Second, these policies benefit corporate and some government users of communication and information because deregulation and privatization expand the number of choices available, including permitting large users to become producers themselves. Hence, a transnational bank like Citicorp can design its own private global communication network and market the data it gathers in the course of conducting its business unrestricted by regulations that aim to protect the public network and the widespread availability of public information. As Schiller (1990) documented, the U.S. government, which once supported universal access to the vast stores of information produced with taxpayers' dollars, now routinely sells that information at market rates or permits private information companies to do so. Simply put, deregulation and privatization promote a world deeply divided between information rich and poor.

Privacy Concerns

The application of computer communications raises concerns about privacy as well. Buying into the information society means more than instant shopping or dialing up videos. It also means providing business and government with enormous amounts of information on how we conduct our daily lives, including what we buy, what we read, how quickly we work, whom we contact, and so on. Because it is increasingly essential for people to use the technology to bank, shop, or work, privacy is becoming an increasingly pressing concern.

The concern about privacy is important, but the problem runs even deeper than individual privacy protection. It is not just a question of individual privacy violations, but of growing potential for *social management*. Electronic communication and information systems—including those that measure and monitor phone transactions, bank deposits and withdrawals, credit or debit card purchases, keystroke counts in the workplace, and so on—make it possible to gather massive amounts of information about the choices of different groups of people, so as to better manage and control group behavior. Consequently, large businesses and government agencies are in a position to manipulate group behavior, even when they guarantee some measure of individual privacy protection. Major interests in social management include governments that want to determine the best means of controlling social behavior and companies that are eager to maintain stable growth in consumer demand and a cooperative work force. One example is the growing number of computer communication systems with built-in surveillance programs that chart networks of contacts among telephone and computer users to identify cliques and other threatening informal groups. Effective social management also means that we change our behavior because we know that the technology *can* monitor it, whether or not it actually does so. The greatest concern is not that we give up our individual privacy, but that we keep it and live in a society in which such privacy is not worth having. As Miller (1988) put it, in such a society, "Big Brother is *you,* watching" (p. 331).

Principles for the Information Age

To address these threats and begin to work toward a more democratic information society, we need to start from a commitment to four basic principles. These principles should guide a social policy for an information age and serve as critical guideposts in working for the peaceful rather than the military uses of communication and information technology.

A social policy for an information age should be based on people's real communication and information *needs,* rather than on what the market simply makes available. Just as we assess people's needs for housing, clothing, and food and struggle to create social movements to meet these needs, so too do we need to develop a systematic assessment of people's needs for communication and information services. What is the right mix of these services necessary for citizens sufficiently skilled to live and work in societies increasingly dependent on communication and information-based skills?

Second, our information age social policy principles should include a broadened conception of *literacy.* Although it is popular to discuss the growing problem of illiteracy in Western societies, including computer illiteracy, the discussion is often vague about just what this means. A democratic social policy should include a commitment to verbal, visual, and information literacy.

The commitment to literacy should include the traditional concern about reading. Well-meaning futurists who argue that computers make reading skills obsolete are actually offering prescriptions for deskilling society. Nevertheless, a renewed commitment to literacy means more than this. In addition to teaching people how to read in the traditional sense, it also means teaching people how to read or understand the wide range of visual materials we are exposed to regularly. This means teaching people how visual material—videos, film, posters, advertising—is put together and used to convey ideas and feelings. Visual literacy includes learning the language that video makers use to speak with their tools. This comprises everything from communicating with camera angles to the different messages that different forms of editing convey. Hampton (1989), executive producer of *Eyes on the Prize,* a 1987 documentary that traced the early years of the civil rights movement, argues convincingly that camera positions went a long way to influencing which side the viewer would take and, more generally, whether blacks and whites would remain at a distance or would be introduced to each other's reality. Literacy also means learning how this happens. By incorporating some of the language and skill of the visual, people would be in a better position to understand, question, take apart, and reassemble for themselves visual messages. You do not have to subscribe to a music video channel to appreciate how we would all benefit by education that makes us less taken (and taken in) by the lure of the video.

Finally, literacy means the ability to read the new systems of electronic communication and information. It is not necessary to learn how a computer is put together or even how to program. Rather, we need to know what these systems can *do*. How do we communicate with them? What communication do they enhance or diminish? What information potential is opened or closed by the development of these systems? What is their relationship to the rest of society? What are the social costs and benefits of developing these systems in different ways, such as the market, government, and the local community? For example, numerous analysts have argued that technology, particularly computers, incorporate the gendered division of power in society. Male qualities of hierarchy, differentiation, and control are built into the structure of both hardware and software so that learning to read technologies such as computers replicates patriarchy (Jansen, 1989; Kramarae, 1988; Rothschild, 1983; Wright 1987). To avoid this requires both a change in the mode of producing and distributing information, as well as a critical pedagogy of consumption that teaches about the shortcomings of traditional literacy and the value of alternative, such as feminist, modes of literacy (Eisler, 1987, pp. 185-203; Wright, 1987, pp. 241-280).

The third building block for an information age social policy is a renewed commitment to *universality*. Reliance on the marketplace is undermining the existing commitment to universal telephone service, postal service, library service, and so on. The typical response of those who oppose the decline of universality is to call for government guarantees of universal access to a particular means of communication such as the telephone. This is a reasonable goal. However, in an age when long-dominant means of communication are changing and evolving in connection with others, it is not enough to guarantee universal access to a specific technology that might itself be facing obsolescence. A useful social alternative would broaden the definition of *universal* to account for changes in communication and information systems and the evolving needs of people for access to such systems.

Specifically, universality should mean access at affordable rates to communication networks that provide a wide range of voice, information, and signaling services. These would include, in addition to local and long-distance telephone use, the availability of basic information about health care, education, and other community services; opportunities to respond electronically to verbal communication; and opportunities to signal for emergency services, information, and other vital communications. Universal service would thereby be redefined to mean access to a public network that provides a range of electronic information services. A "basket" of these services would be available to everyone at an affordable rate. The composition of the basket would be determined by the widest possible public participation and would change with the evolution of social needs in communication and information services. This extension of the underlying principles that guide systems of public education and public telephone service would serve as a useful alternative to the marketplace to guide the development of communication and information services.

Finally, we need new definitions of *self-determination* and *collective determination* that would protect us against the dangers of computerized social management systems by restricting information gathering and surveillance to those areas that communities and their elected representatives determine to be in the public interest. Social management requires, and electronic systems make possible, extending surveillance in breadth across an entire society and in depth into what Michel Foucault has aptly called the "capillary level" of social life. The challenge is not how to protect individual privacy, but rather how to reduce the threat to freedom, to a self-managed life or to a life in which people choose their own form of collective management.

The protection of self-determination in a world of electronic communication and information systems that challenge our common experience of time, space, and selfhood, is difficult in itself. It is made more difficult by the likelihood that *individual* privacy protections may satisfy many people. "What is the problem?" is a typical response. Former Supreme Court Justice Douglas (1987) provided an excellent answer:

> As nightfall does not come at once, neither does oppression. In both instances, there is a twilight when everything remains seemingly unchanged. And it is in such twilight that we all must be most aware of change in the air—however slight—lest we become unwitting victims of the darkness. (p. 38)

Human needs, literacy, universality, and self-determination are the building blocks for an information age social policy, the first steps toward avoiding the negative lessons of old technologies. The next part of this chapter examines how military policy makes realizing these values all the more difficult. It describes the ways communication and information technology are used to reinforce a war system, to impose a military agenda on the information society. This is followed by a description of ways people are trying to turn this around, by using the computer communication revolution to build a system of peace.

Communication and Information
Technology in Support of the War System

As many commentators have noted, the post-World War II period has been marked by the growth of transnational businesses that, with the assistance of Western governments, have promoted mass consumption and militarism worldwide. They have particularly sought to incorporate third world societies into the Western system, but have faced continuous opposition from movements for national and social liberation. In response to these developments, communication scholars have developed a critical school of thought that is guided by the following aims:

1. Challenge established perspectives in communication research.
2. Connect communication issues to the wider social setting.
3. Promote social transformation. (Mosco & Wasko, 1983, p. ix)

Today numerous scholars and media activists identify with the critical school in their work and in their participation in organizations such as the Union for Democratic Communication (UDC) and the International Association for Mass Communication Research (IAMCR). They draw on the analyses of the North American scholars Schiller and Smythe; Europeans Garnham, Mattelart, and Murdock; and Latin Americans Ramero Beltrán and Freire, among others. These are scholars who have long challenged the established view that communication research should serve the profit interests of media businesses and the propaganda needs of government. They uncover the political economic agendas buried within the programs to promote third world acceptance of communication and information technology. They have linked communication research to wider issues of global inequality and authoritarian control. They have also identified modes of building democracy, including democratic communication, as an instrument to achieve, and as an end product of, social transformation.

Some of this work, particularly that of Schiller (1969) Smythe (1981), and Mattelart and Siegelaub (1979, 1983), has addressed the question of militarism, including the use of communication technology in the expansion of military control and in the use of media systems to promote Cold War militarism, particularly as directed against the third world. This analysis of communication and information technology in support of the war system builds on their path-breaking work.

Military priorities have increasingly shaped the development of technology in the United States, particularly the development of communication and information technologies. Fully 70% of all federal government research and development spending is directed to the military. Though it is commonly accepted that U.S. markets are driven *solely* by private firms competing openly, there are enough exceptions to this view to question this conclusion, particularly as it pertains to the information society. For example, the federal government is the single largest user of information systems in the United States. In the 1988 fiscal year, the federal information systems budget was $17 billion or one tenth of the entire market for computers, software, and services. In fiscal year 1991, the army, navy and air force combined to spend more than $7 billion on computers alone; other defense agencies spent an additional $1.5 billion on computer hardware (Lewyn, 1991).

The relationship between the Pentagon and the U.S. computer industry has always been strong (Flamm, 1987). In the 1940s and 1950s, the U.S. government, led by the Pentagon, provided most of the funding for computer research. Furthermore, the Pentagon gave big contracts to commercial firms to build the production equipment needed to create the microchips that have revolutionized the industry. The U.S. military is also largely responsible for underwriting the development of computer software systems. To complete this cycle, the Pentagon has been the major consumer of computer products. It even funded the transition from large, unreliable vacuum tubes to transistors, and eventually, semiconductor integrated circuits. So dependent was the electronics industry on military contracts that one 1957 business analyst worried that " 'Peace' if it came suddenly, would hit the industry very hard," although the analyst concludes that "military electronics is a good business despite the 'risk' of peace" (Harris, 1957, p. 216). Between

1958 and 1974, the military bought 35% to 50% of integrated circuits produced in the United States.

In 1958 the federal government created the Defense Advanced Research Projects Agency (DARPA), to organize military research and development efforts in computers. DARPA, born in the furor raised by initial U.S. failures to launch a space satellite and the Soviet success with its *Sputnik* program, worked with the Massachusetts Institute of Technology (MIT) to build time-sharing computers and with MIT, Stanford, and the University of California at Los Angeles (UCLA) to create packet switching, a system that packages bits of information for efficient and economical distribution over a communication network. These developments led, in turn, to the creation of Arpanet, a computer communications network that has served as the prototype for the development of national information highways. Today, in spite of the end of the Cold War, there is widespread support in government and business for expanding DARPA's mission to, "support high-risk technologies of commercial value, helping the military as well as other federal agencies" (Broad, 1991, p. C11). It is hard to disagree with the science adviser to President Reagan, when, in testimony before a Senate committee, he identified the significance of the computer for U.S. military activity:

> It has been the incredible leaps in data processing, as much as any single area, which has fueled this explosion. . . . It was data processing which overcame John von Neuman's skepticism of ever making the ICBM work in the first place. It was data processing at the heart of the move to MIRVing. It was data processing which tied ICBM fleets together for coordinated execution. It was data processing which has provided the ICBM accuracy necessary for preemptive strikes. And it is data processing which will be at the heart of any defense against ballistic missiles. (U.S. Congress, 1984, p. 8)

The Military and New Technology

As the historian of technology Smith (1985) showed, the U.S. military has exerted strong influence on the general design, dissemination, and management of new technologies. It has influenced design "by establishing standards and specifications for various goods and contracting with private manufacturers for their production" (Smith, 1985, p. 6). Eventually, these technologies, from dehydrated foods to nuclear power plants, have entered the civilian economy. Military support, including the financial backing of government-funded research and development as well as the legitimacy of a government seal of approval, ease the process of technological dissemination. In some cases, such as instant foods, the consequences are arguably benign. In others, such as nuclear power, the impact is quite different.

The military, particularly the U.S. Navy, was a major force in the application of nuclear energy to civilian uses. In fact, in 1953, the navy received the backing of the Atomic Energy Commission to oversee the design and construction of the first civilian nuclear power plant built in the United States. According to Hewlett and Duncan (1974), the navy won out because nuclear power, particularly systems based on light water reactors, worked well on naval vessels. This success helped to inflate the hopes of power companies and reactor manufacturers, including such major defense contractors as General Electric and Westinghouse. These interests used the U.S. Navy's success to argue that energy costs would be reduced to a negligible fraction of a user's budget, if not "too cheap to meter." However, applying the relatively small-scale naval use of nuclear energy to widespread commercial power generation raised enormous technical, managerial, and political problems that continue to cause widespread negative social consequences. In a similar fashion and at around this same time, as Noble (1984) describes, the U.S. Air Force promoted the dissemination of computer-controlled machine tools by going as far as paying prime contractors to learn how to use the new technology. This action was not only far out of line with cost effective ness but contributed to the deskilling of the American machine tool work force.

In addition to its influence on the design and dissemination of technology, the military has set the pattern for the structure and style of corporate management. According to Smith (1985), the centralized and hierarchical structure of the military arms industry was applied to the management of the railroad industry. In fact, he contends that

> the history of every important metalworking industry in nineteenth century America—machine tools, sewing machines, watches, typewriters, agricultural implements, bicycles, locomotives—reveals the pervasive influence of military management techniques. (Smith, 1985, p. 11)

This influence deepened in the 20th century with the application of military regimentation to Henry Ford's automotive plants and the development and application of scientific management practices best identified with the work of Frederick W. Taylor. Taylor was steeped in the management of the firearms and machine tool industries. He drew on this experience for the development of time and motion studies and other techniques for measuring and monitoring work, deskilling craft workers, and concentrating skills in management. Military practice has also funded and legitimized the use of survey research on large populations, one of the more notorious of which was Project Camelot, a $6 million project initiated in the early 1960s to assist the U.S. military in determining the conditions that promote and prevent third world liberation movements.

The Military and the New World Order

The Persian Gulf War gave us the new world order and resurrected Star Wars, the Strategic Defense Initiative (SDI) program. This section situates the new world order in the context of a century of conflicts, dating from the development of the telegraph and deeply bound up with military considerations over who would control the world communication and information order. These include the movement of the 1960s to 1980s that united third world nations in the call for a new world information and communication order. Bush's new world order, buttressed with a revived SDI, is just the latest turn in this history. But can the United States defend a new world order when it cannot maintain its own world economic power or maintain order within its own borders?

Since the 1950s, developing nations, formally organized in the Non-Aligned Movement, forcefully pressed for a new world order of their own. This became known as the *new international communication and information order,* itself an integral part of a new international economic order. These new orders would provide for more equality and democracy in the production and distribution of the world's resources, including mass media and information (Preston, Herman, & Schiller, 1989). The call for a new order in communication culminated in 1980 with publication of the MacBride report, the product of a UNESCO commission, chaired by Nobel-laureate Sean MacBride and charged with identifying problems and proposing remedies. The commission was broadly based with representation from all regions of the world, including novelist Gabriel Garcia-Marquez and communication philosopher Marshall McLuhan. The commission described how media systems in the developed world dominated flows of news and entertainment worldwide and called for a small start to address the problem by strengthening the mass media in the developing world (MacBride, 1984).

The U.S. response was to wage political warfare against this version of a new order. As the book *Hope and Folly* (Preston et al., 1989; see also Roach, 1990) demonstrates, the U.S. government and most major private media in the industrialized world attacked the report by distorting its recommendations. For example, Western media repeatedly attacked a nonexistent proposal to license journalists. The U.S. government demanded the total rejection of its call for equity, balance, and democracy because any policies based on these principles would threaten the free marketplace of ideas, that is, Western-controlled news, information, and data services.

Supporters of the document responded by noting, among other things, that the overwhelming bias and distortion in the media's *own* coverage of the commission showed how Western media monopolies were increasingly able to choke off the flow of ideas that challenged their power. The United States and the United Kingdom gave the final thumbs down to reform by withdrawing from UNESCO, thereby leaving the organization politically battered and with a much-reduced budget. By the time of the 10th anniversary of the commission report, the *New York Times* (Lewis, 1989) could safely declare that even the head of UNESCO was committed to ending what little remained of the new world information and communication order, partly in order to coax back the United States and United Kingdom.

Why was the United States and some of its allies so overwhelmingly opposed to this new order? The principal reason is that global mass media, from Hollywood film to the National Broadcasting Corporation (NBC; now a subsidiary of one of the largest military providers in the world, General Electric) to the *New York Times,* are big businesses *and* the major means to cement a dominant Western view of the world. Any call for a new order based on fairness, balance, equity, and democracy, however slight, would threaten the existing mass media order. A call for a new order is potentially more significant than the nationalization of a copper mine or a steel mill, because the mass media produce ideology as well as a return on investment. And just as significantly, the U.S. communication order is directly connected to its global military hegemony.

The Old Order Versus the U.S. Order

The United States understood the call for a new order very well because it had once been subjected to the domination of a world media order and spent much of the first half of the 20th century overcoming it. In the latter part of the 19th century, international communication, largely telegraph and cable-based press wire services, were dominated by a cartel of European countries, principally the British Reuters, French Havas, and German Wolff (Smith, 1980). In language reminiscent of that used by many developing nations of today, the United States, principally through the State Department and the Associated Press (AP) wire service, protested bitterly about European domination of the world's news and about how the image of America in the world was being filtered through European media. The AP was especially upset that it could not strike deals with newspapers because the big European companies threatened retaliation. Its managing editor protested the "tenacious hold that a nineteenth century territorial allotment for news dissemination had upon the world" (Smith, 1980, p. 44).

The United States fought the European order on numerous fronts starting with what the government called its "chosen instrument," the Radio Corporation of America (RCA), the parent of NBC. The government established RCA by permitting General Electric, AT&T, Westinghouse, and United Fruit to pool their electronics patents and capital, giving the United States one big company with which to beat the Europeans by establishing global dominance in radio-based communication. Recognizing the *strategic* significance of this decision, the U.S. government named a military representative to the RCA board and consistently made the company one of its top defense contractors. Today, as a subsidiary of General Electric, RCA is a major participant in the defense system.

In the 1960s, when communication satellite technology was ready for use, the United States established another chosen instrument to lead the world. The United States set up the Communications Satellite Corporation (Comsat) and the global Intelsat network, made up of non-Communist nations wishing to participate in international satellite communication. The United States managed the system for the world with an executive team filled with military and retired military officials (Kinsley, 1976, p. 196, called Comsat an "old soldiers home") who recognized the strategic significance of dominating the world communication order.

In 1984 the Justice Department approved the creation of the first computer cartel. The Microelectronics and Computer Technology Corporation (MCC) embodied the military-industrial complex by including major electronics defense firms, such as RCA, and was initially headed by a former top administrator at both the CIA and the National Security Agency. It was chosen to take on Japan in advanced computer research.

In 1987, the government approved the final legislation and budget for another computer cartel with a specific mandate to carry out research in microchip design and development. The Semiconductor Manufacturing Institute (Sematech) was founded to arrest "the erosion of the U.S. semiconductor industry and the high technology base on which both the U.S. defense and economy rely" (*Wall Street Journal,* December 10, 1986). In 1991, it operated on a $200 million budget with half of the funding coming from 14 corporate members, including competitors like IBM, Digital, and Hewlett-Packard (Pollack, 1991).

The developing nations call for their own new order was, therefore, seen as a threat to U.S. strategic economic interests (the profits of global electronics and media companies), ideological interests (Western ideas like consumerism, individualism, and private enterprise) *and* military interests (the links between big electronics firms and the war machine). The United States is now prepared to dispose of that threat once and for all by replacing the new order that the developing world so desperately needs with its own version of a new order supported by the same form of military-backed enterprise that established U.S. domination in the first half of the 20th century.

SDI and the New Order

The Star Wars program is central to the new order. After the war in the Persian Gulf, with its Patriot missiles and other "smart" weaponry, the United States revived the view that SDI could become a reality. As President Bush told workers at the high-tech Raytheon company, manufacturer of the Patriot: "For years we've heard that antimissile defenses won't work. The shooting down of a ballistic missile is impossible, like trying to hit a bullet with a bullet. Some people called it impossible; you called it your job. And they were wrong" (Cockburn, 1991, p. 42). Critics have been quick to point out that a few successful attacks on Scud missiles is hardly a test of a global defense against thousands of incoming Intercontinental Ballistic Missiles. Moreover, they note that the Patriot was hardly the efficient defense the news media, dutifully transmitting Pentagon press releases, made it out to be. Most failed to hit their Scud targets. And whether or not they hit, more often than not they caused more damage than they were intended to prevent.

The critics are absolutely right but, however necessary and well meaning, they miss a central point. SDI is not about a worldwide defense against nuclear weapons. It is not a global umbrella. As such, SDI cannot and will not work. Rather, SDI is about other matters that are more central to Bush's new world order and in these respects, SDI is already working. This helps to explain why in November 1991, despite the generally recognized end of the Cold War and the downfall of the Soviet Union, the U.S. government approved the largest annual funding for the SDI program, $4.15 billion and construction of a major antiballistic missile system that could cost as much as $60 billion (Wicker, T., 1991, p. E. 17).

First, SDI is working as an economic program. It is a massive government investment of capital in U.S. multinational businesses. It represents the single largest computer communication research and development program in history. It provides enormous financial benefits to companies like General Motors, which owns Hughes Aerospace and major software firms and General Electric, the parent of RCA and NBC. Hence, despite the trendy rhetoric of laissez-faire, SDI is a program of government assistance to its own transnational businesses.

Second, SDI is working politically. One of the tricky problems for national governments in an era of transnational business is ensuring that those businesses stay "on our side," that they support national government policies as well as their own bottom line. The carrot of big research and development contracts is a major incentive to companies that take globalization too seriously. Or as one Pentagon official put it when asked about IBM's apparent unwillingness to carry out research in areas that the Pentagon deems important: "Either IBM will decide that it will be good to do research in this field and to have a capability in it for defense in the 1990s or it will not. If it does not, there will be many others who will. . . . If IBM does not see that, then in my opinion their market share will decline" (Mosco, 1989, p. 162).

Third, SDI is working as a system of beliefs, what Boot (1989) calls *technopatriotism.* This is an ideology that enshrines defense against the horrors of war as the principal driving force behind U.S. military strategy. According to this view, the Patriot and the accompanying Nintendo battlefield are symbols of a military committed to the clean, automated, morally justifiable goal of knocking offensive weapons out of the skies. The support for the U.S. "defense" of Kuwait suggests that SDI may well be working in this respect as well.

Finally, and most important, SDI is working militarily, but not as a high-tech defensive umbrella. SDI works as a loosely coupled set of military systems that enhance the ability to take offensive action against individual nations that are unwilling to accede to the new world order. SDI is an ideological umbrella for a warfare system based on sophisticated electronics and massive fire power. As the Gulf War demonstrated, here too, it is working.

In essence, Bush's new order is like many new and improved products in an age of advertising hype. It repackages old ideas about military domination and manifest destiny, only in a much more dangerous and destructive form. Nevertheless, even as Bush presents his new order, cracks appear in the U.S. edifice. Europe and Japan represent formidable challenges. The U.S. economy is stagnating under the weight of neglect (leaving its infrastructure crumbling) and crackpot policies like deregulating the banking system, leaving American taxpayers a bill for between $0.5 and $1 trillion dollars. The new order and the renewed commitment to militarization is an attack on America's poor, who are desperate for public housing, health care, and education.

In this respect, the United States could learn many lessons from the principles and proposals in the version of a new order proposed by the developing world. What would such an alternative order look like? According to Mkapa, Tanzania's minister of information, rather than Bush's new world order "based on the respect for the force of might," this would "herald more equal political, economic and cultural relations between states" (Wicker, 1991, p. A29). The West's own underdeveloped peoples are calling for nothing less. The final section of this chapter takes a closer look at this view, one that would use communication and information technology to build a system of peace.

Moving Toward a Peace System

The previous section demonstrated that computers and communication technology are tightly integrated into the global war-making system, coming together in a new world order backed by SDI weaponry. Even when that system is not put to direct military use, it works to the economic, political, and ideological advantage of those who support the war machine. Much is to be done if we are to create an information society built on the values identified earlier: human needs, literacy, universality, and self-determination. The effort to roll back the war system, including the movement toward a military information society, starts from these values and adds both a vision of what the conversion to a peace system would look like, and the construction of local and international networks dedicated to the peaceful uses of technology, including computers and communication systems.

This vision of conversion is examined in this section as well as several of the concrete steps that a wide range of groups are taking to use computers and communication technology in the service of a peace system.

Conversion

One of our most significant jobs is converting the military machine to a peace system. As those who have participated in conversion projects have acknowledged, this is an enormous challenge, because it involves fundamental changes in our thinking about society as well as concrete plans about practical economic change. Information technology will play a central role in the discussion and implementation of conversion projects because technology is central to the war system, because information technology is required to manage the complex process of conversion, and because information technology is indispensable to operate an economy committed to peace.

Conversion can only take place concurrently with an education campaign that explains the costs of the war system and the value of conversion. We have a good foundation for this in the work that such groups as Jobs with Peace and SANE have carried out to inform people about trade-offs between the costs of major weapons systems and the need for schools, hospitals, and housing. This educational effort must incorporate the information technology sector. Commitments to the war system are distorting the development of computers and communication systems in the United States. Reliance on microchips that can survive nuclear combat leads to research and development in narrow areas that show little commercial promise. This makes it more likely that the U.S. lead in the development of advanced microelectronics will continue to erode. Pentagon chosen instruments that are pursuing Pentagon definitions of technologies with enormous civilian economic potential, such as high-definition television, means that it will likely be other nations that develop the productive commercial applications. Military concerns about standardization, automation, control, and surveillance make it more likely that the computer communication systems that are developed contain negative implications for employment and privacy when they are introduced into the civilian economy.

An essential part of the conversion process is teaching people that the war system damages our economy and endangers human rights. The war system is making information technology an object of fear rather than an instrument of peace and prosperity.

Conversion, Political Economy, and
Information Technology

There are numerous examples of conversion projects that offer lessons for the peace movement. Reflecting on these projects, one can draw two major conclusions. First, as the U.S. Council on Economic Priorities put it, "any attempt to convert nuclear weapons production facilities to civilian uses requires a substantial level of planning and financial support at the federal, state and local levels" (Hartung, 1984, p. 88). International studies have confirmed this view (United Nations, 1981). More generally, as Wells (1988) noted, the most successful efforts at military conversion have required significant amounts of political planning and social mobilization. The chief exemplar is the shift to civilian production among those nations with intact military forces, mainly the United States, Canada, the United Kingdom, and the former Soviet Union, at the end of World War II. It is easy to deride this effort because all of these nations remained far more militarized than was necessary. However, the accuracy of this conclusion should not cloud what we can learn from the enormous amount of planning that brought business and government together to shift the world's largest automotive industry to 75% civilian production in a few years time (Wells, 1988).

The numerous unsuccessful local efforts such as the attempt to convert Lucas Aerospace in England and the Cruise Missile Conversion Project in Canada offer lessons in grass-roots organizing. These and similar projects succeeded in mobilizing local organizations for a common planning process. They failed, however, in the conversion effort. One among the numerous lessons from these experiences is that we need to integrate local concerns for alternative use planning with a national strategy that makes building a civilian economy a high priority.

When we raise conversion to the level of a national planning effort, we also raise the concern about excessive centralization and elite planning for the management of a converted national economy. There are real dangers here of eliminating a military economy by substituting militarized planning and production methods. Conversion means more than no longer making bombs; it means eliminating military ways of acting, such as centralized management, extreme surveillance, and the drive to mechanize social life, that increasingly shape the civilian political, economic, and social systems. Mansbridge (1983) points out that there is a great deal to learn from the feminist movement of the 1960s and 1970s about how to establish decentralized and neoanarchist alternatives to bureaucracy.

Computers and information technology can also help in resolving the problem of bureaucratism because they can help free us from the tendency to institute rigid self-perpetuating chains of command. The process of planning for national and ultimately international conversion can thereby provide a major challenge for the peace movement to demonstrate the liberating potential in the technology. This can be done in two ways.

First, the planning process itself can be made far more democratic and decentralized by making use of computers and communication systems to deepen and extend planning networks. The development of electronic bulletin boards, computer communication bridging projects, satellite photograph peace surveillance projects and others that are described in subsequent sections offer opportunities for overcoming the time, space, corporate, and state control constraints that have kept people from building conversion planning networks on a national and global scale.

Second, the conversion planning process should incorporate the beneficial uses of microelectronics into its vision of what alternative economic production would look like in a peace system. Computer communication systems offer the potential for a more democratic workplace by making it possible to give more people more information and involvement in decision making. Zuboff (1988) refers to this as the opportunity to *informate* rather than to automate the work place. Moreover, the declining cost and miniaturization that has come with the growth of microelectronics offers a much wider range of socially beneficial products that an alternative production process would manufacture. For example, to build an information infrastructure for the 21st century, we need to create several systems of products that would expand the national postal, telephone, and cable networks to provide each household with the tools to communicate effectively in a global information society. One of the major values of the British Lucas Aerospace Plan was that planning committees of workers produced detailed designs of alternative products that would make use of advanced information technology to enhance the work of people in the health care, education, and environmental sectors.

I now turn to the concrete ways people are using information age technologies to build a peace system; the increasing involvement of computer communication professionals in the political, including military, implications of their work; and the directions for future action.

Computers Communicating for Peace

> In order to maximize the global impact of local and regional programs, universities should design and implement an international information center and communications consortium. These facilities will support the exchange of information, offer access to computer networks, and afford one- and two-way television linkages among university classrooms in various parts of the world and thereby create a truly "Global Classroom." (Mayer, 1988, p. 23)

This proposal comes from the Talloires Declaration of University Presidents and is the product of a unique meeting of 34 chief university administrators from numerous nations, including China, the United States, Ghana, the former Soviet Union, and Brazil. The purpose of the meeting was to build an integrated, global curriculum in peace studies. The meeting broke new ground by the call to make use of advanced communication and information technology to link students, faculty, libraries, and other information facilities. This principle was given its initial implementation in a model course on the history of the nuclear arms race organized jointly by professors at Tufts University in Boston and the University of Moscow. They put together a common syllabus, linked the two campuses by computer, and arranged for face-to-face meetings at the midterm point in the course. The curriculum schedule included three 2-hour live-by-satellite classes with simultaneous translation to permit students to talk directly to one another. The initial assessment was positive and an international faculty for future global peace studies courses is planned.

At about the same time that the computer-assisted global peace studies program was getting off the ground at the university level, the New York State-Moscow School Telecommunications Project began connecting elementary and secondary school students to promote intercultural understanding and peace. Computers and video speaker phones supplied by the Copen Foundation (a nonprofit organization), Mitsubishi, and the former Soviet government put students in 12 U.S. and 12 USSR schools in regular contact for a planned 3-year project (Malvin, 1988).

These experiments in electronic peace studies education mark an important, if small, step. The most substantial example of what the Talloires Declaration is pointing to is the computer network Peacenet. In a world of for-profit pay-per-bit, information supermarkets owned by corporate giants such as Lockheed, Reader's Digest, and General

Electric, Peacenet stands out as a nonprofit network that connects 2,500 subscribers and 300 organizations in 70 countries for the purpose of communicating about citizen action. Peacenet provides electronic mail, conferences, bulletin boards, data bases, Telex, Fax, and gateway services such as the San Francisco-Moscow Teleport to promote communication and action on peace issues. A typical day on Peacenet includes these items:

—A Beyond War member in Atlanta gets technical details on a satellite downlink of a U.S.-Soviet space bridge he is coordinating for the local chapter.

—A filmmaker in Toronto arranges with her host in Africa for a visit to a local development project.

—A Cambridge, Massachusetts peace researcher works on a mutual security strategy paper for presidential candidates, collaborating with Colorado and California activists.

—The newsletter editor for the Union for Democratic Communication receives submissions online, eliminating the need to retype articles.

—Computer professionals in Costa Rica receive detailed conference entries on computer networks in third world development.

Peacenet is run by the Institute for Global Communications (IGC), a nonprofit company founded in 1987. The IGC acquired Econet, an environmental and appropriate development network in July of that year. In the short period of its existence, Peacenet helped to develop Greennet, a British-based network for peace and environmental groups in Britain, by contributing software and technical support. An essential part of Peacenet's communication function is its computer-conferencing capability. Subscribers have access to legislative update conferences provided by groups such as SANE/Freeze. Southscan offers regular reports on politics in South Africa, and CARnet does the same for Central America. Conferences offer updated information on Star Wars developments and on the peaceful uses of outer space through the Institute for Security and Cooperation in Outer Space. In 1988, Peacenet provided its first full-functioning data bases, including the *Peace Research Abstracts Journal* data base, the largest such peace movement service.

As communications professor Downing (1989) noted, two of the key factors in the success of Peacenet are its low cost and ease of use. The value of low tariffs is clear, but according to Downing, it is just as important that subscribers are provided with an easy to consult (and humorous) user manual for gaining access and conducting searches.

Computer networks can emphasize the telecommunication function; bring people and groups together electronically, as has Peacenet; or act in an information function, finding, packaging, and delivering, in a usable form, important and often inaccessible data. Public Data Access (PDA) chose to concentrate on the latter.

PDA was established in 1986 to overcome problems in gaining access to largely U.S. federal government information. Over the years, accelerating in the Reagan administration, privatization, cutbacks in government information programs, and greater security consciousness have made it more difficult to get information essential for citizen activism. PDA sought to overcome this by securing public data, often in the form of raw computer tapes and packaging it in a usable form on floppy disks. In doing so, PDA demonstrated the power of matching data bases, so often used to increase government and corporate control, for citizen activists.

In its environmental project, PDA made use of Census Bureau and Environmental Protection Agency tapes, acquired through Freedom of Information Act requests, to demonstrate the high correlation between toxic dump sites and minority communities (Downing, 1989, pp. 160-161). This information was used widely, but particularly by the Commission for Racial Justice of the United Church of Christ, which was campaigning against the use of a PCB site in North Carolina. The power of PDA's work rested with its ability to match diverse information sources on a localized basis and provide that information to local activist groups. For example, information on cancer rates in the vicinity of nuclear power plants provides groups with data they can use to take on large companies that claim site location has nothing to do with the geographic incidence of cancer.

Those who would emulate PDA's lead in providing timely electronic analysis and information, need also to understand that those who control information recognize the political nature of this activity and will try to stop it. The Federal Elections Commission (FEC) tried to keep PDA from selling its analysis of the contributions that individuals and companies make to candidates, political parties, and perhaps most important, political action committees. FEC did so by subjecting PDA to a series of complex bureaucratic demands that would make it more difficult for the low-budget organization to carry out its work.

Space Satellites for Peace

In 1985, a group of Swedish journalists decided to overcome the superpower monopoly on space surveillance by setting up the Space

Media Network, an independent company that operates like a news agency by selling information on outer space activities to press and television clients. The network uses pictures that it buys from commercial satellites and government systems such as the U.S. Landsat and the French SPOT. Making use of a 15-year archive of weather satellite photography, the network can identify significant changes in activity at a particular location that might warrant widespread publicity. In 1986, the network provided the first public pictures and details of the nuclear disaster at Chernobyl. It has identified the site for Chinese missiles in Saudi Arabia and a large new cocaine growing region in South America. The network operates as a receiving station in the Swedish town of Kiruna (above the Arctic Circle) and calls on leading scientists around the world to help interpret and verify pictures in return for access to them. As a result of their work, it is considerably more difficult for governments to keep a lid on information that global citizens have a right to know. The Space Media Network will also make it more likely that a decade of discussions among nonaligned nations, France, and Canada to install a similar, though more ambitious, surveillance system, might finally see some positive results (Lewis, 1988, p. A33).

In addition to their significance for observation and surveillance, satellites are central to global communication systems. Just three communication satellites operating in fixed orbits 22,300 miles above the equator can cover the entire surface of the earth. Until recently, communication satellites served the interests of large private media companies and governments, particularly the military and intelligence agencies. There are signs, however, that just as the outer space surveillance field is opening to citizens groups, so too is the critical area of satellite communication. One of the best examples is the Deep Dish Television Network, which, since 1986, has been distributing tapes of citizen interest to cable television systems and those with access to private satellite receiver dishes.

Deep Dish is an outgrowth of the Paper Tiger Productions, an independent video company that for several years has been producing half-hour tapes consisting of critical and satirical readings of print and electronic media; for example, Herbert Schiller reads the *New York Times*. These programs generally air live on a New York City public access cable channel and are distributed on videotape for use in classrooms, meetings, and on other cable outlets.

Deep Dish is an effort to expand the distributional network for alternative video by making use of low-cost space available on underused communication satellites. Its network began in the spring of 1986 with a 10-part pilot series that addressed issues of housing, racism, militarism, women, and access to television itself. The series appeared on more than 250 cable systems in 40 states and featured the work of 200 producers across the country. A 1988 Deep Dish series transmitted 12 shows on similar issues over communication satellites. Since the material is also available to anyone with access to a satellite dish, the distributional network is far greater than this. The result is not unlike the experience of early amateur radio operators who pioneered in citizen use of radio for international communication.

In addition to using satellites for peace, one could cite many other examples of citizens' groups that make positive use of communication and information technology. This is certainly an important dimension of building a peaceful world. At the same time, it is important to acknowledge both the limitations and risks in such activity. Citizen use of computers and communication satellites is a very small part of overall use, which is dominated by the profit goals of private, transnational businesses and the military priorities of major governments. More important, as those who have made extensive use of the technology admit, it is not difficult to become so concerned about technical problems and possibilities, that one loses sight of the social ends that one set out to accomplish.

Networks like Peacenet and Deep Dish are important to study because they are able to put social priorities ahead of the technology. It is also vital to recognize that major social goals can be realized without extensive reliance on advanced technology. For example, Nicaraguans enjoy one of the highest rates of literacy in the world because people were mobilized and sent throughout the country to reach masses of illiterate adults and children. Moreover, scientists have made an important contribution to fighting SDI by supporting petition drives that pledge no cooperation in Star Wars projects. More than 7,000 scientists and science educators have pledged not to accept SDI funding. Mathematicians have been involved in similar actions. In 1988, the American Mathematical Society, with a membership of 20,000, voted to call on its members to refuse SDI work. Even groups of computer experts such as Computer Professionals for Social Responsibility have used traditional means to convey the message that we need to stop high-tech militarism. Each of these organizations and activities carry important consequences for those who support the peace system. Advanced technologies hold enormous potential for constructing a global peace system, but it is important to separate the medium from the movement, the instrument from the goal.

What Is Left to Do?

Computer communication systems are integral to the maintenance and growth of a permanent war system. The leading edge of that system, the SDI, makes the most extensive use of computers, satellites, and related information technology. However, this technology is increasingly being used to promote a peaceful world, one that is not battered by class, gender and race divisions. How can we better advance the latter over the former?

Critics of the war system, particularly those whose expertise is based in the new technology, need to recognize that technical criticisms are useful, but limited. Though the technical criticism of SDI has been strong, making it clear that SDI won't work to provide a protective shield, Star Wars continues to grow because it *is* working economically, politically, and ideologically. Consequently, SDI opponents, including the many scientists, engineers, and computer professionals who refuse to cooperate, need to make part of their critique the ways SDI *works* to maintain a war system, whether or not the hardware or software can ever work to build an impregnable defense.

We need to examine an *appropriate technology* strategy for a peace system. Winner's (1977) work is particularly instructive here. Winner argues that people committed to democracy need to develop "new technological forms" that require a "new sort of inventiveness and innovation" to overcome "the often wrongheaded and oppressive character of existing configurations of technology" (p. 326). According to him, such inventiveness requires "the direct participation of those concerned with their everyday employment and effects" (p. 326). Our guiding principles for the development of information technology should lead to systems that are immediately intelligible to nonexperts, that are highly flexible and mutable, and that minimize human dependence. Finally, development must be guided by a deep sense of the *appropriate*. For, "here, the ancients knew, was the meeting point at which ethics, politics, and technics came together" (p. 327).

In conclusion, a peaceful world requires a commitment to what Siegel and Markoff (1985, p. 12) call *computer citizenship* or "knowing enough about the social, political, environmental, and military implications of computer technology to make personal and social choices." This is far more important than learning how to boot a disk or fax a letter, because societies committed to peace absolutely require open discussion of the potential for information technology to centralize power, violate human rights, deepen divisions, and promote military destruction. At the same time, peace requires planning that promotes the widest possible involvement of people in decisions about the uses of information technology. In essence, information technology is not just an instrument to create a peaceful world, it is a test of our will to achieve it.

References

Bell, D. (1973). *The coming of a post-industrial society.* New York: Basic Books.

Boot, W. (July/August, 1989). NASA and the spellbound press. *Columbia Journalism Review*, pp. 23-24.

Broad, W. J. (October 22, 1991). Pentagon wizards of technology eye wider civilian role. *New York Times*, pp. C1, C11.

Cockburn, A. (July 8, 1991). Beat the devil. *The Nation, 253*(2), pp. 42-43.

Douglas letters cast light on life. (1987, November 29). *New York Times.*

Downing, J. (1989). Computers for political change: Peacenet and Public Data Access. *Journal of Communication, 39*(3), 154-162.

Eisler, R. (1987). *The chalice and the blade.* San Francisco: Harper & Row.

Federal Communication Commission. (1991, January). *Monitoring Report* (CC Docket No. 87-339; prepared by the Federal-State Joint Board in CC Docket No. 80-286). Washington, DC: GPO.

Flamm, K. (1987). *Targeting the computer: Government support and international competition.* Washington, DC: Brookings Institution.

General Accounting Office. (1987). *Telephone communications: Cost and funding information on lifeline telephone services.* Washington, DC: GPO.

Hampton, H. (1989, January 15). The camera lens as two-edged sword. *New York Times*, p. H29.

Harris, W. B. (1957, April). The electronic business. *Fortune*, pp. 137-142, 143, 216, 218, 222, 224, 226.

Hartung, W. D. (1984). *The economic consequences of a nuclear freeze.* New York: Council on Economic Priorities.

Hewlett, R., & Duncan, F. (1974). *The nuclear navy.* Chicago: University of Chicago Press.

Jansen, S. C. (1989, Summer). Gender and the information society: A socially structured silence. *Journal of Communication, 39*, 196-215.

Kinsley, M. (1976). *Outer space and inner sanctums.* New York: Wiley Interscience.

Kramarae, C. (Ed.). (1988). *Technology and women's voices.* London: Routledge & Kegan Paul.

Lewis, F. (October 5, 1988). Little brother watches. *New York Times*, p. A33.

Lewis, P. (September 17, 1989).Unesco chief about to face a showdown. *New York Times.*, p. 2.

Lewyn, M., (September 23, 1991). Meet the world's klutziest computer buyer. *Business Week*, pp. 74, 76, 77.

MacBride, S. (1984). *Many voices, one world* (Report by the International Commission for the Study of Communication Problems). New York: Unipub.

Malvin, T. (December 4, 1988). A computer project links students with Soviet partners. *New York Times*, section 2, p.1.

Mansbridge, J. (1983). *Beyond adversary democracy.* Chicago: University of Chicago Press.

Mattelart, A., & Siegelaub, S. (Eds.). (1979). *Communication and class struggle. Vol. I: Capitalism, Imperialism.* New York: International General,

Mattelart, A., & Siegelaub, S. (1983). *Communication and Class Struggle. Vol. II: Liberation and socialism.* New York: International General.

Mayer, J. (1988, December). Giving peace a chance. *World Monitor.* pp. 20-23.

Miller, M. C. (1988). *Boxed in.* Evanston, IL: Northwestern University Press.

Mosco, V. (1989). *The pay-per society.* Norwood, NJ: Ablex.

Mosco, V. (1992). Dinosaurs alive!: Toward a political economy of information. *Canadian Journal of Information Science, 17*(1), 41-51.

Mosco, V., & Wasko, J. (Eds.). (1983). *The critical communications review, Vol. I: Labor, the working class and the media.* Norwood, NJ: Ablex.

Noble, D. (1984). *Forces of production.* New York: Knopf.

Office of Technology Assessment. (1990, January). *Critical connections: Communication for the future* (OTA-CIT-407). Washington, DC: GPO.

Pollack, A. (April 19, 1991). Sematech starts to make progress. *New York Times,* p. D1, D6.

Preston, W., Jr., Herman, E., & Schiller, H. I. (1989). *Hope and folly: The United States and UNESCO, 1945-1985.* Minneapolis: University of Minnesota Press.

Roach, C. (1990, July). The movement for a new world information and communication order: A second wave? *Media, Culture, and Society, 12*(3), 283-307.

Rothschild, J. (Ed.). (1983). *Machina ex dea: Feminist perspectives on technology.* New York: Pergamon Press.

Schiller, D. (1985, January). The emerging global grid: Planning for what? *Media, Culture, and Society, 7*(1), 105-125.

Schiller, H. I. (1969). *Mass communication and American empire.* Boston: Beacon Press.

Schiller, H. I. (1973). *The mind managers.* Boston: Beacon Press.

Schiller, H. I. (1990). *Culture, Inc.* New York: Oxford University Press.

Siegel, L. & Markoff, J. (1985). *The high cost of high tech.* New York: Harper & Row.

Smith, A. (1980). *The geopolitics of information.* New York: Oxford University Press.

Smith, M. R. (Ed.). (1985). *Military enterprise and technological change.* Cambridge: MIT Press.

Smythe, D. (1981). *Dependency road.* Norwood, NJ: Ablex.

UNESCO chief about to face a showdown. (1989, September 17). *New York Times.*

Unfriendly Users. (April 23, 1988). *The Economist, 307*(7547), 26.

United Nations, Group of Governmental Experts on the Relationship between Disarmament and Development. (1981). *Study on the relationship between disarmament and development.* New York: United Nations.

United States Congress, Senate Committee on Foreign Relations. (1984, April 25). *Strategic defense and anti satellite weapons* (98th Cong., 2nd sess). Washington, DC: GPO.

Wells, D. (1988, Autumn). Politics and the economic conversion of military production. *Studies in Political Economy, 27,* 113-136.

Wicker, T. (June 5, 1991). A not-so-new order. *New York Times,* p. A29.

Wicker, T. (November 24, 1991). Why another ABM? *New York Times,* p. E17.

Winner, L. (1977). *Autonomous technology.* Cambridge: MIT Press.

Wright, B. D. (Ed.). (1987). *Women, work, and technology.* Ann Arbor: University of Michigan Press.

Zuboff, S. (1988). *In the age of the smart machine.* New York: Basic Books.

3

Dealing With Reality:
The News Media and the Promotion of Peace

PETER BRUCK with COLLEEN ROACH

In addition to communication technology, the mass media play an essential role in war and peace. Bruck's chapter picks up where Chapter 1 left off, by providing us with more details on the structural-organizational elements of capitalist-based media systems. He argues that there are certain inherent elements of the mass media that, by and large, promote war much more than peace.

For example, the very mode of organization of the news media— hierarchical and centralized—mirrors the military paradigm that, according to Mosco, has marked modern-day industrial production. Factors such as the increasing corporate concentration of the media and their all-consuming search for profits are also shown to have special consequences for coverage of war and peace.

Bruck, however, is not a Chicken Little, screaming that the sky is falling because our media horizons are defined by capitalism's "captains of consciousness." He feels that although the structural organization of the media precludes profound changeover to a peace system there is still room for maneuver. In other words, the media are not monolithic, or to use his phrase, there are still "discursive spaces" that allow dissident messages to get through. Bruck believes that this perspective is essential in answering the query "What is to be done?" because an extreme dominant ideology position may lead to political paralysis. His chapter provides proof that it is possible, as suggested in the first chapter, to find a middle position in the contentious debate on ideology that has divided critical researchers.

Introduction

Today we live in a media world. The means of communication that we use have developed over hundreds of years and have altered the ways in which we relate, think, and feel. As the Canadian economist and

71

cultural historian Innis (1951) observed more than 40 years ago, our media of communication and our ways of using them determine the kind of civilization in which we live. They determine the character of knowledge and influence the distribution of power in our societies. The shapes and contents of government, religion, education, and even the building and destruction of empires depend largely on the available kinds of communication media, their efficiency, their durability, and their speed (Innis, 1970).

While Innis saw the largest transformations in social and political life in the history of the West (and we may add, of the north) as the result of the transformations following the invention and development of writing and printing, McLuhan (1964), another Canadian thinker, suggested that modern culture is even more profoundly affected by the electronic media. He argued that the serial logic of the written word and print is fading out before the intuitive mosaic of instantaneous communication, thus altering subtly and constantly our perceptual senses.

McLuhan was enthusiastically optimistic about these changes and their direction. He saw on the horizon a society returning to the intimate interactions of tribal existence and hoped for the emergence of a global village where human beings are freed from alienation, anxiety, and loneliness by the cool media of instant communication such as television (McLuhan, 1964, pp. 36-46).

However, McLuhan's optimistic vision of a new society and an age of peace generated by communication technology has not materialized. True enough, television informs and entertains us, radio is all around and travels with us. Our work life and our leisure time are structured by the media of mass communication, and we need them, pay for them, and enjoy them. But they do not deliver the promised land. Rather, as Postman (1985) argued, we are amusing ourselves to death, ignoring much of what goes on around us, and becoming oblivious to the challenges posed by a civilization of ever increasing complexity. Television and the other electronic media thus appear not to be the means of salvation but the plug-in drugs, offering escape from the realities of the arms races, world hunger, ecological destruction, global inequalities, and concrete injustices (Winn, 1977).

Communication scholars and cultural analysts share with ordinary people in embracing a fundamental contradiction: high hopes and deep despair regarding the means of communication and the opportunities they might present. Both emotions combine in many judgments about the function of mass media.

No doubt, the mass media are an essential part of present-day complex societies. No contemporary society can function without them. Be it information about children's medication laced with poison or the review of a new movie, we require the mediation of the mass media in our daily lives.

But the ways and the degree to which we can influence how the media operate and function are far from clear. Rather, it seems that we are given little else than the opportunity to make consumption choices. We can pick from the vast offerings without being able to increase the range or diversity of choices that we have. The media are owned and operated by others. It seems, therefore, that we can react and seek liberty only in the freedom to refuse.

The impression that we have little choice and even less influence is grounded in the fact that our economic, social, and political systems build on the media system and vice versa. The way the social exchanges of information are organized structures all aspects of modern life. Stock prices rise and fall under the influence of media reporting; politicians get voted in or out, depending on their media presence and personality. And the media provide and distribute information in ways that are largely congruent with the values and social order of society. They are the keys for making sure that the social system can operate, that it is maintained and reproduced. In this function, the media have pushed aside and partly replaced traditional institutions such as the school, the church, and the family.

The Media System: Capitalism, Industry, and Bureaucracy

The operations of any given media system, what it can do and how it proceeds, depend on a constellation of factors: who the owners are, how the media production is organized, who the producers are, and how all of these elements influence the creation of mass media knowledge (Bagdikian, 1983; Schiller, 1973, 1981).

In North America, the media are capitalistically organized and privately owned by ever fewer multinational corporations. The mass media are run as commercial enterprises and are thus governed by the logic of profit accumulation. The trend is toward increasing conglomeration; mergers; and vertical, sectorial, and regional monopolies (Murdock, 1982). In 1979, the conglomeration purchase of a billboard and television company by the Gannett newspaper chain broke the records as $362 million changed hands. When Rupert Murdoch less than 3 years later bought TV Guide and other magazines from the Triangle Publications Corporation, he wrote a check of $3 billion. And in 1989, we witnessed the merger of the century when Time, Inc. and Warner Communications, Inc. (WCI) decided to join an unprecedented $18 billion in assets and operations.

The new media giants have as their main goal of business to take over smaller companies, to eliminate competition and grow ever bigger (Bagdikian, 1989). The top position is now firmly occupied by Time Warner, Inc., with subsidiaries in Australia, Asia, Europe, and Latin America. It calls itself "the world's leading direct marketer of information and entertainment" and boasts a worldwide readership of an estimated 120 million. Time Warner's media products include periodicals like *Time* magazine, *Sports Illustrated, Fortune,* and *People* magazine. It also owns publishing houses such as Little Brown, Time-Life Books, and the Book-of-the-Month Club; and runs WCI, the world's second largest record company, and the second largest cable television operation, including Home Box Office and Cinemax (Bagdikian, 1989).

Corporations such as Time Warner and its second-place rival in the world, the German Bertelsmann conglomerate, and the third-place News Corporation Ltd. of Murdoch do business in much the same way. The bottom line dictates what is good and valuable. Profitability supersedes all other objectives, and a year's success is measured in terms of the number of acquisitions, and increases in revenue and profitability.

Australian-born Murdoch's empire also encompasses vast media holdings. Murdoch started out with his News Corporation by running successfully a number of newspapers in his home country. A quite obsessive empire builder, he bought up dailies all over the English-speaking world and now owns prestigious papers such as the *London Times* and the London *Sunday Times,* the *South China Morning Post,* and tabloid rags like the London *Sun.* He now controls the fourth American network, Fox Broadcasting, *TV Guide,* and 20th Century Fox movie studios (Bagdikian, 1989; Simon & Wagenhauser, 1988).

On a global scale it is no exaggeration to state that a media oligopoly is in the making that operates according to the principles outlined above (Compaine, 1985). McLuhan never thought that the global village would be dominated by a few media lords in whose vocabulary and conceptual world terms like *universal understanding* have little or no place. Intent on staking out markets, winning audiences, and expanding wherever there seems to be a profitable opportunity, these corporations talk the language of the marketplace and use this language in the media they own.

It is implicit to the logic of capital that the mass media seek to cater to the largest possible audiences with the highest available income. And the North American media operators have perfected before others the strategies and tactics of how to attract, measure, and maintain these mass audiences. The goal is to reach as cheaply as possible ever larger audiences, and to sell them off to as many advertisers as possible. The products of Time Warner Inc., Capital Cities/ABC Inc., or the Gannett company include not only the magazines, books, and television shows they produce but also the audiences whose attention they can get, which in turn they can then sell to advertisers. Mergers, conglomeration, and integration all have as a net result that audiences can be sold many times over.

This principle of maximizing audiences and turning them into commodities is fundamental to the operation of the North American mass media (Smythe, 1981). Audience maximization has been and still is the driving force behind the North American standard of reporting and journalistic objectivity. It is the key factor in the invention and development of television forms like soap operas and prime-time serials and determines the news and production values of the media.

The ratings chase so typical of North American television can also be explained in terms of the search for profits. It is the outcome of the use of advertising during programming. Unlike their print counterparts, electronic media have no direct means of knowing the number of receivers. Print media can roughly calculate this number on the basis of the number of copies they sell, although readership exceeds the number of copies sold often by as much as one to four.

The ratings chase becomes ever more crucial as the electronic media in North America, (with the exception of the Public Broadcasting System in the United States and the Canadian Broadcasting Corporation), are entirely advertising supported. Within this form of institutional organization, the measurement of the number of viewers is an operating requirement. The price of advertising time depends on the size of the audience. It is, therefore, quite fair to say that program-interrupting commercials are the outcome of the North American ownership organization of television and that the importance of ratings is directly linked to the overriding incentive to get the largest possible audiences in order to sell them off at the highest possible rate of return.

In Europe, many television stations still work more in the tradition of public service broadcasting and do not have commercials that interrupt programming every six or seven minutes. But the privatization of much of the public systems in Italy, France, and Spain has changed this and will continue to do so unless new regulatory initiatives come into play (Fisher & Schapiro, 1989). Within North America, however, commercials that interrupt programming are systemic to the degree that they are considered normal. And it is this impression of normalcy, or naturalness, that hinders analysis and change. For someone who has grown up with a media culture characterized by advertising-driven television it is difficult to imagine a different form of television and a different organization of the mass media, let alone work for specific changes.

Commercials that interrupt programming do, in fact, alter the nature of television. They tie the production of programming, be it entertainment or news, directly to the size of the audience that can be reached. This process works as an ever-present imperative that influences virtually each and every consideration on script writing, staging, directing, and editing of a program. Ratings become the final arbiter of program success and quality, focus groups replace creative judgments, and fashion designers and effects specialists become the leading members of the production staff.

The consequences of television's ownership organization and advertising support illustrate the difficulty of converting the mass media to a peace system. As long as profit is the key goal, all other values, including peace, will take a back seat in the production and distribution of television programming. As long as commercials can interrupt programming, broadcast executives will judge a program almost exclusively in terms of the size of the audience it is able to produce. As long as the audience size is the main point of interest, programming will be judged in terms of the advertising rates and revenues, and not in terms of content or cultural expressiveness.

Advertising-supported broadcasting turns audiences into commodities that are produced and sold. As Smythe (1981) argued, programming in this system is hardly more than the filler between commercials. Programming is needed to entice the largest possible audience with the highest disposable income. This not only places narrow limits on creativity in terms of programming genre, format, and content but also prevents a genuine expression of diverse views and conceptions of the world.

Even electronic media enterprises that are not privately owned, such as the Canadian Broadcasting Corporation (CBC) or Public Broadcasting System (PBS) stations in the United States, face the pressures of audience maximization. Because they must work within the general media system, they are also subject to the very pressures of the private media: Greatest audience appeal is specifically articulated in the demands and imperatives to justify and legitimate programming, corporate plans, and resource allocation choices. Within this framework, a large audience still turns out to be the best argument. Little else will be as convincing to decision makers and critics who view a privately owned and advertising-supported media world as the natural way to organize social communication.

Industrialism and Bureaucratic Dependency

Conceptualizing the conditions for peace and the mass media has to also take into account the fact that our media not only are capitalistically organized but operate in an industrial mode. This industrial organization places further constraints on the work that can be done, a point that has been especially well documented in regard to the news media (Fishman, 1980; Tuchman, 1979).

When we talk about an industrial-capitalist form of production, the first element is the separation between owners of the means of production and those who work in production. The production plants—in the case of mass media things such as cameras, computers, archives, printing presses, and transmitters—are thus not owned by the people who work in the mass media but by the investors of capital. Furthermore, the production work is organized with a high degree of division of labor between, for instance, reporters on the scene, desk personnel, assignment and copy editors, managers, editorial writers, columnists, archivists, and publishers. Complex systems of machinery are employed, and characteristically, the labor of news workers becomes productive only in interaction with this machinery. In their operation, a specific series of detailed working steps have to be carried out by an interlinked chain of people and machines. Today, the reproduction and distribution of the media products of news workers are largely automated. The entire working process has been and is continuously subject to increasing rationalization and automation through, for instance, the use of integrated text processing and typesetting computers, and systems that allow the design of a newspaper right on the editorial screen.

The separation of the intellectual powers of production from manual execution has not progressed—and possibly cannot—as far in the media industry as in other industrial sectors. Rather, the latest computer inventions tend to reverse the process of increased division of labor to the degree that journalists have to do more than most of them want to in terms of copy production, layout, and page design.

Moreover, it is quite clearly in the interest of the media owners to rearrange the entire organization of industrial production. This observation found vivid demonstration in the flight of the British press entrepreneurs from Fleet Street in the 1980s, or late in that decade, the restructuring of American network news operations by the accountants of their new owners. In each and every case, a greater profitability was sought by the elimination of certain job categories or work functions, be it typesetters, layout personnel, production assistants, or researchers.

Analysis of the industrial form of organization of media work also suggests another factor that must be taken into consideration: the continuous nature of production demands. This is most evident in broadcasting, where the need for an uninterrupted flow of programming, the volume and regularity of production, and program schedules all necessitate both a complicated division and interrelation of labor. Media production work has thus long ceased to be the effort of creative individuals developing out of their imagination or factual knowledge a well-crafted message. Rather this production is best understood as an assembly-line process of churning out well-packaged products. What counts is not individual effort or input, but reliable and continuous output.

In light of this industrial organization of media production, concepts for change cannot merely focus on individual journalists, journalist education, or consciousness raising. Such conceptions miss the point of the systemic organization of media and all the factors of production overriding individual influence or ability.

Another aspect of the systemic nature of media is the bureaucratic organization of production. Taking again the example of the news media, a number of studies have shown how journalists are directly dependent on a stock of regular sources, how they habitually scan and check the same institutional sites, and how they depend on information subsidies and the documents released to them by their sources (Fishman, 1980; Gans, 1979; Tuchman, 1979). By *bureaucratic organization* we mean that journalists give preference to views of the world that come from people who have official positions in established institutions and who make available to them written records of what is taking place. In stories of disarmament or peace this means then not only that the spokespeople of government departments or established institutions will have easier means of getting into the news but that journalists and news workers covering disarmament will structure their workdays around what state department officials, diplomats, and members of government have to say and when they choose to say it.

News workers construct their work practices around offices and organizational hierarchies, their pace and places of operation, and their divisions of labor. Offices and institutions make it easier for journalists to do their work. They produce part of the paper trail that journalists need to have documentation and proof for what they write up as facts. A press release from the office of an arms control negotiator supplies enough information to make half a newspaper story. A press conference creates the event required for having an actuality angle on the story (journalists call this a *hook* or a *newspeg*). Journalists constantly work under the pressure of deadlines. They have to meet the cut-off time when editors start composing the pages or when newscasts get on the air. Bureaucratic sources aid journalists in meeting the deadlines and thus have come to be indispensable to the ongoing, routine production of news. Without them no news organization could function.

News work thus consists largely of the routinization of production of texts and images about what is going on in the world. News work makes the world known according to its imperatives and logic of industrial and bureaucratic production. The bureaucratic organization of news work ties journalistic practice and media production to operational modes and agendas of the management apparatuses of the state and the economy. Having on first sight a proclivity for the sensational, and therefore the unbureaucratic, the news media on closer examination are an integral part of present-day social administration.

Authorities and Democracy

The above description of the media culture and system in North America sets out the structures and dynamics of operation as constraints and challenges to the project of creating a peace culture. However, the identification of the news media as part of the dominant system, as a key element in the processes of reproduction and legitimization, marks but the starting analytical point of such a project.

Two points need to be considered here. To begin with, the media system does not operate and reproduce itself in a noncontradictory or conflict-free fashion. Second, there are factors that decide the success and/or failure of reproduction. The following questions must be asked: Is there room for movement? What are the opportunities for and limits of change? How can these limits be altered? More specifically, what room for maneuver do the established news media allow for nonestablishment organizations and movements to become politically effective?

Our discussion of these questions will concentrate on the analysis of news reporting, although they also should be asked about the media system in general. In recent years, critical scholars produced a number of studies that argue that the mass media produce and/or impose a dominant ideology (e.g., Gans, 1979; Gitlin, 1979; Glasgow University Media Group [GUMG], 1982, 1985; Hall, 1978, 1980; Knight, 1982; Tuchman, 1972, 1973, 1979). These studies, however, have not helped much to identify the possibility for alternatives or change. Most of the studies are examinations of media content, which consider, after the fact, the outcome of what is often quite a contradictory journalistic accomplishment, thus making it difficult analytically to distinguish between success and domination. Or to pose the question in another way, is any story carried by a mainstream news organization necessarily part of the dominant ideological perspective, and if not, how can one identify deviations and their significance? Or to put it most bluntly and reductionistically, does the capitalistic, industrial, and bureaucratic nature of media production determine the media content? If not, what factors mediate the deterministic pressure?

The problem of the relation between the overall social organization of media production and the shape and form of media content is most often phrased as the problem of media ideology and media bias. Both conservatives and Marxist positions tend to view the relationship in mechanistic and often quite simplistic terms that leave out much of the structures, influences, and logic that make the media and their production work the complex and fascinating fabric of modern society that they are.

Analytical efforts to determine solely from textual data the existence of a dominant ideology or news bias tend to have a formalist, ahistorical, and in the end, very theoretical tendency. They blur concrete historical changes, struggles, and most important, action alternatives. Such arguments lead to considerable difficulties for social movements, minority groups, and nonestablishment organizations attempting to assess the chances for, and measures of, effective work through the mass media. These social actors face daily an ambiguous situation: They depend on the establishment media for the dissemination of their messages, and yet they have learned to be fundamentally suspicious of the media and any interaction with them. The conclusions of critical media research do not suggest any alternatives. The result has been a continuous tug of war within these movements, groups, and organizations between those who promote a more or less wholesale adoption of establishment techniques and procedures to sell advertising-like images and those who prefer to circumvent the established media or even try to do entirely without them.

Evidence supports, for instance, the assertion that American network television news usually acts as the mouthpiece for the U.S. administration. Yet I would argue that we need to come to terms with the additional evidence that television news, and even more often the press, do not always behave in this fashion. In our analysis, it is important to allow for the fact that the media do their work in different ways at different times depending—among other things—on topic, administration, and I would argue, on the alternative social and discursive pressures exerted at a given time.

The case of Vietnam can illustrate how popular myths and selective recollection combine to create popular, commonsense theories of the media's effectiveness in regard to war and peace. Popular mythology holds that television news and the reporting in the opinion leader press of the East Coast were instrumental in ending the war, eroding public support, and undermining military efficiency. This mythology has a liberal and conservative side, the former seeking to heroize the press by invoking legendary episodes of journalistic independence and the latter seeking to blame the perceived adversary stance of the media and arguing for stricter state controls on reporters if not outright censorship. (Recall the Reagan administration's total news black out during the first days of the Grenada invasion in November 1983.)

Research into the American media coverage of the Vietnam War contradicts this popular mythology and its key empirical assumptions (Hallin, 1989). To the contrary, it has been shown that the media were not the adversaries to the American policy of waging a bloody proxy war on the backs of Vietnamese peasants, nor were the media, including television, the decisive factor in the outcome of this war. Hallin's study substantiates what the Museum of Broadcast Communications in Chicago convincingly illustrated in its spring 1988 exhibit called Vietnam on Television/Television on Vietnam 1962-75. A careful review of broadcast material, both on the national and local level, shows that television did not show graphic portrayals of violence, gory images of atrocities, and overpowering illustrations of injustice. Rather, television largely toed the government line. Even the U.S. Army's official history of the war acknowledges that the media never exceeded the boundaries set out in the voluntary guidelines for the protection of military information. With the exception of the famous icons (most of which were still pictures on *Life* magazine covers or newspaper front pages), such as the terrified peasant girl running screaming down the country road in a desperate attempt to escape, or the South Vietnamese colonel coldbloodedly executing his kneeling prisoner, coverage of the war tended to be sanitized. What changed American policy was not the media's coverage but the failure of the American government to rationalize the increasingly high casualty figures, the inability of the military to suggest to bereaved families that the deaths of their sons had any meaning that could console, and the collapse of the moral justification of the war apologists to explain the human suffering and hardship of war.

Television played some role in bringing the war into the proverbial living room. The arrival of the new filming technology of lightweight, hand-held, single-operator videocameras did allow more access to the battlegrounds. Reporters were able to get out of the transport aircraft flying over combat zones and get down on the ground away from fortified camps and patrol highways into the jungle, close to the action. This clearly altered the point of view of television news. The stark close-up of the sweating face and the mangled limbs replaced the trivializing aerial panning shots, and the new gear allowed reporters and cameramen to drop into the front-line misery in a routine way (Groen, 1988). The technology helped to individualize the consequences of an abstract and general policy developed thousands of miles away, and it put this policy under pressure to justify and legitimize the efforts and costs, the victims and slain. In the end, the policy failed either to justify or to legitimize the war. As the mood in the army camps changed, cameras and reporters were there to document it and give the lie to Pentagon announcements and presidential press briefings.

The news media speak in their own particular ways about the world, and news talk consists of particularly structured accounts of what is going on in the world. In Vietnam and in many other cases, this news talk follows the way governments, elite spokespersons, and institutional and established news actors speak the issues. News talk also presents the contradictions inherent in these forms of discourse and their failures to justify and legitimate their goals and objectives.

With very few exceptions indeed, the news media report about plane crashes, wars, elections, and inflation on the basis of information they receive from authorities and networks of established institutions. These networks designate the people whom reporters pay attention to and listen to. Using what these people have to say, the media then have their specific ways of presenting events, making their stories work, seeking their audience's assent, and rendering their messages intelligible.

In a recent study for the New York-based organization Fairness and Accuracy in Reporting (FAIR, 1989), Hoynes and Croteau showed that the news makers, policy experts, and analysts who appear on programs such as ABC News *Nightline* belong to these networks of sources and authorities. *Nightline* limits its range of guests overwhelmingly to white, male spokespeople of powerful institutions. Current or former government and military officials, professional "experts," and corporate representatives make up 80% of the show's guests. Public interest, labor, and ethnic and racial leaders make up less that 6%. While no labor leader has appeared more than twice, Ted Koppel, the show's host, shook hands more than 10 times with people such as Henry Kissinger, Alexander Haig, Elliott Abrams, Jerry Falwell, and Lawrence Eagleburger. Not only are nine out of ten guests male, but men are given more time to speak than women.

While *Nightline* had on occasion people who presented other than the "official" American view, these cases remained restricted to foreign policy crises. Only then were people such as Daniel Ortega or Robert Mugabe allowed to take the studio floor. On the whole, the study concludes, *Nightline* serves as an electronic soapbox from which white, male, elite representatives of the status quo can present their case, expound their political positions, and legitimize their actions (FAIR, 1989). The show evokes a worldview that sees the United States as "number one," albeit under siege from without. *Nightline's* fundamentally conservative political program is largely the result of the people it selects for its programs and thus nominates as interpreters for what is going on at home and abroad.

In doing their reporting work, the media employ set codes and conventions. The material they work with is not their own. Rather, their reports of what happens in the world build on and around the accounts of other people, be they eyewitnesses, police officers, spokespersons, experts, lobbyists, politicians, or business leaders. What these people have to say, enters into the media accounts either as unacknowledged background information or as acknowledged and attributed source/interview. Either way, what they say and how they say it has considerable influence on the angle of the news story, the structure and the flow of the story, and so on. They form a hierarchy of information based on social standing, functional relation, routine availability, and circumstance. This hierarchy decides the usefulness, credibility and news value of a point of view on the basis of who utters it. Similarly, the media have preferred documents and texts that they work with and that they treat as reliable sources.

We can speak of the media reprocessing the discourses spoken by their sources. They reassemble the information, rearrange different parts, and thus create their own particular way of telling the events in the world. It is, therefore, useful to distinguish between discourses of the media and the discourses they use as material to build on, process, and deliver.

The Coverage of Disarmament Stories and Peace Issues

An analysis of the coverage of peace, disarmament, and security issues in 13 English-language Canadian newspapers in late 1985 and early 1986 can illustrate these different kinds of discourses. One of the major stories in the sample concerned the testing of the U.S. Air Force's cruise missiles over the Northwest Territories and Alberta. Since their inception, the cruise missile tests had been vigorously opposed by Canadian peace and disarmament groups, and "Refuse the Cruise" became the rallying cry for a resurgence of mass demonstrations, public education, and political lobbying. Much of what Canadians look back on as the peace movement of the 1980s in their country was organized around opposition to the cruise testing. The story began in 1982 with the publication of the announcement of the testing agreement between Canada and the United States. The agreement was signed in 1983. News coverage of the story peaked in the periods of the demonstrations against the agreement and around the first number of test flights in 1984 and 1985. During our sample period, the tests had become a continuing news story.

In the analysis of the coverage of the cruise missile story we distinguished between actor sources and institutional sources. We conceptualized actor sources to be those narrative characters who were not only accessed for quotation and reference but also portrayed as actively involved in the story action, that is, their activities were part of the material reported. Institutional sources are those sources that were supplying story material by quotation or reference but were not portrayed to be among the main actors. Generally, people who are used as institutional sources are always identified in relationship to the organization they speak for.

The analysis of the cruise missile story shows that the leaders of the state are the only actors in the entire news story; they are the only characters who are not only quoted and referred to but also described doing things and setting actions.

Actor	Quoted	Referred to
Harve Andre, assistant minister of Defense	78	9
Ed Broadbent, leader of the New Democratic party (NDP)	17	4
Jean Chretien, liberal foreign affairs critic	11	0
Pauline Jewett, NDP foreign affairs critic	11	0
Joe Clark, minister of External Affairs	7	3
Len Hopkins, liberal defense critic	4	7
Erik Nielsen, minister of defense	0	1
Brian Mulroney, prime minister	0	10

The cruise missile story was also dominated by institutional sources speaking the bureaucratic-technical discourse. Of the total of 90 story items only 32.2% had an actor in the lead topic of the report. However, 91.1% had an institutional voice in the lead topic. Armed forces spokespeople were the lead source in 73.4% of the items. A tally of the total number of quotes and references further illustrates this point.

Institutional Source	Quoted	Referred to
Canadian Armed Forces spokespeople	202	27
U.S. Air Force officials	132	10
Greenpeace spokesperson	46	36
Government leader of the Northwest Territories	15	8
Operation Dismantle spokesperson	11	2
Canadian Centre for Arms Control and Disarmament	9	1
Assistant Mayor Inuvik	8	0
Peace Association for Nuclear Awareness (Grande Prairie) president	8	0
U.S. ambassador to Canada	6	1
Chief of the Assembly of First Nations	6	0
Alberta Citizens Anti-Cruise	5	0

Institutional Source (continued)	Quoted	Referred to
Cold Lake town council	4	0
Lakeland Coalition for Nuclear Awareness	4	1
Former adviser to George Schultz	3	1
Toronto Disarmament Network spokesperson	3	1
Women at Greenham Common	2	2
North American Aerospace Defense Command (NORAD)	1	5

These findings suggest the extent to which the bureaucratic-technical discourse spoken largely by military spokespersons, diplomats, and other experts of state and governmental institution, dominated the coverage of the story. The discourse generally feeds on the knowledge and ways of speaking of international law, military strategies, and weapons technology; it is replete with acronyms and specialized vocabulary. Sincere-sounding treaties and solemn declarations serve as standardized references, supplementing the categories of national security with concerns for state sovereignty and territorial integrity, aiming at *international accords, mutual efforts* and *deterrence*. In this discourse, *security* is understood only as the result of well-functioning weaponry. No concrete actors are named. History is decided by anonymous subjects such as military strength or the arms race in general, and much is done to avoid identifying any other subjects of history. When it comes to the question of disarmament, by and large this discourse becomes bogged down in its own maze of technical detail and administrative textualizations. It can only follow its course but is unable to reverse itself.

The news media tend to use, but not to focus on, this discourse. They often simply make it their own. The discourse's predictability, stemming from prescheduled events, makes it good material, because it produces hard news. Yet, it is rarely cited outside an event context. Institutions or institutional arrangements rather than individuals are displayed as authors and few if any visuals are provided.

The bureaucratic-technical discourse was evidently the dominant way in which the media reported on the cruise missile story during the sample period. But it neither went unchallenged nor was without a need for support. Rather, it was, and is, to a considerable extent a discourse that derives its legitimation from another, more authoritative way of representing the issue, the discourse spoken by the leaders of the state.

Alternative positions to these dominant points of view of the leaders of the state, and their associates in the military and diplomatic bureaucracies, were covered mainly when the fifth cruise test under the 1983 weapons agreement failed on January 25, 1986. The unexpected crash reopened for discussion the conceptual terrain of "speaking the event." On the following day, newspapers across Canada covered positions alternative to the military-technical view that had dominated the reporting leading up to the test. Three papers even carried a photograph of a Greenpeace protester challenging an officer of the Royal Canadian Mounted Police at the entrance gate to the cruise missile test site in Cold Lake. Generally, the test's failure positioned the spokespeople of peace groups across the country as the "other side" in the story (see the above figures for their use as third most used institutional source). Thus the dynamic of routine press coverage via quotation of, and reference to, two contrasting positions provided alternative views with space to speak about and articulate a different logic regarding the arms race.

The majority of the reports in our sample address this opposition at least once, as shown in an analysis of the themes of the cruise missile coverage. On the one hand, we find that the majority of themes used in the 90 reports clearly belong to the bureaucratic-technical discourse. More interesting, however, is the fact that the opposition to the cruise testing turns out to be the most frequently used theme over 6 months of "talking" the cruise missile story in the English-language Canadian press.

Theme	*Frequency*
Opposition of peace groups against the military and the government	50
Necessity of preparing war fighting skills	29
The danger of relying too much on technology is too great (e.g., the shuttle)	20
Cancel 1983 Testing Agreement with the United States (effective until 1988)	16
Cancellation necessary to guarantee public safety	15
The cruise is safe to test because of the advanced monitoring systems used during testing	15
Canada provides landscape similar to the Soviet Union	10
Delay tests	8
More tests needed to avoid future crashes	7
Flight corridor not a danger to the public because it is largely uninhabited, carefully monitored	7

Theme (continued)	Frequency
Cruise missile test record looks good: 8 failures out of 54 tests	6
Necessary to prove allegiance to United States	4
Change flight corridor to less populated area	2
Verification regarding arms testing	2

In analyzing these data it is important to recognize the fact that a good number of the challenges to the testing program also must use elements of the bureaucratic-technical discourse and that this discourse is the dominant way in which the press spoke of the entire issue. Oppositional views thus must often insert themselves within the established framework, and in many cases only when they do so can they offer perspectives that challenge the larger bureaucratic technical discourse.

Discursive dominance must, therefore, be understood as the result of the ownership and organizational structures of the media *and* of the ongoing social and ideological struggles. This dominance is never permanently established but faces challenges and requires constant maintenance and repair. Our examples also show the importance of specific events that can considerably alter the way a story is processed and talked about by the news media. Thus stories develop not only according to the operating dynamics of the media but according to the social and factual pressures under which the media must carry out their reporting work.

Peace Activism and Mass Media

Peace activists know that the mass media are in many ways crucial to their work. The daily reporting in the press, on radio, and on television produces the information environment in which we work, and on which we have to depend. Moreover, the if and how of reporting is quite decisive for our political effectiveness as well as the public perception of the relevance of peace issues to the political agenda and other key events of the day.

But we also know that neither peace issues nor peace views dominate the reporting of the news media. The tendency of the media to pick up on the sensational, dramatic, disastrous and dangerous, and on the negative in general, leads many peace activists to become generally skeptical if not hostile toward the media. The media are consequently seen as one of the main, if not *the* main, obstacle to the creation of a peace culture.

We have seen above the structures and logics that create these sentiments and the situations from which they stem. We have placed the media in the economic and social contexts of production, and argued that blaming the mass media is not only too simplistic and ultimately erroneous but also leads peace work into a dead end. The mass media are not the universal culprit for the development of social systems, war or peace oriented as they may be. A differentiating analysis—example of which is provided by our study of the cruise missile reporting—shows that the mass media, in this case news reporting, are as contradictory as the society to which they belong.

In this sense it is important to realize that while the coverage of peace activities is clearly insufficient, a different coverage is no substitution for different social relationships. Views and issues, and the ways in which the mass media organize them, are part and parcel of the overall system. The mass media form an essential part of present-day complex society. Alternate information provision and distribution is in the long run only possible if the larger system is also changed. This interdependence cannot be overlooked in the calls for media reform, improved coverage, and new national and international information orders. It should not deter us, however, from looking for the steps within the media system that can be taken to advance a culture of peace and from supporting the many media reform groups active across the continent. These groups range from organizations monitoring press coverage such as FAIR in New York City, Media-Watch in Vancouver, and the Women's Institute for Freedom of the Press in Washington, D.C., to organizations working to help and develop critical reporting such as the Canadian Association of Journalists in Ottawa, the Center for War, Peace, and the Media at New York University, and Investigative Reporters and Editors (IRE) in Columbus, Missouri, as well as organizations addressing structural issues of the media system such as the Telecommunication Research and Action Center in Washington, D.C., and the Friends of Canadian Broadcasting in Toronto (see the Appendix).

How to Think Peace and Communication[1]

When considering the relationship between peace and mass communication, many people repeat the same mistake during most of their thinking lives: They forget that both peace and communication are processes and not fixed states.

As peace is not a far-removed goal or the distant state of affairs of the one good society, but a particular way of living, doing things, and interrelating so is communication not a thing or a media product. Communication is to be understood as the processes of interrelating with the use of meaningful symbols. The processes almost always involve at least two parties, a sending and a receiving one. It is the distinct feature of the development of modern mass media that our social communication mainly involves not the interrelation of individuals but of groups and corporate entities as in the case of a daily newspaper for which a group of professionally working journalists communicate with a large and mostly anonymous public. Sending a communication in this sense is not one act but a well-coordinated set of multiple activities structured by a complex division of labor. Receiving is not an immediate act, as in interpersonal communication, but an activity quite removed from the situation of sending. Despite this considerable mediation, the people involved in mass communication on the consumption as well as production side participate in processes in which they assume concrete positions as *addressees* and *addressers,* and they make sense of communication on the basis of this assumption.

It is useful to consider this dimension of social interaction. The point is that peace and communication are related insofar as there are peaceful ways of communicating, and that these ways have less to do with the images and messages (i.e., the contents) that are exchanged than with the social relationships of mass communication. Images of violence and cruelty are, therefore, not objectionable in themselves, but rather their use for simple commercial benefits. The pictures of children starving to death in the desertlike plains of Eritrea or of the distorted bodies in the bombed-out buildings of Beirut have an information value, but they can also be used in a sensationalist way as short, high-energy clippings to promote a television station in its ratings war with its local competitors. This reasoning also applies to entertainment programming and magazines. The images of violence, suffering, and injustice are not, strictly speaking, objectionable but their deliberate and strategic exploitation for greater profits and market shares. In sum, the cynical calculation of the number of jolts per minute is part and parcel of commercial, advertising-supported television.

A structural, organizational, and institutional analysis of the mass media and their audiences is thus central to a peace project. We need to find forms of social communication and build institutions of mass communication that are peaceful for ourselves, for others, and for the groups and communities in which we live. This project will never be fully achieved. Rather, I take it to be part of our basic human condition that we must always begin with the task of communicating peacefully, and that, in principle, it can never be completed.

The abstract idea that peace as such can be accomplished is antihuman, and the will to completely realize peace in this world is a dangerous fantasy that denies the development of life and history and the essential tension of light and dark. This fantasy is quite dangerous, because it is the first step away from concentrating on the process—on the way of communication—and the first step toward privileging an end that might justify the means. We are always tempted to move in this direction, in the small and personal ways, as well as in the big, institutional, and political ways. If we give in to this temptation, most of the time we end up not recognizing ourselves and others in the cruelty, totalitarianism, and inhumanity that stand along this road.

These considerations are quite important to communication. The way humans produce, use, store, exchange, and receive symbols is and must be an open process, with flexible structures and varied means. Meanings are never fully realized, nor are they exhausted. Communication is never a closed affair, but it always goes on and continues, without having one definite starting point. This means that the intentions of the communicators are not sufficient to explain the meaning of a text, nor is the understanding of the recipients tied simply to these intentions or the text itself.

Peace activists, like other people interested in bettering this world, are often tempted to disregard this relative openness of communication, including mass communication processes. In their analyses as well as in their proposed remedies, they often rely on assumptions of precise communicative intentions, fixed meanings, determined understandings, and invariable effects. But these assumptions are wrong and misleading. Which is not to say—obviously—that there are not powerful institutions, dominant and preferred meanings, common understandings, and quite general effects. All of these do exist, but not in an absolute way. Rather, they exist in relation to specific historical, social, cultural, and biographical circumstances. Thus we have to be aware that we are seeking peaceful ways of mass communication in the specific conjuncture of the early 1990s in the Western, northern, industrial, capitalist societies of the United States and Canada with their particular gender and class stratifications, their religious and spiritual traditions, and their environmental destruction and international competition.

Civilizing Arms Control and Verification

Creating the conditions for a peace culture is clearly a process that can be started in many ways and in many places. Yet it cannot be achieved without the progressive demilitarization of all sectors of society and state. A crucial aspect of this process is the lifting of secrecy and the creation of *publicness* regarding military affairs and defense matters. Freedom of information in this area prepares the conditions for a peace system. The provisions of the Helsinki Accords of 1975 and the ongoing process of the Conference for Security and Cooperation in Europe (CSCE) have set out a useful framework for a transnational regime of information freedom.

The demand for a reversal of the arms race is crucial for beginning demilitarization. In the current process of arms reduction negotiations and arms control agreements between the United States and the former Soviet Union, a strange oddity persists and contradicts the stated goals of the process. The control and verification of the agreements is left exactly to those agents and structures whose interest lies in the preservation of the militarization of societies and states. We need to make arms control and verification a civilian task, and we ought to involve the news media in this process.

Arms control and verification might at first appear to be primarily technical subjects and of concern mostly to military analysts and diplomatic negotiators. Yet the disarming of the present-day nuclear regime and the "builddown" of the plethora of conventional weapons amassed in the Northern Hemisphere over the last decades of the 20th century can only be realized if effective arms control agreements are reached and adequate verification measures are allowed. And we all have a survival interest in this being done as soon as possible.

The above discussions of the media system suggested that censorship and other measures of direct and overt control of the social information flows do not represent the most important issues within present capitalist, democratic societies. The direct manipulation and control of news was considered to be the exception rather than the rule, and in fact a number of features of the existing media system are in place to counter such tendencies by the power elites in state and society at large. Moreover, liberal democratic structures are quite able and apt to deal with direct and overt exertions of power regarding media coverage. And while there is always a continuing social and political need to consider this possibility and to counteract such infringements on the reportorial work of the news media, they do not constitute the key constraints of the capitalist media system. The exception, however, is the military complex and the national and international state security where the restriction of information is still the rule (Bruck, 1988a, 1988b).

Verification is key to arms control and disarmament. Treaties can be concluded logically only if their compliance can be ensured, and such a guarantee depends on the use of specific means to check that specific actions are undertaken or omitted (Sanders, 1988). Generally, verification is considered to be a task undertaken by governments and their various military or intelligence agencies. It is part of the information gathering considered vital for the ability to act militarily.

Proposing a role for the media in this area violates the traditional conception of verification and challenges the prerogative of the military and intelligence apparatus (Schear, 1988; Schneider, 1988). However, as long as verification means and data remain the preserve of the military and intelligence agencies, civil society will be dependent on their interest and activities. It follows that making verification a civilian task will be the critical factor in taking control from the military apparatus and also increasing public interest in and support for arms control.

Rendering verification a nonmilitary activity is only logical if one considers the fact that it is the public at large in every nation state who have the most to gain from more arms control, stricter compliance, and a reversal of the arms race. The vested interests of the military obviously run counter to efforts to reduce armament expenditures and the share of general social resources allocated to war making and defense. However, if people around the world want to tackle the social and economic issues facing them, then verification must also become a civilian task and enterprise. Verification involves two aspects: the examining of the behavior of a treaty partner by another, and the demonstration of good behavior and will to allay fears and strengthen mutual confidence. An increase in the news media's involvement in verification would create relatively independent actors in a game in which hitherto every player had a strong vested interest. It would also free demonstration of good behavior from suspicions of self-service and possibly tie it more to the common good (Cleminson, 1988).

Currently, technologies exist that can be used by the news media to undertake verification tasks. New remote-sensing equipment and high-resolution satellites that are in geostationary orbit or pass in short intervals over territories of newsworthiness could already be used routinely were it not for governments and their restrictions. In exceptional cases, such as the ABC News satellite photographs of the movements of the military front in the Iraq-Iran war, the capability and interests in such information gathering has already been demonstrated. In the United States, the contest between state interest in maintaining national security and the First Amendment right of the media to gather news information is being fought out in the courts (Aamoth, 1988).

ABC News, which is pursuing this case, argues that the collection of satellite-procured data for possible verification purposes by the media is part of news gathering and thus protected under the First Amendment to the U.S. Constitution. This position holds that regulations and restrictions by the U.S. government on the deployment of a MEDIASAT can only operate within the accepted framework of First Amendment rights.

Conclusion

This chapter has presented a dual perspective on the mass media. On the one hand, we have argued that the capitalist media must be understood as a system with built-in limitations based on such factors as their industrial and bureaucratic organization as well as their increasing tendency toward conglomeration. But we have also presented, on the other hand, a case against the totalizing argument that the media are all-powerful, monolithic complexes that allow no room for maneuver. Research has shown that in certain cases, the media offer, albeit usually on their own terms, discursive spaces that peace activists can exploit. In addition to making use of the media's contradictions, and creating alternative media and watchdog groups, it has also been suggested that even large establishment media such as ABC should not be entirely written off. The components of a genuinely public peace culture based on active participation from civil society are to be found in several different directions.

Note

1. There is a rich literature on the relationship between the mass media, communication, and peace. For works not already cited, see Becker (1983), Bruck (1989), Bruck, Hargadon, Servage, Scott, and Allan (1987), Bruck, Langille, and Vardy (1986), Fabris (1986), GUMG (1985), Hackett (1988), Manoff (1988), Peringer (1987), Raboy and Bruck (1989), Schlesinger, Murdock, and Elliot (1983), and Varis (1986).

References

Aamoth, R. J. (1988). From Landsat to Mediasat: The development of remote-sensing technology and the first amendment right of the press. In P. A. Bruck (Ed.), *A proxy for knowledge: Arms control, verification and the news media* (pp. 125-144). Ottawa, Ont.: Norman Paterson School of International Affairs.

Bagdikian, B. H. (1983). *The media monopoly.* Boston: Beacon Press.

Bagdikian, B. H. (1989, June 12). The lords of the global village; Cornering hearts and minds. *The Nation,* pp. 805-818.

Becker, J. (1983). Methodological problems of dealing with disarmament in the press. *Current Research on Peace and Violence, 1,* 29-51.

Bruck, P. A. (Ed.). (1988a). *A proxy for knowledge: Arms control, verification and the news media.* Ottawa, Ont.: Norman Paterson School of International Affairs.

Bruck, P. A. (Ed.). (1988b). *News media and terrorism* (CCCS Discussion Documents). Ottawa, Ont.: Carleton University.

Bruck, P. A. (1989). Strategies for peace, strategies for news research. *Journal of Communication, 39*(1), 108-129.

Bruck, P. A., Hargadon, R., Servage, J., Scott, J., & Allan, S. (1987). *CCCS report: Arms control and the media.* Ottawa, Ont.: Centre for Communication, Culture and Society.

Bruck, P. A., Langille, D., & Vardy, J. (1986). *Bibliography on media/peace/security.* Ottawa, Ont.: Carleton University, Centre for Communication, Culture and Society.

Cleminson, R. F. (1988). The media's role in the verification process. In P. A. Bruck (Ed.), *A proxy for knowledge: Arms control, verification and the news media.* (pp. 119-120). Ottawa, Ont.: Norman Paterson School of International Affairs.

Compaine, B. M. (1985). The expanding base of media competition. *Journal of Communication, 35*(3), 81-96.

Fabris, H. H. (1986). Research traditions on the media, peace and disarmament. In T. Varis (Ed.), *Peace and communication.* (pp.30-42). San Jose, Costa Rica: Editorial Universidad para la Paz.

Fairness and Accuracy in Reporting (FAIR). (1989). *Are you on the* Nightline *guest list? An analysis of 40 months of* Nightline *programming.* New York: FAIR.

Fisher, W., & Schapiro, M. (1989, January 9-16). Four titans carve up European TV. *The Nation,* pp. 1, 52-58.

Fishman, M. (1980). *Manufacturing the news.* Austin: University of Texas Press.

Gans, H. (1979). *Deciding what's news.* New York: Pantheon.

Gitlin, T. (1979). Prime time ideology: The hegemonic process of TV entertainment. *Social Problems, 26*(3), 251-266.

Glasgow University Media Group (GUMG). (1982). *Really bad news.* London: Writers and Readers Publishing Cooperative Society Ltd.

Glasgow University Media Group (GUMG). (1985). *War and peace news.* Milton Keynes, UK: Open University Press.

Groen, R. (1988, March 26). Clearing the air: The politicians and generals, not television, lost the conflict in Vietnam. *Globe and Mail,* p. C1.

Hackett, R. (1988). The disarmament movement and the Canadian media: The case of Vancouver's Walk for Peace. In P. A. Bruck (Ed.), *A proxy for knowledge: Arms control, verification and the news media* (pp. 59-72). Ottawa, Ont.: Norman Paterson School of International Affairs.

Hall, S., et al. (1978). *Policing the crisis: Mugging, the state, and law and order.* London: Macmillan.

Hall, S., et al. (1980). *Culture, media, language.* London: Hutchinson.

Hallin, D. C. (1989). *The uncensored war: The media and Vietnam.* Berkeley: University of California Press.

Innis, H. (1951). *The bias of communication.* Toronto: Toronto University Press.

Innis, H. (1970). *Empire and communications.* Toronto: Toronto University Press.

Knight, G. (1982). Myth and structure of news. *Journal of Communication, 32*(2), 141-161.

Knight, G. (1988). Stratified news: Media, sources and the politics of representation. In
P. A. Bruck (Ed.), *A proxy for knowledge: Arms control, verification and the news media* (pp. 15-24). Ottawa, Ont.: Norman Paterson School of International Affairs.

Manoff, R. K. (1988). Who speaks and how: Some notes on nuclear discourse. In P. A.
Bruck (Ed.), *A proxy for knowledge: Arms control, verification and the news media* (pp. 41-58). Ottawa, Ont.: Norman Paterson School of International Affairs.

McLuhan, M. (1964). *Understanding the media: The extensions of man.* New York:
Mentor Books/The New Amercian Library.

Murdock, G. (1982). Large corporations and the control of communications industries. In
M. Gurevitch, T. Bennett, J. Curran, & J. Wollacott (Eds.), *Culture, society and the media* (pp. 118-150). London: Methuen.

Peringer, C. (1987). *How we work for peace: Canadian community activities.* Dundas,
Ont.: Peace Research Institute.

Postman, N. (1985). *Amusing ourselves to death: Public discourse in the age of show business.* New York: Viking.

Raboy, M., & Bruck, P. A. (Eds.). (1989). *Communication for and against democracy.*
Montreal: Black Rose Books.

Sanders, B. (1988). The concept of verification. In P. A. Bruck (Ed.), *A proxy for knowledge: Arms control, verification and the news media.* Ottawa, Ont.: Norman
Paterson School of International Affairs.

Schear, J. A. (1988). Verification: A role for the media? In P. A. Bruck (Ed.), *A proxy for knowledge: Arms control, verification and the news media.* Ottawa, Ont.: Norman
Paterson School of International Affairs.

Schiller, H. (1973). *The mind managers.* Boston: Beacon Press.

Schiller, H. (1981). *Who knows: Information in the age of the Fortune 500.* Norwood NJ:
Ablex.

Schlesinger, P., Murdock, G., & Elliott, P. (1983). *Televising terrorism: Political violence in popular culture.* London: Comedia.

Schneider, H. (1988). Arms control, verification and compliance: The role of the media
in the Federal Republic of Germany. In P. A. Bruck (Ed.), *A proxy for knowledge: Arms control, verification and the news media* (pp. 121-124). Ottawa, Ont.: Norman
Paterson School of International Affairs.

Simon, S. A., & Wagenhauser, D. (1988, February 13). Can Rupert Murdoch have it all?
Hubris and hypocrisy. *The Nation,* pp. cover, 200-202.

Smythe, D. (1981). *Dependency road: Communication, capitalism, consciousness and Canada.* Norwood, NJ: Ablex.

Tuchman, G. (1972). Objectivity as a strategic ritual: An examination of newsmen's
notions of objectivity. *American Journal of Sociology, 77*(4), 660-679.

Tuchman, G. (1973). Making news by doing work: Routinizing the unexpected. *American Journal of Sociology, 79*(1), 110-131.

Tuchman, G. (1979). *Making news.* New York: The Free Press.

Varis, T. (Ed.). (1986). *Peace and communication.* San Jose, Costa Rica: Editorial
Universidad para la Paz.

Winn, M. (1977). *The plug-in-drug.* New York: Viking.

4

Not Yet the Postimperialist Era

HERBERT I. SCHILLER

Imperialism is most often defined as the military, political, or economic structures that undermine a country's sovereignty. The term is usually applied to characterize northern industrialized countries' relations with the south (or third world). By
the beginning of the 1970s, a new element was added to our understanding of how
this domination works: cultural imperialism. A generation of researchers, whose
work is cited throughout this book (Smythe, Schiller, and Mattelart) made essential
connections between cultural domination through the mass media and mass culture,
and the other forms of imperialism.

However, by the 1980s, a not uninfluential group of researchers within the
critical tradition began to contest the underpinnings of the cultural imperialism
arguments: dominant ideology, the political economy of the media, and structural analysis. Schiller singles out two variants of this research tradition that
emerged in the 1980s: the active audience and globalization.

Schiller does not believe that the basic thrust of the cultural imperialism
argument is negated by the observation that different people can interpret
messages differently (the active audience theory). In this regard, he would take
issue with Bruck's arguments about discursive spaces, offering the possibility
of resistance. Nor does he believe that the globalization rhetoric reflects anything really new: If anything, it signals the tentacular growth of Western-based
cultural industries around the globe. The war in the Persian Gulf is cited by
Schiller as a stark metaphor for the enduring age of imperialism. The exercise
of military might—the most naked form of imperialism—is thus complemented
by the widespread growth of a total cultural package that includes far more than
television.

AUTHOR'S NOTE: An earlier version of this article was published in 1991 in *Critical
Studies in Mass Communication, 8,* 13-28. Copyright by the Speech Communication
Association, reprinted by permission of the publisher.

Apart from the persistent explanatory and semantic efforts in recent years to minimize or discredit the idea of cultural domination (Ang, 1985; Liebes & Katz, 1990), changing conditions make it desirable to reassess the original thesis.

Two governing circumstances strongly influenced the early elaboration of the theory of cultural dominance in the mid-1960s. The first was the then-existing world balance of forces. About 25 years ago, the international order could be divided into three major groups. The most powerful of these was the so-called first world, including essentially those countries that were grounded in private propertied relations and whose production was undertaken by capitalist enterprise. The second world comprised those nations that were organized along state owner-ship of property lines and were socialist. The last category (in every sense) was the third world, containing those countries that had just emerged from the collapsed European colonial empires. In the case of Latin America, these nations continued to suffer economic exploitation although they had been nominally independent for over a century. In most of the third world states, national liberation movements still existed, and the social structures had not yet been completely captured by new, privileged elites. In this general map, the United States was by far the most powerful individual state in the first world and in the other two categories as well. Although the Soviet Union, after World War II, claimed super-power status on the basis of possessing nuclear weapons, its economic and technological position was decidedly subordinate.

The other determining feature of this period in the cultural realm was the rapid development of television and its capability for transmitting compelling imagery and messages to vast audiences.

These geopolitical and technological conditions provided the social landscape for the era's cultural domination perspective. The essential assumptions undergirding it were (and are) few and relatively straight-forward: Media-cultural imperialism is a subset of the *general* system of imperialism. It is not freestanding; the media-cultural component in a developed, corporate economy supports the economic objectives of the decisive industrial-financial sectors (i.e., the creation and extension of the consumer society); and the cultural and economic spheres are indivisible. Cultural, no less than automobile, production has its polit-ical economy. Consequently, what is regarded as cultural output also is ideological and profit serving to the system at large. Finally, in its latest mode of operation, in the late 20th century, the corporate economy is increasingly dependent on the media-cultural sector.

The thesis assumed that the state socialist (second) world was, if not immune to Western cultural-informational pressure at least to some degree, insulated from it and would, under certain circumstances, support limits on its advance. The third world, in contrast, was seen as an extremely vulnerable and deliberate target of American cultural exports. At the same time, it also was viewed as a potentially organizable force—not yet frozen in class relationships—that might give leadership to a comprehensive restructuring of the world information system. The movement for a new international information order was one vehicle for such a mobilization.

The charge that American-produced cultural commodities—television programs in particular—were overwhelming a good part of the world hardly needed documentation. But the data were there (Nordenstreng & Varis, 1974).

Changes in the International Geopolitical Arena

Now, 25 years later, some of this map has changed. Most important, the second world (the socialist camp) has all but disappeared. With the (temporary?) exceptions of China, Albania, North Korea, Vietnam, and Cuba, there is no longer a state socialist sphere in the global arena.

The Eastern European states, along with the former Soviet Union, are in varying stages of capitalist restoration. Rather than providing an oppositional pole to the first world, they are now eager adherents to that world as well as its supplicants. They offer national space to the marketing and ideological message flows of their former adversaries.

In a material sense, the strength and influence of the first world, especially that of its most powerful members, are less restrained than they were in the preceding period. This is observable not only in regard to the erstwhile socialist bloc but even more so with respect to the people and nations of Africa, Asia, and Latin America.

Actually, the condition of the third world vis-à-vis the north (Western Europe, Japan, and the United States) is one of near desperation. Now under the control of elites that accept and benefit from the workings of the world market economy, the African, Asian, and Latin American nations are deeply in debt and stalled for the most part in efforts for improvement. Most of the third world nations seem more helpless than ever to resist the demands of their creditors and overseers. Despite some variability in this condition and occasional balking by a recalcitrant ruling group, the general situation reveals practically an abandonment of the challenging economic and cultural positions this group advanced not so long ago.

The role of television in the global arena of cultural domination has not diminished in the 1990s. Reinforced by new delivery systems—communication satellites and cable networks—the image flow is heavier than ever. Its source of origin also has not changed that much in the last quarter of a century. There is, however, one significant difference. Today, television is but one element, however influential, in an all-encompassing cultural package.

The corporate media-cultural industries have expanded remarkably in recent decades and now occupy most of the global social space. For this reason alone, cultural domination today cannot be measured by a simple index of exposure to American television programming. The cultural submersion now includes the English language itself, shopping in American-styled malls, going to theme parks (of which Disney is the foremost but not exclusive example), listening to the music of internationally publicized performers, following news agency reports or watching the Cable News Network in scores of foreign locales, reading translations of commercial best-sellers, and eating in franchised fast-food restaurants around the world. Cultural domination also means adopting broadcasting systems that depend on advertising and accepting deregulatory practices that transform the public mails, the telephone system, and cable television into private profit centers (Engelhardt, 1990).

Alongside this all-service-supplying cultural-media environment, the relative economic and political power of the United States continues to diminish. This suggests that American cultural domination is not guaranteed in perpetuity. Yet irrefutably that domination has been preeminent for the last four decades and remains so to this date, though subsumed increasingly under transnational corporate capital and control. The cultural primacy that the ruling national power in the world economy historically exercised may now be changing.

The commanding position of American media products in the post-World War II era, the expertise derived from more than a century of successful marketing activity, and the now near-universal adoption of English as the international lingua franca still confer extraordinary influence on U.S. produced cultural commodities. How long this influence can be sustained while American systemic power declines is an open question. But in any case, American *national* power no longer is an exclusive determinant of cultural domination.

The domination that exists today, though still bearing a marked American imprint, is better understood as *transnational corporate cultural domination.* Philips of The Netherlands, Lever Brothers of the United Kingdom, Daimler-Benz of Germany, Samsung of Korea, and Sony of Japan, along with some few thousand other companies, are now the major players in the international market. The media, public relations, advertising, polling, cultural sponsorship, and consultants these industrial giants use and support hardly are distinguishable from the same services at the disposal of American-owned corporations. Still, a good fraction of these informational-cultural activities continue to be supplied by American enterprises.

These developments leave most of the peoples and nations in the world more vulnerable than ever to domination—cultural, military, and economic. Former oppositional forces have collapsed.

Unsurprisingly, at this moment, there seems a barely contained euphoria in Washington and other centers where capital rules. George Bush, speaking at the United Nations General Assembly in New York in October 1990, proclaimed "a new era of peace and competition and freedom. He saw *a world of open borders, open trade and, most importantly, open minds*" ("Transcript," 1990, p. A6).

How aptly expressed are the current objectives of the for-the-moment unrestrained global corporate order—open borders, which can be transgressed; open trade, which enables the most powerful to prevail; open minds, which are at the mercy of the swelling global flows of the cultural industries. At least for now, the celebratory mood seems justified. Still, the currently triumphant corporate juggernaut is not on an open freeway with no stop lights and road checks. Possible sources of slowdown will be considered later.

Cheerful Surveyors of the Current Scene

Not all view the developments described above with skepticism or dismay. Indeed, some see the phenomena that now characterize daily life in a very large, and growing, part of the world as evidence that cultural domination no longer exists, or that what appears as domination actually fosters resistance to itself.

The idea of cultural diversity, for example, enjoys great popularity among many cultural observers. The central assumption—that many

diverse cultural tendencies and movements operate, with no one element dominating—is the familiar pluralist argument, now applied to the
cultural field. A more recent construct is the notion of *globalization*. In
this proposition, the world is moving, however haltingly, toward a
genuinely global civilization. There is also the very widely accepted
hypothesis of an active audience, one in which viewers, readers, and
listeners make their own meaning from the messages that come their
way, often to the point of creating resistance to hegemonic meanings.
Most comprehensive of all is the postmodern perspective. Whatever
else this approach offers, it insists that systemic explanations of social
phenomena are futile and wrong headed. Featherstone (1990) writes:

> Postmodernism is both a symptom and a powerful cultural image of the
> swing away from the conceptualization of global culture less in terms of
> alleged homogenizing processes (e.g. theories which present cultural imperi-
> alism, Americanization, and mass consumer culture as a proto-universal cul-
> ture riding on the back of Western economic and political domination) and
> more in terms of the diversity, variety and richness of popular and local
> discourses, codes and practices which resist and play-back systemicity and
> order. (p. 2)

Each of these presently prevailing ideas asserts that

1. Imperialism no longer exists. (A variant is that U.S. imperialism, in
   particular, is a spent force.)
2. A new global community is now emerging—global civil society, so to
   speak—that is independent of the interstate system. It is busily constructing alternative linkages and networks that provide space for new cultural
   environments.
3. Finally, it is of little consequence if cultural outputs from one source
   occupy a preponderant share of an audience's attention, because individuals reshape the material to their own tastes and needs. In this schema, the
   individual receptor takes precedence over the cultural producer.

How do these propositions stand up when examined against the actual
context of observable conditions?

Imperialism's Vital Signs Are Unimpaired

Is imperialism dead? Is the United States a declining imperialist
power? These are two separate though connected questions.

Imperialism, understood as a system of exploitative control of people and resources, is alive and well. At the same time, opposition and resistance to imperialism are far more intense now than at the end of the 19th century. The existence of 125 new nations testifies to the fact that many relations of domination have been broken. But powerful means of control still exist. Most of the African, Asian, and Latin American nations continue to experience economic, financial, and even military domination.

Although the term *imperialism* rarely appears in Western media, the word seems to befit the deployment of more than 500,000 U.S. troops in Saudi Arabia. It is also a signal that people's efforts to arrange their affairs without regard for the interests of current controllers (of oil, real estate, or good geographical bases) will be met with overpowering force. Moreover, the Middle East situation reveals another aspect of contemporary imperialist strategy: the ability to mobilize international organizations—now that the Soviet presence has been integrated into the West—for imperialist aims. President Bush explained it this way: "Not since 1945 have we seen the real possibility of using the United Nations as it was designed, as a center for international collective security" ("Transcript," p. A6).

A good part of the world's population lives in desperation, often below the subsistence level. A recent dispatch from Mexico City starkly described the appalling conditions in the capital city of the country directly south of the United States (Guillermoprieto, 1990). Hundreds of millions of people on all continents are similarly affected.

When efforts are made—as they continuously are—radically to change these awful conditions, invariably there is foreign intervention to maintain the arrangements that offer advantage to one or another global governors and their local surrogates, the so-called national elites. In recent years, Central and South America serve as models of this process. Chile, Guatemala, El Salvador, the Dominican Republic, Nicaragua, Panama, and Cuba have felt the force of U.S. intervention— economic, military, ideological—when they have tried to create new living conditions. Similar treatment has been meted out across Africa (e.g., Angola, Mozambique, and Zaire) and Asia as well (e.g., Vietnam, and Afghanistan).

The U.S led war in the Persian Gulf is only the most recent instance of imperialism. This action takes place amid growing contradictions, however. The relative position of the United States in the world economy seems to be declining, yet it embarked on a costly and potentially disastrous adventure to maintain control of an economically and strategically valuable region and a source of colossal profitability. One explanation, one most pleasing to officialdom, is that American power is still dominant. It is expressed best by Joseph Nye, a former top-level State Department official and currently a professor of international relations at Harvard University, who finds the fall in auto sales hardly enough to conclude that the entire economy is faltering. "We still have a lot more strengths that weaknesses" (Nye, 1990, p. A33).

Interestingly, Nye finds some of these strengths in what he calls *soft power.* "Soft power—the ability to co-opt rather than command—rests on intangible resources: culture, ideology, the ability to use international institutions to determine the framework of debate" (p. A33). Soft power, as Nye defines it, is essentially the control of communication and definitional power. This is cultural imperialism with a semantic twist.

Nye may be overly sanguine about the capabilities of soft power to do the job, but he is not totally off the mark, especially with respect to "hard power." *Fortune*'s 1990 list of the Global 500 (the 500 biggest industrial corporations in the world) reveals that "the U.S. leads all countries, with 167 companies on the list. That's more than Japan, West Germany, and Canada combined. . . . Americans are No. 1 in 14 of the 25 industries on the Global 500." Still, the magazine notes, "Impressive as these figures are, U.S. dominance is slowly giving way. In 1980, 23 U.S. companies made the top 50, compared with only 5 Japanese. Now there are 17 American and 10 Japanese" ("The Global 500," p. 265).

But other factors must be considered in evaluating the present strength or weakness of the American global imperial position. One momentous development is the breakup of Communist Eastern Europe as well as the accelerating restoration of capitalist forms and practices there and in what was the former Soviet Union. Removed thereby is an oppositional pole that served to limit severely, though not fully check, the exercise of American power in the postwar years. One (possibly too extravagant) reading of this situation is that "Washington may enjoy a greater freedom of action in foreign affairs than at any time since the end of World War II" (Toth, 1990, p. A6).

Certainly, the Persian Gulf War would have been inconceivable a few years ago. In any case, whatever the extent of the expanded range of American power, for the poorer people and countries in the world, the new situation is a disaster (Ramirez, 1990). The unrestrained use of what is called *low-intensity warfare,* against desperate people, now moves closer to realization as American military power no longer has to be concerned with Soviet counterforce (Klare, 1990). Whether it can disregard the financial cost of such undertakings is another matter.

Domination is further strengthened by the enfeeblement of the Non-Aligned Movement of the nations of Africa, Asia, and Latin America, established in Belgrade in 1961. Its present weakness can be attributed, in large part, to the enormous growth of transnational corporate power in the last 20 years, the collapse of the nonmarket sector of the world, and its own internal class stratification. Today, the ruling strata in the periphery have nowhere to turn except to the reservoirs of corporate capital. And they are doing just that.

Once assertive and insisting on national sovereignty, governments on all continents—including Brazil, India, and Mexico—headed by their dominant classes are enlisting the support of Western banks and the flow of Western-Japanese capital. One-time stalwarts of independence have demonstrated their new accommodationist outlook by engaging in sweeping denationalizations and privatizations.

Some still believe that these vast regions soon will be the vanguard of a new revolutionary upsurge (Amin, 1990). Perhaps, if the time frame is long enough, this will prove true. But in the meantime, their integration into the world market economy moves ahead. As part of their integration, the people are exposed to the drumbeat of corporate consumerism, no matter how limited the ordinary individual's spending power. The consumerist virus is an inseparable element in the rising global volume of marketing messages. This virus will impair the ability of leaders, still unborn, to act for the national community's social benefit.

A new hope for overcoming the deepening economic and social disparities around the world is seen in what is called the trend to globalization. This development, according to Featherstone (1990), one of its proponents, "emphasizes the autonomy of the globalization process, which should be seen not as the outcome of inter-state processes, but to operate in *relative* independence of conventionally designated societal and social-cultural processes" (p. 6). Contributing to this movement are "the increase in the number of international agencies and institutions, the increasing global forms of communication, the acceptance of unified global time, the development of standard notions of citizenship, rights and conception of humankind" (p. 6). It is emphasized that "the focus on the globe is to suggest that a new level of conceptualization is necessary" (p. 4). This new conceptualization can be comprehended in what it wants to dispose of: the center-periphery model of analysis and the very notion of intense social conflict. "From the vantage point of the late twentieth century it seems that the era of revolution is now finally over" (p. 4).

In short, globalization is defined to exclude domination, cultural control (soft or hard), and social revolution. The growth of the global institutions enumerated above is supposed to make these relationships and processes irrelevant, if not obsolete.

Globalism or Corporate Transnationalism?

It is indisputable that extranational cultural and political relationships have expanded spectacularly in recent decades. But what has been the engine of this growth? Is it a multifaceted outpouring of impulses toward a still-distant but slowly emerging world order? Do the forms and structures, however embryonic, indicate a looming era of universality?

It would be comforting to believe this. It would also be profoundly delusionary. The genuine character of the globalization drive can be appreciated by examining the fate of United Nations structures in the last 15 years and the apparent reversal of their prospects since the Persian Gulf War.

Until the fall of 1990, the experiences of the World Health Organization (WHO), the Food and Agriculture Organization (FAO), and, especially, the United Nations Educational, Scientific and Cultural Organization (UNESCO)—the entity established to encourage education, science, and culture on a world scale—tell a uniform story. Each of these organizations, as well as the United Nations itself, has been harshly attacked by the U.S. government and the American media. Each has been financially disabled for pursuing goals unacceptable to powerful American interests, i.e., the media, right-wing anti-abortion and anti-environmental groups, and the military-industrial complex. In mid-1990, the United States owed $750 million to the UN overall, exclusive of unpaid dues to WHO and FAO *(The New York Times,* September 13, 1990, p. A10).

Such massive withholding of funds has crippled major health, agricultural, and educational programs worldwide. UNESCO has been a special target of Washington's anger because it served as a forum— nothing more—to express the complaints of 125 nations against the prevailing international information order. The United States withdrew from UNESCO in 1984 and has remained outside that organization since (Preston, Herman, & Schiller, 1989).

Now, however, a new era seems to be opening up. It was inaugurated with UN support (thus far) for the U.S. initiated embargo of Iraq and the American pulverization of that country. A newfound appreciation of the international organization has emerged in Washington and across the American media.

Does this suggest a better-late-than-never response to global organization and international cooperation? More realistically, what the new spirit reveals is the current U.S.-Russian accommodation, achieved on the collapse of the Soviet economy and consequent Soviet eagerness to acquiesce in whatever initiatives its former adversary may propose—embargoes, aid termination to Angola and Cuba, and unification of Germany and its adherence to NATO.

Equally important in this era of seemingly widespread international agreement is the indebtedness and paralyzing weakness of the third world and its resultant inability to express any serious opposition to current developments. This species of *internationalism,* based on either the weakness or the opportunism of most of the participants, can hardly be viewed as a movement toward global equilibrium and social peace.

The actual sources of what is being called globalization are not to be found in a newly achieved harmony of interests in the international arena. To the contrary, the infrastructure of what is hopefully seen as the first scaffolding of universalism is supplied by the transnational corporate business order, actively engaged on all continents, in all forms of economic and cultural organization, production, and distribution. Many of the actual international structures that monitor these activities are staffed and managed or advised by personnel on leave from the major (mostly American) companies in the system (Schiller, 1985).

This worldwide system now enlists American, Japanese, German, Korean, Brazilian, English, and other nationally based but globally engaged corporations. These private giant economic enterprises pursue—sometimes competitively, sometimes cooperatively—historical capitalist objectives of profit making and capital accumulation in continuously changing market and geopolitical conditions.

The actual practices of individual companies vary from one national setting to another, and there is no general coordination of the system at large. (This does not mean that there is an absence of uncoordinated ensemble action. Capital flight, for example, demonstrates how many groups and companies, acting independently when there is a perceived threat to their interests, can cripple the economy from which the capital flows.) Still, with different specific interests and objectives, and often rival aims, harmonization of the global business system is out of the question. Yet the *generalized interest* of some thousands of super-companies is not that different. In their quest for both markets and consumers, they adopt fairly similar practices and institutional pro-cesses—technological, economic, political, and cultural. They are at one in maintaining the existing global hierarchy of power, though individual positions in that hierarchy constantly change. They utilize the communication and telecommunication systems, locally and glob-ally, to direct their complex and geographically dispersed operations. They have pressed for and obtained privatization of communication facilities in one national locale after another, enabling them to have the greatest possible flexibility of decision making and allowing them a maximum of social unaccountability. They fill the media circuits with their marketing messages. Their combined efforts in the places they exercise the greatest influence have produced the consumer society, of which the United States stands as model.

Although the supercompanies are owned for the most part by national groups of investors and are based in specific national settings, national concerns are not necessarily primary in the calculations and decisions of these enterprises. As the chief executive of Fiat, Italy's largest industrial corporation, pointed out "reasoning in nationalist terms does not make sense anymore" (Greenhouse, 1990, p. C11). This seems to be the case for at least some of the transnational corporate companies.

How this works itself out in the world at large is still unclear, and not all transnationals behave identically. Still, the question of national sovereignty has become quite murky in the intersection of national interest and the profit-driven activities of these economic colossuses.

Insofar as the visible slippage of the U.S. economy in the global hierarchy of advantage is concerned, American companies' constant search for low-cost sites of production has contributed considerably to this con-dition. Yet there is one sector in which American dominance remains, if not intact, at least very considerable: the media-cultural arena.

U.S. Media-Cultural Dominance

American films, television programs, music, news, entertainment, theme parks, and shopping malls set the standard for worldwide export and imitation. How long this dominance can endure alongside a receding economic primacy is uncertain. Already, many U.S. media enterprises have been acquired by Japanese (film and television), German (publishing and music distribution), British (advertising), and other competing groups. Yet even when this occurs, the new owners, at least for the time being, usually are intent on keeping American creative and managerial media people in executive positions.

American cultural domination remains forceful in a rapidly changing international power scene. It is also undergoing transformation. This occurs by acquisition and, more important, by its practices being adopted by the rest of the transnational corporate system. What is emerging, therefore, is a world where alongside the American output of cultural products are the practically identical items marketed by competing national and transnational groups.

For some time, critics of media-imperialism theory have offered as evidence of the doctrine's fatal flaw the emergence of new centers of media production. Brazil, in particular, is hailed as a strikingly successful example of this development. Its achievement in television production and export is supposed to demolish the notion of a single center of cultural domination (Rogers & Antola, 1985; Straubhaar, 1989; Tracy, 1988).

In reality, according to the work of Brazilian researcher Oliveira (1990), Brazilian television now broadcasts a minimum of U.S. programming. The biggest audiences watch and prefer Brazilian shows, which are widely exported abroad. Globo, the main Brazilian private television network, currently exports shows to 128 countries. "Its productions outnumber those of any other station [*sic*] in the world." Oliveira writes that American researcher Straubhaar (1989) concluded that Brazilian television programs have been "Brazilianized almost beyond (American) recognition." U.S. researchers Rogers and Antola (1985) see Brazil's exports as "reverse media imperialism." And Tracy (1988) writes that "in Brazil one sees a television devoted to national culture."

In Oliveira's reading of the same evidence, Brazilian programming is "the creolization of U.S. cultural products. It is the spiced up Third World copy of Western values, norms, patterns of behavior and models of social relations." He states that "the overwhelming majority of Brazilian soaps have the same purpose as their U.S. counterparts, i.e., to sell products"—and, it should be emphasized, to sell goods made by the same transnational corporations that advertise in Brazil as well as in the United States. The "local" sponsors are Coca-Cola, Volkswagen, General Motors, Levi's, etc.

"In most Brazilian soaps," Oliveira notes, "the American lifestyle portrayed by Hollywood production reappears with a 'brazilianized face.' Now we don't see wealthy Anglos any more, but rich white Brazilians enjoying standards of living that would make any middle class American envious." Oliveira concludes, "Glamorous as they [television series] are— even outshining Hollywood—their role within Brazilian society isn't different from that of U.S. imports. Unfortunately, the refinements applied to the genre were not to enhance diversity, but domination."

Domination is precisely what cultural imperialism is all about. With that domination comes the definitional power, Nye's "soft power," that sets the boundaries for national discourse.

Meanwhile, despite the developments already noted, the global preeminence of American cultural products is being not only maintained but extended to new locales. U.S. media incursions into Eastern Europe and the former Soviet Union are assuming the dimensions of a full-scale takeover, albeit shared with German and British media conglomerates.

American-owned and -styled theme parks, with their comprehensive ideological assumptions literally built into the landscape and architecture, are being staked out across Europe and Japan. "Euro-Disneyland will open its first park at Marne la Vallee in 1992, with a second possible in 1996. Anheuser-Busch [the second-largest theme park owner after Disney] has launched a theme park development in Spain, and other U.S. corporations are exploring projects elsewhere in Europe" (Sloan, 1990, p. D3).

It must be emphasized that the corporate takeover of (popular) culture for marketing and ideological control is not a patented American practice, limited exclusively to U.S. companies. It is, however, carried to its fullest development in the United States. Cultural-recreational activity is now the very active site for spreading the transnational corporate message, especially in professional sports, in which American practice again provides the basic model.

In the United States, practically no sports activity remains outside the interest and sponsorship of the big national advertisers. The irresistible lure of big sponsorship money has become the lubricant for a sport's national development. Accordingly, sports events and games have become multibillion-dollar businesses, underwritten by the major corporations that stake out huge television audiences. The hunt for sports events that can be made available to advertisers now includes university and, in increasing instances, high school games. Assuming the mantle of moral concern, the *New York Times* editorialized, "College athletic departments have abandoned any pretense of representing cap and gown and now they roam the country in naked pursuit of hundreds of millions of television dollars" ("Bright Lights," 1990, p. A22).

Unsurprisingly, the practice has become internationalized. A report from Italy describes the frenzied pursuit, by the largest Italian corporations, to own soccer and basketball franchises. "A growing trend in Italy . . . [is] the wholesale takeover of a sport by the captains of industry in search of new terrain from which to promote a corporate product or image" (Agnew, 1990, p. 14). The new patrons of Italian sports include the agrochemicals giant Montedison, which also owns the widely read Rome daily *Il Mesaggero;* the Agnelli family, owners of the giant Fiat company, who also own the successful Juventa soccer club; and Silvio Berlusconi, the Italian television and film mogul, who owns the AC Milan soccer club and other teams.

Recent developments in the former East Germany illustrate the extent to which sports have become a venue of corporate image promotion and an aggressive marketing instrument. *Business Week* reports that

> the women's Grand Prix tennis tournament scheduled for the final week of September [1990] is moving from Mahwah, New Jersey to Leipzig, East Germany. . . . The tournament [is] the first successful effort to lure big corporate sponsors into a major tourney behind the old Iron Curtain. . . . A number of heavyweight sponsors . . . include Volkswagen, Isostar, Sudmilch, Kraft-General Foods and American Airlines. ("Look Out Wimbledon," 1990)

Major sports are now transmitted by satellite to global audiences. The commercial messages accompanying the broadcast, ringing the stadia, and often worn on the uniforms of the athletes constitute a concerted assault of corporate marketing values on global consciousness.

The Total Cultural Package and the Active Audience

The envelopment of professional and amateur sports for transnational corporate marketing objectives and ideological pacification is a good point at which to return to another one of the arguments contradicting the cultural imperialist concept. This is the belief in the existence of an *active audience,* a view supported by a good number of Anglo-U.S. communication researchers.

According to this view, the audience is supposed to make its own meaning of the messages and images that the media disseminate, thereby playing a relatively autonomous role that is often interpreted as resistance to these messages and meanings (Budd, Entman, & Steinman, 1990; Schiller, 1989). Active audience theorizing has been largely preoccupied with the analysis of individual cultural products—a program or a television series, a movie, or a genre of fiction. The theory follows closely in the tradition of *effects research,* although not necessarily coming to the same conclusions.

Leaving specific studies aside, it can be argued that one overarching condition invalidates, or at least severely circumscribes, the very idea of an active audience, to say nothing of one resisting a flow of messages. This is the current state—impossible to miss—of Western cultural enterprise. How can one propose to extract one television show, film, book, or even a group, from the now nearly seamless media-cultural environment, and examine it (them) for specific effects? This is not to say there are no *generalized* effects—but these are not what the reception theorists seem to be concerned with.

Media-cultural production today has long left the cottage industry stage. Huge conglomerates like Time-Warner, with nearly $20 billion in assets, sit astride publishing, television production, filmmaking, and music recording as well as book publishing and public classroom education. Theme park construction and ownership, shopping malls, and urban architectural design also are the domain of the same or related interests.

In this totalizing cultural space, who is able to specify the individual source of an idea, value, perspective, or reaction? A person's response, for example, to the television series *Dallas* may be the outcome of half-forgotten images from a dozen peripheral encounters in the cultural supermarket. Who is to say what are the specific sites from which individual behavior and emotions now derive?

In 1990, even actual war locales become the setting for the marketing message. *Business Week* announces: "Welcome to the New World Order, Marketing Dept. where companies are using history-making events as occasions to promote their products." The magazine then explains that American companies are vying to supply U.S. troops stationed in Saudi Arabia with everything from nonalcoholic beer to video cassettes. The rationale: "If a soldier is going to be photographed sipping a cold drink or playing poker, most marketers agree that he or she might as well be using their product" ("Publicity?" 1990). In this new world of pervasive corporate message making, the dispatch of over 500,000 troops provides an opportunity to cultivate this or that taste for consumption, along with a powerful patriotic backdrop for the company and the product. How does the audience engage this spectacle of democracy and consumption? And what is one to think about audience resistance after the torrential, one-sided television news reporting of the Gulf War?

There is much to be said for the idea that people do not mindlessly absorb everything that passes before their eyes. Yet much of the current work on audience reception comes uncomfortably close to being apologetics for present-day structures of cultural control.

Meaningful Resistance to the Cultural Industries

There is good reason to be skeptical about the resistance of an audience, active or not, to its menu of media offerings. Yet this does not mean that the cultural conglomerates and the social system they embody are without an opposition. It is a resistance, however, that differs enormously from the kind of opposition that is supposed to occur in reinterpreting the message of a television sitcom.

Some may believe in the end of history and others may insist that the era of revolution is finally over and that social (class) conflict is obsolete. The daily newspaper headlines tell a different story (though of course they don't explain it). What is apparent is that aroused people, if not their leaderships, all around the world are protesting their existing living conditions.

In the United States itself, still the most influential single unit of the world market economy, numerous oppositional elements force at least minimal acknowledgment, and some limited accommodation, from the governing crowd. For example, the congressional fight over the national budget in the fall of 1990 was essentially a class conflict, however obscured this was in its media coverage. To be sure, the class most directly affected— the working people—was largely absent from the deliberations. But the main question at issue was which class would be compelled to shoulder the burden of America's deepening crisis. This debate, and others under way, reveal the fragile condition of the dominating power in the country.

Between 1980 and 1990, the wealthiest 1% saw their incomes rise by 75%, while the income of the bottom 20% actually declined. The richest 2.5 million Americans' combined income nearly equaled that of the 100 million Americans at the bottom of the pyramid (Meisler, 1990).

It is the still growing disparities between the advantaged and the disadvantaged countries, as well as the widening gap *inside* the advantaged and disadvantaged societies, that constitute the fault line of the still seemingly secure world market economy. To this may be added the ecological disaster in the making, which is the inevitable accompaniment of the market forces that are roaring triumphantly across the continents.

A routine headline in the Western media reads: "Indonesia: The Hottest Spot in Asia." Elaborating, *Business Week* rhapsodizes, "With a 7% growth rate, a population of 182 million—the world's fifth largest—and a wealth of natural resources, Indonesia is poised to be the region's new success story" ("Indonesia," 1990, pp. 44-45). As the 20th century winds down, success presumably is achieved by adopting the long-standing Western industrialization model, profligate with resource use and wastage, and exploiting the work force to satisfy foreign capital's search for the maximum return.

Indonesia, with an average wage of $1.25 *a day,* is an irresistible site. The chairman of the American Chamber of Commerce in Indonesia explains, "Indonesia will have a cheap labor supply well into the 21st century. . . . Nobody else in Asia except China can offer that." Not unexpectedly, "The income gap between affluent business people and the millions of impoverished who eke out a living in the villages and Jakarta's teeming slums is widening" (*Indonesia,* 1990, p. 45).

The Indonesian "success story," and others like it, are hardly confirmation for the end of social conflict perspective. Much more convincing is the expectation that the 21st century will be the truly revolutionary era, accomplishing what the 20th began but could not finish. In any case, communication theory—tied to the assumptions of political and cultural pluralism, harmonization of interests between the privileged and the deprived, resistance to domination residing in individualized interpretation of television shows and film, and overall, the long-term viability of capitalist institutions—is and will be unable to explain the looming social turbulence.

Certainly, there are no grounds for complacency about the prospects of the first and third worlds (the latter now including the once-second world states) in the years ahead. Yet Western communication researchers seem intent on holding on to these assumptions. Curran (1990), surveying the British and Continental research scene over the last 15 years, concludes that a major change has taken place. The most important and significant overall shift has been the steady advance of pluralist themes within the radical tradition, in particular, the repudiation of the totalizing, explanatory framework of Marxism, the reconceptualization of the audience as creative and active and the shift from the political to a popular aesthetic. . . . A sea change has occurred in the field, and this will reshape—for better or worse—the development of media and cultural studies in Europe. (pp. 157-158)

The same tendencies are well advanced, if not dominant, in the United States, though they have not totally swept the field as they seem to have done in the UK. There is still more than a little life left in those who look at the material side of the economy in general and the cultural industries in particular. Expressing this perspective is Harvey (1989). Reviewing the same years that Curran surveyed (from the 1970s on) and relying on many of the same basic sources (although not as focused on the field of communication research), Harvey (1989) also finds that "there has been a sea-change in cultural as well as in political-economic practices since around 1972" (p. vii). He concludes that these changes and the rise of postmodernist cultural forms, "when set against the basic rules of capitalist accumulation, appear more as shifts in surface appearance rather than as signs of the emergence of some entirely new post-capitalist or even post-industrial society" (p. vii).

Yet these "shifts in surface appearance" have contributed greatly to the capability of the corporate business system to maintain, and expand, its global reach. For this reason, the acknowledgment of and the struggle against cultural imperialism are more necessary than ever if the general system of domination is to be overcome.

References

Agnew, P. (1990, September 4). Italy's sport madness has a very business like basis. *International Herald Tribune*, p. 14.

Amin, S. (1990). The future of socialism. *Monthly Review, 42*(3), 10-29.

Ang, I. (1985). *Watching "Dallas": Soap opera and the melodramatic imagination.* London: Methuen.

Bright lights, big college money. (1990, September 13). *New York Times*, p. A22.

Budd, M., Entman, R. M., & Steinman, C. (1990). The affirmative character of U.S. cultural studies. *Critical Studies in Mass Communication, 7,* 169-184.

Curran, J. (1990). The new revisionism in mass communication research. *European Journal of Communication,* 5, 135-164.

Engelhardt, T. (1990). Bottom line dreams and the end of culture. *The Progressive, 54*(10), 30-35.

Featherstone, M. (Ed.). (1990). *Global culture.* London: Sage.

The global 500, the world's biggest industrial corporations. (1990, July 30) *Fortune,* p. 265.

Greenhouse, S. (1990, October 5). Alliance is formed by Fiat and French company. *New York Times,* p. C11.

Guillermoprieto, A. (1990, September 17). Letter from Mexico City. *The New Yorker,* pp. 93-104.

Harvey, D. (1989). *The condition of postmodernity.* Oxford, UK: Basil Blackwell.

Indonesia: The hottest spot in Asia. (1990, August 27). *Business Week,* pp. 44-45.

Klare, M. T. (1990). Policing the gulf—and the world. *The Nation, 251*(12), pp. 1, 416, 418, 420.

Liebes, T., & Katz, E. (1990). *The Export of meaning: Cross-cultural readings of "Dallas."* New York: Oxford University Press.

Look out Wimbledon, here comes Leipzig. (1990, September 24). *Business Week,* p. 54.

Meisler, S. (1990, July 24). Rich-poor gap held widest in 40 years. *Los Angeles Times,* p. A11.

Nordenstreng, K, & Varis, T. (1974). *Television traffic—A one-way street* (Reports and Papers on Mass Communication, No. 70). Paris: UNESCO.

Nye, J. S., Jr. (1990, October 3). No, the U.S. isn't in decline. *New York Times,* p. A33.

Oliveira, O. S. (1990, October 8-10). *Brazilian soaps outshine Hollywood: Is cultural imperialism fading out?* Paper presented at the meetings of the Deutsche Gesellschaft fur Semiotik, Internationaler Kongress, Universitat Passau.

Preston, W., Jr., Herman, E., & Schiller, H. (1989). *Hope & folly: The United States and UNESCO, 1945-1985.* Minneapolis: University of Minnesota Press.

Publicity? Why it never even occurred to us. (1990, September 24). *Business Week,* p. 46.

Ramirez, A. (1990, September 14). 2 American makers agree to sell Soviets 34 billion cigarettes. *New York Times,* p. A14.

Rogers, E., & Antola, L. (1985). *Telenovelas:* A Latin American success story. *Journal of Communication, 35*(4), 24-35.

Schiller, D. (1985). The emerging global grid: Planning for what? *Media, Culture and Society, 7,* 105-125.

Schiller, H. I. (1989). *Culture, Inc.: The corporate takeover of public expression.* New York: Oxford University Press.

Sloan A. K. (1990, August 22). Europe is ripe for theme parks. *Los Angeles Times,* p. D3.

Straubhaar, J. (1989, May 25-29). *Change in asymmetrical interdependence in culture: The Brazilianization of television in Brazil.* Paper presented at the International Communication Association, San Francisco.

Toth, R. C. (1990, September 12). With Moscow crippled, U.S. emerges as top power. *Los Angeles Times,* p. A6.

Tracy, M. (1988, March). Popular culture and the economics of global television. *Intermedia,* 19-25.

Transcript of president's address to U.N. General Assembly. (1990, October 2). *New York Times,* p. A6.

5

The Culture of Western Bureaucratic Capitalism: Implications for War and Peace

SHEILA COLLINS

With Collins' chapter, we now turn to an analysis of the culture of the war system. Her wide-ranging concept of culture is very similar to what was laid out by Roach in Chapter 1. The connection of her work to the other chapters is also evident: First of all, she takes up some of the same themes, such as globalization and multiculturalism; second, whereas Mosco, Bruck, and Schiller identify the essential features of the mass media, communication technology, and cultural imperialism, Collins takes these same features and relates them to the entire *ensemble* of capitalist culture.

Thus, while Mosco's chapter analyses the increasing commodification of information, Collins shows how the commodification process is also cultural, in that it pervades all aspects of human relations and values. Likewise, the objectivity and bureaucratic organization of the news media, analyzed by two of the other authors, are taken one step farther: Both are shown to be essential components of modern-day Western culture. The argument of biological determinism, used to rationalize war, is here shown also to be intimately connected to the justification of racism and sexism.

Collins's chapter looks in new directions for the elements of a peace culture. She calls for a cultural-spiritual conversion that would not exclude insights based on intuition, dreams, and poetry. In this conversion, the best hope for new, emerging cultural paradigms lies with the native Americans. Collins suggests that we have much to learn from the disinherited of this country.

To elaborate the elements of a peace system, it is essential to understand the elements of Western bureaucratic capitalism, a culture that has dominated a large part of the world for the last 500 years and is currently incorporating most of the world into its orbit. With the now-near globalization of the economy under the hegemony of Western multinational corporations, the culture of Western bureaucratic capitalism is fast becoming the lingua franca of the modern world system.

Culture is defined here as that ensemble of values, myths, beliefs, customs, norms, expectations and habits that encapsulate the way of life of particular groups of people living in historical-specific times. Culture is the framework, or paradigm, that holds a people together, giving them a shared understanding of the world, of the place and purpose of people and objects, of their origins and destiny.

For about the last three centuries, the culture that will be described here was associated first with the Western European nation states and later with the United States. It was molded and tempered by values, myths, and institutions that preexisted the development of the capitalist economy and were adapted in varying ways by it. As this culture came into contact with others, through the process of colonization, it established a dialectical relationship between two societies, two national cultures, in which the dominating power stamped the conquered peoples with certain distinctive features, but that, in turn, was influenced in that colony by the preexisting culture's values, myths, and institutions. Thus, while British, French, Dutch, Portuguese, and Spanish colonialism shared certain general features, each differed from the others in significant respects (Worsley, 1984, p. 3).

Until the rise of capitalism, cultures were primarily generated and reinforced by kinship-based, religious, and political-juridical relations and institutions. With capitalism, however, a new source of cultural generation arises: the capitalist market, with its insistent laws of supply and demand. Capital's insatiable search for raw materials, cheaper labor, and new markets translates the ideas of a few philosophers—Newtonian physics, Cartesian rationalism, Comteian positivism, and Lockean property rights and contract theory—into powerful political and juridical institutions. It is the capitalist market that destroys ancient kinship systems, domesticates the transcendent God of medieval Europe, and either domesticates or destroys the numen of land-based peoples in the European colonies.

Marx's apocalyptic description of this great cultural transformation is probably more relevant today than when he wrote it in 1848:

> The bourgeoisie, wherever it has got the upper hand, has put an end to all feudal, patriarchal, idyllic relations. It has pitilessly torn asunder the motley feudal ties that bound man to his "natural superiors," and has left remaining no other nexus between man and man than naked self-interest,

than callous "cost payment." It has drowned the most heavenly ecstasies of religious fervor, of chivalrous enthusiasm, of Philistine sentimentalism, in the icy water of egotistical calculation. It has resolved personal worth into exchange value, and in place of the numberless indefeasible chartered freedoms, has set up that single, unconscionable freedom—Free Trade. In one word, for exploitation, veiled by religious and political illusions, it has substituted naked, shameless, direct, brutal exploitation. (Marx, 1969, p. 111)

Marx's critics have pointed out that the determinative role given to the "structure" of economic relations over the "superstructure" of cultural and political institutions was reductionist and, therefore, a misreading of reality. Feminists have pointed to the persistence of preexisting patriarchal myths and relations not only in the structures of capitalism but also in the socialist systems that were supposed to have overthrown the capitalist order. Some African-American theorists have claimed a sui generis role for white racism, which is certainly made use of by capitalism but that cannot be reduced to a mere epiphenomenon of the economic system (West, 1988). Still others assert that all attempts to reduce cultural phenomena to a single class of determining relations is bound to be false.[1]

While there is merit to each of these arguments, the sheer concentration and magnification of power that exist today in the interlocking web of transnational corporations that invest, allocate labor and other resources, and reap profits on a global scale suggests that there may be a qualitative change taking place in the relationship between the economic, political, and kinship spheres. Some have spoken of the decoupling of economic decision making from the political and spatially oriented strictures of the nation-state. Lash and Urry (1987) posit three stages in the development of capitalism, the first two of which were defined by capital that was "nationally owned and clearly tied into the fortunes of the country in which it was owned and to which it was indissolubly bound." In the third (present) stage, capital's "attachment to any single economy becomes more tentative, as capital expands (and contracts) on a global basis" (pp. 89-90). Sassen (1988) speaks of the creation of a new *transnational space* for the circulation of capital. Others see a fusion of the economic and political. Miller (1989) speaks of the United States as having a new social order, which he labels the *corporate state,* that is, a government corporation symbiosis. Gramm (1989), looking at similar data on the concentration of economic power, labels the system *oligarchic capitalism,* with characteristics bordering on fascism. Still others have referred to the system as *corporatism.*

Whatever the label, it is clear that wherever transnational corporations prosper, the political has ceased to function as an autonomous realm that conditions and structures economic decision making, and it has long since been the case that kinship roles condition and structure either economic or political decision making. Almost everywhere Western capitalism has penetrated, traditional kinship patterns have been, if not destroyed, then severely eroded, while patriarchal gender roles have been transformed into rationales for the inequitable allocation of economic costs and benefits.

During the centuries in which capitalism was structured by the destinies and needs of nation-states, the purely economic laws of the market could not totally dominate the civil and political spheres. Within Western capitalist societies, the idea of bourgeois democracy and individual freedom always threatened to break out of the property relations that held their application in check. The uneasy tension that existed between the laws of the market and the political realm allowed trade unions, socialist parties, and various social movements to appeal to state power to intervene in the economy on behalf of a more just and equitable regulation of the market. While the state usually did the bidding of those with economic power, it had to give lip service, at least, to nationalist and universalist sentiments and moral values. The British empire was erected to extend "civilization" to the untutored natives. *Noblesse oblige* was a characteristic concomitant of a *nationally* structured world economy. When the United States took over the function of empire building from the British, its many interventions in the third world had to be legitimized by the rationalization that it was "saving the world for democracy."

Profound changes have been wrought by the collapse of communist governments as the vehicle for oppositional ideals, values, and habits as well as the accelerated concentration of capital. The transnational corporation, through its monopoly of advanced telecommunications technology and fiber optics, has become the bearer of a culture that is more purely a projection of economic relations than of economic relations tempered by kinship, ethnic, national, religious, or political values.

Of the Western capitalist cultural ensemble, we need to ask (1) What are the dominant values and myths embedded in this culture that are being embraced by peoples all over the world and how do they contribute to oppression, exploitation, and war? (2) How are these values structured conceptually so that they form a logic that is accepted as the way things are? (3) What values, insights, and knowledge has Western capitalism in its relentless pursuit of world dominance suppressed or destroyed that could be helpful in shaping a new system of world peace? (4) What are the cultural dimensions of a new peace system and where do we see it emerging?

A culture can be characterized by what it holds holy, or sacred. In Western capitalist societies, five values stand out:

> private property and its extension as commodities, money, and capital
> individualism
> competition, rather than cooperation, as the chief civic virtue
> European or Western cultural superiority, which is often expressed as white male supremacy
> Western scientific objectivity

Private Property in the Culture of Capitalism

The concept of private property—in things and in people—is not unique to capitalism. It existed in the ancient world.[2] However, such a concept was foreign to the peoples who inhabited the North American continent before its conquest by Europeans. Indeed, it was the native Americans' inability to comprehend the idea of private property or its implications that made them more vulnerable to the Europeans. State sanctioning of the concept of private property made possible the near extinction of the indigenous peoples of the Americas—called by some the greatest demographic catastrophe in history.

Although private property is not peculiar to capitalism, what is new is the fetishism with which it is invested.[3] Raw materials that are transformed into commodities take on a metaphysical reality that, as the volume of their exchange increases, diminishes the autonomy and subjectivity of their human creators. As commodities are turned into money and money into the even more abstract symbol *capital,* those who control it come to look on capital itself, as the "fount of life" (Hinkelammert, 1986, p. 33).[4]

Marx (1977) dramatically analyzed the effects of the fetishism of money as the highest form of commodity fetishism:

Everything becomes saleable and purchaseable. Circulation becomes the great social retort into which everything is thrown, to come out again as the money crystal. Nothing is immune from this alchemy, the bones of the saints cannot withstand it, let alone more delicate *res sancrosanctae, extra commercium hominum.* Just as in money every qualitative difference between commodities is extinguished, so too for its part as a radical leveler, it extinguishes all distinctions. (p. 229)

One doesn't have to look very far today to see in the capitalist world the consummation of Marx's vision. Individuals with rich histories and personalities have become consumers, and people identified by some ascriptive label such as income, skin color, gender, or the census track in which they live have become markets. Harvard economist Reich (1991) cites the example of the founder of a direct-mail business who bragged, "Tell me someone's ZIP code and I can predict what they eat, drink, drive, even think" (pp. 17, 24). Where collectivities of people lack the resources to be markets, they are given another label—the underclass—and read out of the acceptable human polity.[5] In such a world, community becomes the act of bonding together to protect one's particular economic enclave from those who do not share it. Says Reich (1991), "generosity and solidarity end at the border of similarly valued properties" (p. 42).

The commodification, or privatization, of functions and services that used to be performed by the family or provided by the state as part of its obligation to provide for the common welfare or to socialize the polity has accompanied the more frenzied circulation and concentration of capital. The world of leveraged buyouts, corporate mergers, and the junk bond market—through which paper profits are piled on one another like a house of cards, resulting in the obscene wealth of a few and the unemployment and impoverishment of many—is a reflection of the triumph of the fetishism of money. So too is the savings and loan scandal, which will mortgage the future of generations to come, while the international drug trade destroys for the sake of money all traditional communal ties between human beings and causes elected governments to become mockeries of the idea of democracy.

In effect, the fetishism of money produces a social relationship between products and a material relationship between producers. The fetish also obscures from the human producers and capitalists alike, the connection between human labor and the products it produces as well as the connection of workers to each other and their interdependence. In advanced capitalism human beings are labeled *human capital* (a term used easily and uncritically even by leftist sociologists and economists in capitalist culture). Their labor capacity is quantified and factored in as just one of the many material variables that go into extending the value of the owners of these means of production. The extent to which humans have become *things* and human creations *human* is found in the definition of a corporation as a *person* in American jurisprudence. Although the Fourteenth Amendment was added to the Constitution to provide equal protection of the laws to black people, corporations, under their definition as persons, have made more extensive use of the amendment to protect themselves from public scrutiny and regulation.

Through the same logic, individual workers in capitalist societies measure themselves and others by means of the material return they can command for their labor power. In his elegy to the common laborer, "El Pueblo," Neruda (1972) portrays not only the low status but the invisibility, in the consciousness structure of dominator systems, of those common laborers whose basic work cleared the fields, built the cities, and provided the bread for the tables of the rich:

> *In the comings and goings of families,*
> *at times he was my father or my relative*
> *or (it may have been, it may not)*
> *perhaps the one who did not come home*
> *because water or earth devoured him*
> *or a machine or a tree killed him,*
> *or he was that funeral carpenter*
> *who walked behind the coffin, but dry-eyed*
> *someone who never had a name*
> *except as wood or metal have,*
> *and on whom others looked from above,*
> *unable to see*
> *the ant for the ant-hill;*
> *so that when his feet no longer moved*
> *because, poor and tired, he had died,*
> *they never saw what they were not used to seeing—*
> *already other feet walked in his place.*

(pp. 445-447)

Those excluded from participation in the labor market (the unemployed and subemployed) or discriminated against within it because of preexisting biases that capitalism has found useful to maintain (African-Americans, immigrant or "guest" workers, and women) are of little or no value compared with those whose labor can command high salaries or whose position within the market enables them to command the labor power of others. Such undervalued workers then become the cannon fodder (one of the factors of production) for wars fought to preserve the prerogatives of capital. A case in point is the cost-benefit analyses conducted by military strategists as they planned for a war in the Persian Gulf, glibly talking about the number of casualties they could sustain in order to protect the world oil markets.

In the colonial era and later during the Cold War, undervalued workers rationalized their own destruction by believing that they were fighting for the glory of God, king, and country; civilization; the white man's burden; or democracy. With the diminution of the nation-state as the determining unit in world affairs and the disappearance of the Communist menace, workers' internalization of their *thingness* becomes more apparent. This was revealed in the numerous interviews of American soldiers deployed in the Persian Gulf in 1991. One was struck by how often they referred to their lethal mission as the "job they had to do."

While capitalist forms of domination and labor exploitation might not be qualitatively worse than earlier forms of human oppression, the architecture through which they are assembled is much more intricately obscured from human consciousness. In previous systems in which classes and state are clearly crystallized (systems that Amin, 1989, refers to as tributary modes of production), the character of economic exploitation is more transparent; that is, precapitalist societies are more directly governed by the political, to whose constraints the other aspects of social reality, including the economic, have to conform (Amin, 1989, p. 5).

The mystification of the means of exploitation under capitalism, when coupled with the Enlightenment myth of the ability of all people to rise to their potential, makes it harder for the victims to recognize not only the source of the violence and oppression with which they live but *the very fact of their exploitation and oppression*. Their undervaluing and exploitation is attributed to universal laws that operate independently of any human agency, or to the victims themselves who are thought to lack the drive, intelligence, or genetic makeup to get ahead.

Moreover, the illusion of class permeability coupled with the ideal of universal equality of opportunity leads almost inevitably to the scapegoating of those lower down the economic ladder when economic conditions become precarious for the middle and working classes. This phenomenon was at work in Nazi Germany and can be seen in the contemporary rise of the radical right in the United States as the American Dream sours for more and more lower-middle- and working-class whites.

The human costs of the working out of the inexorable laws of capitalism—industrial illnesses, social rupture, and ecological destruction—are never accounted or compensated for in the systems used to measure and evaluate the market. In all major economic accounts systems they are considered *externals.*

With the globalization of the capitalist economy, the obscuring of the social relationship among workers in one country—which to some extent was exposed by the trade union and socialist movements during the early part of this century—is made more obscure by the internationalization of the labor market. Now, displaced workers in the Rust Belt of the American Midwest instead of recognizing their connection with workers in the third world and thus their need for solidarity with them, are likely, instead, to experience them as rivals who are "taking away our jobs." The potential for exploiting such misperceptions and fears to generate *enemy thinking* and justify U.S. military intervention abroad is not hard to see.

Commodity fetishism is premised on the acceptance of a norm carried over from a previous age: private property. But private property is only the basis for another basic norm sacred to capitalism: the contract as the medium by which the ownership of commodities changes hands.

> From commodity relationships and their state of development are derived legal relationships and norms of behavior. Commodity relationships are the crucial factor for determining the property system, the legal and state system and the system of behavioral norms. . . . Commodity relationships not only set down the rules for social relationships between human beings. Dating from the appearance of money [which, according to Marx is the king of the commodity world, its highest form] at the very latest, human destiny itself is interpreted on the basis of commodity relationships. The values that propel commodity development are seen to come from money. It is precisely money that paves the way for a change in human perspectives. (Hinkelammert, 1986, p. 21)

In capitalist societies, the only contract that is held sacred is that in which money changes hands. Loss of life, loss of limb, or in the case of indigenous peoples, loss of the land that is the very lifeblood of their cultures are compensated by a money transaction. Actuarial tables valorize human life in terms of its money value. A nation's development is valued in terms of the sum total of goods and services produced as expressed in their exchange value. Those who are brought before the law and do not have money are incarcerated, while those who can make bail are given their freedom.

Just as commodity fetishism obscures the relationship between humans and their labor, between humans and the products of their labor, and between one human being and another, so does this fetish also obscure the relationship between human beings and the land, the original source of all wealth. Land itself and now even air and water, become commodities that are bought and sold on the market. The conception of the earth as a living organism and humans as intimately related to and dependent on the rhythms of nature is utterly unthinkable inside the logic of Western capitalism.

Individualism: The Snake
That Swallows Its Tail

The concept of individualism, which started off as an enlightened reaction to the caste rigidities of the feudal order, has, under the conditions of advanced transnational capitalism, become another contributor to the war system. People at every level of American society are experiencing a deeper level of atomization and disassociation from religious, ethnic, kinship, workplace, and political ties that once held them to wider human obligations and responsibilities.

The wealthier inhabit a transnational world linked by jet, fax, satellite, and fiber optic cable. Their encounters with others are quick and superficial, measured in terms of hours, minutes, and bytes. Those who are outside the electronic circuits that bind them together simply do not exist. The *noblesse oblige* of the wealthy of an earlier era has given way to a kind of ruthless forgetfulness of the less fortunate.[6]

The overworked, declining middle class is isolated in a different way. With two or more family members having to earn money to maintain a middle-class life-style and with success secured through the operation of individual achievement unfettered by family or other group affiliations (Bellah et al., 1985, p. 148), they have little time or incentive for the communal obligations of family nurture, community maintenance, or political participation. Hence dinners are at fast-food restaurants, children are stuck in front of television sets or Nintendo games—where they are programmed into the habits of thought and affective responses needed for the prosecution of electronic warfare—and elderly parents are sent to nursing homes.

The poor, who once got by through strong community survival networks made up of extended families, churches, and other institutions are increasingly isolated in their poverty and thus subject to the allure of drugs, crime, teenage pregnancy, and random violence.

For many young men and women of the ghetto, the solution to the breakdown of communal ties and the desire to aspire to middle-class affluence is found in the criminal gang or the military. There they find a collective purpose and a way out of economic misery. But they also become part of the war machine that destroys others as well as those it recruits. Those who mimic middle-class life-styles through gang membership or involvement in crime inevitably end up in the prison system. Today, the United States has the highest per capita rate of incarceration in the world (*New York Times,* January 7, 1991, p. A14). It is the volunteer army that enabled the U.S. government to assemble the most formidable military machine ever arrayed in the Persian Gulf. In both cases, individualism carried to its logical conclusion in advanced capitalism becomes the snake that devours its own tail.

Competition as Civic Virtue

Flowing from the fetishism of money capital is the virtue through which it is assumed to be accumulated: continual competition to outmaneuver, outmarket, outbuy others in the same game. Competition is continuous and unending, because not to be in the circle of competition is to deny capitalism's very ground of existence. Marx described the human being defined by capitalist relations as a Sisyphus, a "conqueror whose conquests lead only to new frontiers, who makes into the greatest virtues the norms of behavior appropriate to his race. . . . One formulates the goals in such a way that they can never be reached" (Hinkelammert, 1986, p. 26).

Competition as civic virtue generates continuous levels of anxiety and frenzy in those who have internalized the quest for the eternally unsatisfied goal. Competition generates the reproduction of ever greater quantities of unnecessary and wasteful goods and services. More and more of life is converted to commodity relationships as the market takes over the functions once performed by the family, the religious sphere, the community, or the state—such as child and elder care, food preparation, healing, punishment and rehabilitation, and even the rituals and decisions surrounding the primal events of life and death.

Engelhardt (1989) demonstrates that in the advanced capitalist countries every bit of available physical and psychic space has been filled by the advertising industry, to the extent that new space—in the form of microspace, or ads within ads, is now being created. Under such a relentless drive to sell products, human life itself and thoughts that do not conform to the advertising mode begin to seem artificial in comparison to the "reality" of the fantasy world created by the ad (Engelhardt, 1989).

War is the logical result of competitive anxiety on a national and international scale. It is the attempt to resolve and master, once and for all, the terrible anguish of never being good enough, never having arrived. In the statements of American leaders on the war in the Persian Gulf, one caught this anxiety just below the surface of the bravado displayed in the recounting of ordinance dropped and battles won.

European Superiority

The fourth value Western capitalist culture holds sacred is the conviction of its own superiority over all other forms of social organization. This sense of superiority is expressed as European ethnocentrism, which often takes the form of a belief in and practice of white supremacy.

Amin sees Eurocentrism as the reason why the Renaissance marks such a qualitative break with previously existing cultures. According to Amin (1989), "it is from this time on, that Europeans become conscious of the idea that the conquest of the world by their civilization is henceforth a possible objective . . . even if the actual submission of other peoples hasn't yet taken place" (pp. 72-73).

Eurocentrism plays a legitimizing role for capitalism, hiding its actually existing nature and distorting awareness of its contradictions (Amin, 1989, p. ix). As such, Eurocentrism is not just one among many forms of ethnocentrism that stem from the ignorance of other peoples, but a totalizing paradigm that claims that "the imitation of the Western model by all peoples is the only solution to the challenges of our time" (p. vii).

Amin dissects the ideology of Eurocentrism but is unable to account for its etymology. In the *Protestant Ethic and the Spirit of Capitalism,* Weber (1958) offers one possible explanation in the complex of religious attitudes and beliefs that were generated by the Protestant Reformation, through which the religious virtues of abstinence and self-sacrifice were transmuted into the virtues of thrift and saving, while God's mark of election became the accumulation of worldly capital.

In Marx's anatomy of commodity fetishism, however, we may find a more important clue to the particular arrogance that Eurocentrism and its correlate white supremacy exhibit. Once buying and selling are separated by the capitalist market and money becomes the depository of value and, therefore, the gateway to all values, there arises

> an image of infinity connected to money and the power associated with it, not only because everything produced seems purchaseable, but the producers themselves and indeed the whole world seems purchaseable. Hoarding or accumulating seem to be the precondition for having access to everything; and beyond the limit of all that is possible there appears the reflection of transcendent infinity. Gold can even enable souls to enter paradise. (Hinkelammert, 1986, p. 24)

Thus the rising bourgeoisie came to think of themselves and the civilization they were creating as the apex of world development and as the only means by which the world could be saved from ignorance, fear, and poverty. Such an attitude, when coupled with the use of the gun, provided for a "conquering dynamism," greatly disproportionate to all earlier societies (Amin, 1989, p. 73).

In positing itself as the end product of all human development, European culture erected an ideology that denied the economic, political, spiritual, philosophical, and technological contributions of other peoples and cultures to world development. Says Amin (1989):

> This dominant culture invented an "eternal West" unique since the moment of its origin. This arbitrary and mythic construct had as its counterpart an equally artificial conception of the Other (the "Orients" or the "Orient"), likewise constructed on mythic foundations. (pp. 89-90)

Western history removes ancient Greece from the Orient in which it unfolded and annexes it to Europe, to provide a claim for the predisposition of Europe to the rationality that emerges as democratic capitalist civilization. It also erects the myth of separate races—at various points in history the inferiority of other peoples being rationalized by reference to biology, religion, or geography—in order to claim continuity between ancient Greece and modern Europe (Amin, 1989, pp. 90-100).

The cultural arrogance and superiority characterizing Western societies is seen in the concept *white man's burden,* which legitimized British colonialism in the 19th century; in the attitudes of missionaries and military men alike to the indigenous peoples of North America, considered either childlike or savage; and in their attitude toward Africans as subhuman. It is demonstrated in the concept of Manifest Destiny and in the pious assumption that American intervention in the third world is saving these countries for freedom, democracy, and the rule of law.

The Myth of Western Objectivity

Critical to the worldview of Eurocentrism is the central place that Western science and technology hold. The myth of objectivity on which Western science and technology are based holds that the world is made up of discrete objects that have properties independent of any people or other beings who experience them. We get our knowledge of the world through observing, manipulating, and experimenting with these objects, then categorizing and labeling their properties. Western science and the scientific method provide us with a methodology that calls us to achieve understanding from a universally valid and unbiased point of view. Science can ultimately give a correct, definitive, and general account of reality, and through its methodology it is constantly progressing toward that goal (Lakoff & Johnson, 1980, pp. 186-188; see also, Adas, 1989).

The myth of scientific objectivity denies the validity of knowledge derived from any other source but observation and experimentation. It invalidates the insights obtained through intuition, dreams, feelings, relationships, and the creative imagination. The language of poetry and religion—metaphor, symbol, simile—is cast into the realm of denigrated subjectivity and irrationality.

Lakoff and Johnson as well as Kuhn (1970) demonstrate that Western scientific objectivity is a myth or paradigm—just one of many that can be used to describe the world. Berry (1988) describes the industrial age, based on this myth, as "a period of technological entrancement, an altered state of consciousness, a mental fixation that alone can explain how we come to ruin our air and water and soil and to severely damage all our basic life systems under the illusion that this was 'progress' " (p. 82).

In spite of the fact that modern quantum physics and ecologists—as well as Eastern and native American worldviews—revealed a picture of the world that is far more complex, organic, and unpredictable than the picture given us by Western science, the myth of scientific objectivity continues to dominate Western capitalist culture because it plays a significant legitimizing function for the economic system. The arrogance of scientism was demonstrated in the comments of military experts as they analyzed U.S. prosecution of the war in the Persian Gulf and bragged about the smart bombs that could home in on the air shafts in buildings.

The instrumental use of nature through which capital accumulation is accomplished is validated by the Western scientific paradigm that views nature as dead matter that is available to be harnessed to the Western engine of progress. Every new lode of ore that was discovered, every new product or technology made possible through the instrumental use of nature only served to prove the validity of the thesis. Only now, as the cumulative ecological crisis looms, are alternative conceptions of nature gaining some credence in the Western world. As the stepchildren of the Enlightenment, Marxist systems have also shared in this flawed (because partial) and ultimately destructive myth of scientific objectivity.

Not coincidentaly, the kind of science and technology idolized in both capitalist and Marxist systems has been capital intensive. Reliance on such technology reinforces the power of large capital owners—in capitalist societies, private corporations, and in Marxist systems, the state and its managers. Small-scale technology, intermediate technology, and scientific methods that reflect the wholeness of organic systems and the interdependence of their parts are treated as unscientific in Western culture.

The logic of Western science not only legitimized the destructive pillage of natural resources but served to mystify the exploitation of human labor. In his genealogy of white racism, West (1982) showed how the Western scientific community's penchant for observation, measurement, comparison, and ordering—when regulated by the aesthetic and cultural ideals of ancient Greece—led it to conclude that Africans were inferior because they had smaller foreheads or larger noses than Europeans. Similar biological explanations have been offered for women's social inferiority in Western cultures. In this case, Western biological determinism replaced the older orders of creation through which an earlier society, dominated by the "sacred canopy" of androcentric Christianity, rationalized its social subordination of women. Such supposedly scientific evidence provided the rationale for American slavery and later the use of African-Americans as a cheap, secondary labor source as well as the exclusion of women from participation in public life and wage work or their relegation to a secondary, gender-typed labor market.

Contemporary examples of supposedly scientific authority to legitimize economic exploitation and structural unemployment and underemployment are seen in Taylorism and Harvard Business School theories of scientific management, through which working-class aspirations for economic democracy have been thwarted and calls for policies of full employment or family-oriented workplace arrangements have been ignored.

Western social science has also purported to have discovered that the poverty in the third world is due to the inherent underdevelopment or *development lag* of third world countries, which can be relieved by adopting the Western development model. More recently, a body of positivist social science has begun to develop theories that rationalize the emergence of an underclass in the heart of the industrialized West. Since the emergence of this third world in the heart of the first world is an anomaly, this new body of scientific logic is beginning to legitimize the permanent marginalization of these sectors of the population through a new version of social Darwinism. In its crudest version, the new social Darwinism asserts that those labeled as members of the underclass are held to be ineducable, pathological, and inherently vulnerable to drugs and crime. The rationale is, therefore, in place to invade their homes and arrest, imprison, or kill them as threats to the educable, rational, and more civilized sectors of the population.

The Structuring of Western Cultural Values and Myths

While in capitalist societies political and social values, beliefs and institutions arise from economic relationships in dialectical interaction with previously existing values, beliefs, and institutions, they eventually assume a life of their own, becoming embedded in language and institutional arrangements that structure the consciousness of the society's members. They provide the lenses through which subsequent generations literally see the world. Because Western languages—especially English—have become the bearer of capitalist culture, we must look at the structure of the language to understand how it both reinforces the values we have been describing and excludes other ways of seeing.

Feminists and those who have sought to understand the anatomy of racism have pointed to the dichotomous logic at the heart of modern English discourse. This logic divides much of reality into antinomies. Dichotomous logic can be explained by lining up under positive and negative signs all those words that in everyday use are invested with either positive or negative significance relative to the other. The following list illustrates the logic.[7]

+	−
human	animal
male	female
white	black
Western	Eastern
rich	poor
civilized	barbaric
north	south
private	public
capitalist	communist
good	bad
first world	third world
developed	underdeveloped
Christian	pagan
healthy	sick
culture	nature

These antonyms and others that could be added reflect the actual unequal property relations that exist in capitalist societies and the qualities that are associated with those who are on the winning and losing side. By positing reality as a zero sum equation and by excluding other conceptual categories that would make the words above into not antonyms but points along a conceptual spectrum, the very structure of the language both obscures the more complex reality that it seeks to represent and reproduces the system of inequitable property relations.

In contrast to dichotomous logic we see a different conceptual framework in the cultures of native Americans, who refer to humans as *two-leggeds,* indicating their place along a spectrum of sentient life. The dichotomy between *human* and *animal* in English allows those labeled humans to domesticate, mutilate, kill, and even destroy whole species of those labeled animals, without any feeling that humans are in any way affected by, connected to, or dependent on the objects of their destruction. Native Americans, constrained by their language and by a more organic worldview, took from the animal world only what they needed to survive and, in the process, asked forgiveness of the "sisters" and "brothers" whom scarcity forced them to kill.

Dichotomous logic is not peculiar to capitalist cultures. It originated in the cultural dualism of neoplatonic philosophy that Europe adopted along with Constantinian Christianity. Such logic has proven useful to this form of economy, however. Because capitalism is based on continuous accumulation and growth, the dichotomy between human culture and dead nature has allowed the continued pillage of the natural world to feed the capitalist growth machine. Dichotomous valorization is also useful to a system that is structured so that most must lose so that a few can win. Dichotomous logic keeps other ways of arranging economic goods and services, and rewards and punishments not only from being socially valued but even from coming to collective consciousness. If private ownership is positively valorized and public ownership is its negative opposite, then the public sector is seen as a negative drag on private enterprise and as an impediment to capitalist accumulation. The public sector is then made to compensate or cover for the mistakes, waste, and inequalities generated by the private sector and then blamed for not being efficient in accomplishing this impossible task.

In addition to the dichotomous parameters that circumscribe thought in Western languages, capitalist culture is also reproduced by bureaucratic organization—the institutional arrangement best suited to the accumulation of private profit and the application of capital-intensive technology.

For Weber, bureaucracy was the highest form of human development because it conformed to the precision and rationality of Western science. Critical organization theorists, however, have pointed out the irrationality of large bureaucracies; their failure to live up to the rule-directed, politically neutral meritocratic ideal type outlined by Weber; and their function as forms of social control—control of the workers by owners and managers as well as control of potentially rebellious classes and subcultures. Though bureaucracy is not unique to capitalism—large-scale organizations existed in previous empires and bureaucracies have also existed in socialist systems—the modern capitalist world is unique in the extent to which it is penetrated by bureaucracy. While bureaucracy everywhere induces conformity, stifles democratic participation, and keeps human beings from realizing their potential as political actors, it does so in a particular way in capitalist societies.

Feminist theorist Ferguson (1984) points out that bureaucracies in capitalist societies exist in a context in which social relations between classes, races and sexes are fundamentally unequal: "Bureaucracy, as the 'scientific organization of inequality,' serves as a filter for these other forms of domination, projecting them into an institutional arena that both rationalizes and maintains them" (pp. 7-8).

According to Marglin (1974), the social function of hierarchical work organization is not technical efficiency, but accumulation. "By mediating between producer and consumer, the capitalist organization sets aside much more for expanding and improving plant and equipment than individuals would if they could control the pace of capital accumulation" (p. 62).

Although bureaucracy is rationalized by the need to manage large groups of people, products, and markets, bureaucratic organization— the specialization of tasks and the routinization of functions—took place before the advent of sophisticated mechanization and the application of fixed capital. The writings of Taylor, the father of scientific management, make it clear that the purpose of such organization was to wrest knowledge of and control over the work process from workers and to put it into the hands of managers.

Today, bureaucracy works at two levels to stifle creative thought and deviant political power. First, it separates workers from one another and segments the consciousness of workers at both the lower and management levels. To quote Ferguson (1984):

> Bureaucracy imposes the simultaneous isolation of individuals from one another and the depersonalization of the channels still linking individuals together. Relations among members of a bureaucracy are impersonal and rule-governed in order to maintain the organization and to "prevent the disintegration of the bureaucratic structure . . . should these be supplanted by personalized relations." Thus managers who break these rules and seek to humanize, perhaps even democratize, relations within their offices are posing a fundamental threat to the organization; even if their offices function effectively, they are subverting the hierarchy, undermining the official value system, and attacking the organizationally defined identity of other managers, and propagating relationships within the organization that are antithetical to the legitimated ones. (pp. 12-13, reprinted by permission of the publisher)

This isolation and segmentation of human life has onerous consequences for both personal and political development.

> If we see that the human self is created by a process of interaction with others, in which individuals arrive at their own unique identity through

viewing themselves from the perspective of others, then the destruction of personal relations through bureaucratization threatens the foundation of self-identity. . . . The structures that isolate us undermine politics itself in that they undermine our sociality; they harm our capacity to take the perspective of others onto ourselves and our situation, to imagine alternatives that come from shared experience, to project different futures and redefine past experiences on the basis of other possibilities for individual and collective life. (Ferguson, 1984, pp. 13-14)

Second, bureaucracies also develop their own language systems that simultaneously mystify the real (and unequal) power relations that lie at the heart of bureaucratic organization by rendering all human relations in terms of ostensibly neutral administrative jargon. They thus develop their own semisecret language to allow the personnel to maintain control over their objects and procedures. According to Ferguson (1984), secret language performs several related functions:

It allows the organization to monopolize information, safeguard the actions of its members from protest or supervision by outsiders. In order to do business with bureaucrats, one must engage in conversation with them; this requires that one learn their language, play their game, and come onto their turf. (p. 15)

Bureaucratic language, whether used by multinational corporations, defense intellectuals, or lawyers is not simply language *about* a reality that everyone has access to; such language literally creates its own reality. Feminist legal scholars, for example, have demonstrated how the abstract, rule-governed language of the legal profession denies the way in which most women have been socialized to come to ethical decisions through taking into account the context of relationships in which such decisions are embedded (Lewin, 1988, p. 39).[8]

Cohn (1988), who spent a year living and working with defense intellectuals (all men), describes how the language of this profession began to change her very relationship to reality:

I had previously encountered in my reading the extraordinary language used to discuss nuclear war, but somehow it was different to hear it spoken. What hits first is the elaborate use of abstraction and euphemism, which allows infinite talk about nuclear holocaust without ever forcing the speaker or enabling the listener to touch the reality behind the words. . . . Defense analysts don't talk about incinerating cities: they talk about "countervalue attacks." Human death, in nuclear parlance, is most often referred to as "collateral damage." (p. 85)

Beyond this superficial recognition of the function of this language, Cohn (1988) came to yet a deeper understanding of its significance.

> Technostrategic language articulates only the perspective of the users of nuclear weapons, not the victims. Speaking the expert language not only offers distance, a feeling of control, and an alternative focus for one's energies; it also offers an escape from thinking of oneself as a victim of nuclear war. (p. 92)

The more immersed she was in the language, the more Cohn found herself unable to connect with the reality she had previously known.

> The better I became at this discourse, the more difficult it became to express my own ideas and values. While the language included things I had never been able to speak about before, it radically excluded others. . . . If I was unable to speak my concerns in this language, more disturbing still was that I also began to find it harder even to keep them in my own head. No matter how firm my commitment to staying aware of the bloody reality behind the words, over and over I found that I could not keep human lives as my reference point. (p. 93)

Technostrategic language and the thought patterns it employs came out of the war colleges and into the home of every American via television coverage of the Persian Gulf conflict. In the daily Pentagon briefings, millions of Americans were mesmerized by explanations of smart bombs, laser-guided missiles, by announcements of so many thousand sorties, missions, and kills. The video demonstrations of bombs hitting their targets with pinpoint accuracy found a ready audience in young people long conditioned by video games to view war as an antiseptic process—a matter of pushing buttons and making targets disappear in a puff of electronic smoke.

Lifton (1991), the psychologist who has studied the process of psychic numbing, observed that there is a *technological euphoria* that happens as one watches smart bombs home in on their targets. It is a deceptive substitute for people getting maimed and killed, and it doesn't work perfectly. Sometimes, other images of war's costs break through. Once this happens, there is a reassertion by the high-tech experts who become our teachers in a sort of classroom in which we feel we're being initiated into the secrets of a mystery cult.

The language of the defense establishment is not very different from the language to be found in other kinds of bureaucracies—including those of the former socialist bloc—that share the myth of objectivity with the West. All bureaucratic language is abstract, one-directional and acausal. "The language of technics replaces the language of human action; 'feedback,' 'input,' and 'output' replace dialogue, debate, and judgement. The linguistic tendencies of technocratic society suppress the processes of open conflict and compromise that constitutes meaningful publics" (Ferguson, 1984, p. 15).

So pervasive is bureaucratic discourse with its ability to deny alternative realities, that to be involved in public life today "is to be embedded within bureaucratic discourse; to be firmly grounded in the nonbureaucratic is to be removed from the arenas of available speech" (Ferguson, 1984, p. 23).

Still a third way bureaucracies function to maximize social control, stifle political dissension, muzzle creativity and destroy diversity is through the functionalist and panoptical ordering of space, as seen in the aesthetics of modern industrial, residential, public, and even leisure design.[9] Some examples are the corporate office tower, with its chillingly impersonal glass and steel facade outside and rows of standardized cubicles inside, designed for maximum observation and control of the work force; the condominium development, where even the color of one's mailbox is regulated; the public housing projects, public school buildings and asylums that resemble prisons; the Holiday Inns, which look and feel identical everywhere in the world; and even the store mannequins, with their featureless faces, menacing poses, and clothes that mimic the lines and colors of steel, iron, and chrome. Our culture's fascination with the robot and the robotized images of humanity portrayed in so much of the children's toy industry, not to mention television images, are an extension of the bureaucratic aesthetic. All serve the same function as the abstract, acausal language of the defense intellectuals: to create a reality that denies human feeling, the reality of human suffering, the connection between image and sensuous reality, the individuality of persons and the diversity of cultures. According to Ewen, it is a culture of surfaces and images, without depth and texture, a culture in which politics is sold by the advertising industry and dissenting social movements are coopted and sold back to the public as the latest fashion (Ewen, 1988).

Toward a Culture of Peace

Because the bureaucratic capitalist culture is so encompassing, we must look for signs of a peace culture among sectors of the population and subcultures that have not been fully drawn into its orbit. Scattered across the Western industrialized world are pockets of peace cultures—spaces—sometimes physical, sometimes simply psychic—in which numbers of people are forging the dimensions of an alternative culture. Such groups include native American communities, feminist communities, African-Americans who are rediscovering the Afrocentric ethos long denied by Western culture, holistic health and healing practitioners, environmentalists and peace activists, bioregionalists, the Green party movements, and scientists who have discovered the mystical at the heart of their own professions.

Perhaps it is the native Americans, most directly linked to ongoing oppositional ways of knowing, that provide us with the richest elements for inventing a culture of peace. Native American communities across the country and throughout the hemisphere are listening with greater intent than at any time since the late 19th century to the teachings of their elders and shamans, who have predicted a turning point for human culture—a time of decision—that they believe the world has now entered.[10] In native American teachings, the Western cultural, economic, and political project has reached an end point the conclusion of which will be the destruction of life on earth. What is required of human beings to avert this catastrophe is nothing less than a cultural/spiritual conversion—an unlearning of the ways that lead to death and an opening to a new understanding of ourselves, our relations to one another, and to the universe.

The native American worldview demands that we put on a different set of lenses, that we see the world and the universe as an organic unity whose parts—human, animal, vegetable, and mineral, living and dead—are intricately interconnected. It is the vision of the mystic and seer that must become practical, concrete, and institutionalized.

Berry (1988), a cultural historian and one of a new breed of ecotheologians, has attempted to bring native American wisdom into dialogue with developing discoveries in the scientific and countercultural disciplines. Berry asserts that we need a new historical vision of the earth to guide us to a more creative and peaceful future. Such a vision must be of a greater order of magnitude than any of the visions that have guided previous epochs, because we have changed in a deleterious manner not simply the structure and functioning of human society: we have changed the very chemistry of the planet, we have altered the biosystems, we have changed the topography and even the geological structure of the planet, structures and functions that have taken hundreds of millions and even billions of years to bring into existence. Such an order of magnitude has never before entered into earth history or into human consciousness. (Berry, 1988, p. xiii)

In keeping with the native American insight that the floods, volcanic eruptions and climatic changes we are experiencing are warnings from Mother Earth, Berry (1988) asserts that the earth itself

is mandating that the human community assume a responsibility never assigned to any previous generation. . . . We are involved in a process akin to initiation processes which have been known and practised from earliest times. The human community is passing from its stage of childhood into its adult stage of life. . . . What we need, what we are ultimately groping toward, is the sensitivity required to understand and respond to the psychic energies deep in the very structure of reality itself. (pp. 47-48)

Berry's (1988) book *The Dream of the Earth* lays out the dimensions of a culture of peace, with insights drawn from native American teachings; quantum physics and biology; Asian, Middle Eastern, and Western religious traditions; the discoveries of ecological scientists; the insights of feminists; and the lessons to be learned from a detailed study of world history. Berry's vision suggests a reconstruction of all of the major disciplines from economics to politics to theology and history. Some of his suggestions include

- A postpatriarchal dictionary that would establish a new sense of reality and value throughout the entire structure of the Western language
- An economics premised on the sustainability of all of the life systems of the planet, rather than on the zero sum assumptions of capitalist economics
- A social-planning model that realigns human dwelling and human divisions of the earth with the local biosystems, thus providing a primary biological identity, rather than a primary political, social, or ethnic identity
- Technologies that function in an integral relationship with earth technologies, not in a despotic or disturbing manner or under the metaphor of conquest— technologies that incorporate the participation of every component of the human community; that take care of their own waste products; that are healing, preventive, and defensive; and that function on a bioregional scale

- Drawing from the work of feminist scholars, a new historical myth that encompasses a longer view of human history including the prepatriarchal matricentric period as well as a wider lens that sees Western culture within the context of a diversity of cultures and periodicities
- A constitution for the North American continent, not simply a constitution for the humans occupying this country—a *United Species,* not simply a United Nations.
- A new college curriculum that enables students to understand the immense story of the universe and the role of the student in creating the next phase of the story
- A new spirituality grounded in listening to and learning from our genetic coding, the earth, and the universe—the inner voice

While Berry's voice points us to a path of cultural reformation, he does not tell us how to get there. Many people, however, have embarked on that journey in varying ways. In the image of feminists at the Greenham Common peace encampment in England dancing on the nuclear silos and hanging pictures of their children on the gates to the compound, we were offered the model of a new way of opposing these weapons of mass destruction that was not coopted by the technostrategic framework in which they are embedded. Similar peace encampments have followed—at the U.S. missile base in Sicily when cruise missiles were being deployed; in the Kuwaiti desert, as the war between Iraq and the United States was about to unfold; in Nicaragua, El Salvador, Guatemala, the West Bank, and Gaza, where groups of North Americans and other nationals risked their lives to accompany, stand with, and otherwise bear witness to the suffering and injustice of the victims of the war machine.

An international gathering of indigenous peoples from all over the Western Hemisphere met in Quito, Ecuador, in 1990 to make plans for the appropriate commemoration of the 500th anniversary of Columbus's so-called discovery of the Americas. A national network of North American educators, artists, librarians, musicians, historians, writers, and others have embarked on a similar venture, with a call to a new cultural transformation of the Americas.

In the last quarter century, scientists and physicians have formed new international organizations (like Physicians for Social Responsibility) to promote an ethic of peace and to work for the abolition of the instruments of war and ecological destruction. A group of maverick ecological economists is beginning to map the outlines of the kind of economics proposed by Berry, challenging traditional economics on its own turf, accusing economists of mismeasuring development, underestimating the intangible costs of pollution, and ignoring society's responsibilities to future generations (Passell, 1990).

More and more groups across the United States are demanding multicultural education as a recognition of the changing demographics of the country and the interdependence of the world community. People-to-people diplomacy efforts, just in their infancy, indicate a growing willingness to flout the bureaucratic control of the political technocrats.

In the movement against the war in the Persian Gulf, there was a new maturity among those who worked for peace. Having learned the lessons of Vietnam, the new peace activists were more careful about mimicking the war system even as they opposed it. The effort not to blame the troops but to focus on the policy that sent them to the Gulf was an indication of such maturity.

Though the war machine appears to be stronger than ever, appearances may be deceptive. The United States, the world's foremost military power, had to go begging to fund its prosecution of war. The international financial system that has funded wars is extremely fragile and may have run out of room to maneuver. A new paradigm is emerging from the bowels of the old system.

Notes

1. Albert and coauthors (1986) posit the existence of four separate but interacting spheres of life—the economic, political, community, and kinship—which through their complex interactions define social life and social change. Worsley (1984) takes a more eclectic posture, examining human cultures in the concrete and attempting to define the sources of their complex mixtures.

2. According to Eisler (1987), there was a centuries-long transformation of originally peaceful, egalitarian Neolithic societies into violent, male-dominated, hierarchical societies through conquest by warring Indo-European tribes. If this account is correct, then the concept of private property may have been an outgrowth of this process—not a natural evolutionary development as Western mythology would have it.

3. Marx (1977) demonstrates how a fetishism of commodities develops through capitalism's particular property relations, that is, through the fact that value is added to raw materials through the "labor of private individuals who work independently of each other" (p. 165) and then exchange the resultant commodities through an impersonal market.

4. An early form of such fetishism and the relationships that flowed from it is seen in Columbus's attitude toward gold. He wrote in a letter, "Gold is a wonderful thing. Its owner is master of all he desires. Gold can even enable souls to enter paradise" (quoted in Hinkelammert, 1986, p. 22).

5. The term *the underclass* has achieved a wide currency over the last decade among journalists and social scientists as a way of describing and defining classes of people who have become permanently marginalized from participation in mainstream labor markets. Sometimes, the underclass is defined spatially (as all those living within certain low-income zip codes) and, at other times, psychosocial indicators (such as unwed mother-hood, criminality, and welfare dependence) have been used to define the population. The use of the term *to write off politically* population strata (particularly inner-city minorities) that the productive system can no longer accommodate has been severely criticized by other social scientists (see Gans, 1990; Stafford & Ladner, 1991).

6. Studies indicate that most of the charitable acts that the wealthy engage in are on behalf of the places and institutions that entertain, inspire, cure, or educate the wealthy (Reich, 1991, p. 43).

7. I am indebted for this schema illustrating dichtomous logic to Daniel Buford, from whom I first heard it used in a training session of the People's Institute for Survival and Beyond.

8. Feminist legal revisioning has extended the analysis of Gilligan (1983), whose studies of women's ethical decision making revealed the difference between the relational orientation of women's ethics and the rule-governed ethics of male culture (see also Gilligan et al., 1988).

9. The term *panoptical,* or *panopticism*—coined by Foucault (1977)—derives from Bentham's 18th century design for the prison (see Atkinson, 1969, pp. 84-87). It was a building or apparatus designed to serve as a machinery of power. Using no other instruments than "architecture and geometry," panopticism, says Foucault, gives those occupying the centralized "all seeing" location the "power of mind over mind" (quoted in Ewen, 1988, p. 201).

10. The work of Thunderhorse and Le Vie (1990) combines insights from native American shamanic cultures and Western science as well as reflections on the usefulness of the wisdom of tribal peoples to the current civilizational dilemma facing the world.

References

Adas, M. (1989). *Machines as the measure of man: Science, technology and ideologies of Western dominance.* Ithaca, NY: Cornell University Press.
Albert, M., Cagan, L., Chomsky, N., Hannel, R., King, M., Sargent, L., & Sklar, H. (1986). *Liberating theory.* Boston: South End Press.
Amin, S. (1989). *Eurocentrism* (R. Moore, Trans.). New York: Monthly Review Press.
Atkinson, C. M. (1969). *Jeremy Bentham: His life and work.* New York: A. M. Kelley.
Bellah, R. N., Madsen, R., Sullivan, W. M., Swidler, A., & Tipton, S. M. (1985) *Habits of the heart: Individualism and commitment in American life.* New York: Harper & Row.
Berry, T. (1988). *The dream of the earth.* San Francisco: Sierra Club Books.
Cohn, C. (1988). Sex, death and the rational world of defense intellectuals. In D. Gioseffi (Ed.). *Women on war* (pp. 84-99). New York: Touchstone.
Eisler, R. (1987). *The chalice and the blade.* New York: Harper & Row.
Engelhardt, T. (1989, August 30-September 5). Eternal invasion of privacy: The good, the ad and the only. *In These Times, 13,*(32), 18-21.
Ewen, S. (1988). *All consuming images: The politics of style in contemporary culture.* New York: Basic Books.

144   *Communication and Culture in War and Peace*

Ferguson, K. E. (1984). *The feminist case against bureaucracy.* Philadelphia: Temple University Press.

Foucault, M. (1977). *Discipline and punish: Birth of the prison.* New York: Random House.

Gans, H. J. (1990, January). *The dangers of the underclass: Its harmfulness as a planning concept* (Working Paper No. 4). New York: Russell Sage.

Gilligan, C. (1983). *In a different voice: Psychological theory and women's development.* Cambridge, MA: Harvard University Press.

Gilligan, C., Ward, J. V., Taylor, J. M., & Bardige, B. (1988). *Mapping the moral domain: A contribution of women's thinking to psychological theory and education.* Cambridge, MA: Harvard University Press.

Gramm, W. S. (1989). Oligarchic capitalism: Arguable reality, thinkable future? In M. R. Tool & W. J. Samuels (Eds.), *State, society, corporate power* (pp. 353-374). New Brunswick, NJ: Transaction Publishers.

Hinkelammert, F. J. (1986). *The ideological weapons of death.* Maryknoll, NY: Orbis Books.

Kuhn, T. (1970). *The structure of scientific revolutions* (2nd ed.). Chicago: University of Chicago Press.

Lakoff, G., & Johnson, M. (1980). *Metaphors we live by.* Chicago: University of Chicago Press.

Lash, S., & Urry, J. (1987). *The end of organized capitalism.* Madison: University of Wisconsin Press.

Lewin, T. (1988, September 30). Feminist scholars spurring a rethinking of law. *The New York Times,* p. 39.

Lifton, R. J. (1991, February 2). [Interview by Paul Gorman.] New York: WBAI-FM.

Marglin, S. A. (1974, Summer). What do bosses do? The origins and functions of hierarchy in capitalist society. *Review of Radical Political Economy, 6,* 60-112.

Marx, K. (1969). Manifesto of the communist party. In K. Marx & F. Engels, *Selected works* (Vol. I) (pp. 108-137). Moscow: Progress Publishers.

Marx, K. (1977). *Capital* (Vol. I; B. Fowkes, Trans.). New York: Vintage Books.

Miller, A. S. (1989). Legal foundations of the corporate state. In M. R. Tool & W. J. Samuels (Eds.), *State, society and corporate power* (2nd ed. rev., pp. 79-99). New Brunswick, NJ: Transaction Publishers.

Neruda, P. (1972). El Pueblo. In P. Neruda, *Selected Poems* (pp. 445-447; N. Tarn, Ed.). New York: Dell.

Passell, P. (1990, November 27). Rebel economists add ecological cost to price of progress. *New York Times,* p. C1.

Reich, R. (1991, January 20). Secession of the successful. *New York Times Magazine,* p. 16ff.

Sassen, S. (1988). *The mobility of labor and capital.* New York: Cambridge University Press.

Stafford, W. W., & Ladner, J. (1991). Political dimensions of the underclass concept. In H. J. Gans (Ed.), *Sociology and critical American issues* (pp. 138-155). Newbury Park, CA: Sage.

Thunderhorse, I., & Le Vie Jr., D. (1990) *Return of the thunderbeings.* Santa Fe: Bear & Co.

U.S. has highest rate of imprisonment. (January 7, 1991). *New York Times.* p. A14.

Weber, M. (1958). *The Protestant ethic and the spirit of capitalism.* New York: Scribner's.

West, C. (1982). *Prophecy deliverance.* Philadelphia: Westminster Press.

West, C. (1988). Toward a Socialist theory of racism. In C. West, *Prophetic fragments* (pp. 97-108). Grand Rapids, MI: Eerdmans.

Worsley, P. (1984). *The three worlds: Culture and world development.* Chicago: University of Chicago Press.

6

From Domination to Partnership:
The Foundations for Global Peace

RIANE EISLER

This chapter presents an analysis of how culture contributes to the war system and how the process of "cultural transformation" may lead us (back) to peace. *Culture* is here used in the same wide-ranging anthropological sense adopted in Chapter 1. Although most of the other authors encountered so far have integrated gender concerns into their work, the very basis of Eisler's text is what she calls a *gender-holistic* approach.

This chapter serves to remind us that feminist peace researchers have very important things to say about the war system. Eisler traces its roots back to prehistoric times, when peaceful partnership societies were replaced by male-dominator models of society. Through the prism of cultural transformation theory, she argues that the entire development of Western culture can be viewed as a struggle between these two forms of social organization.

In this chapter, we find that the author treats themes that resonate in the rest of the book. Like all of her cohorts, she singles out the mass media as powerful shapers of our myths and values and notes the connection between violent television images and real-life aggression. She joins with several of the authors in supporting the south's call for a new world information order, but emphasizes that this cannot be constructed "as long as one half of humanity remains excluded." The primacy of Greek culture in the Eurocentric vision, also dealt with by Collins, is treated here within a gender context. Eisler also seconds the call for a new *remything* process voiced in two of the other chapters.

Eisler's answer to the question of what to do is, on a practical level, the transformation of daily relations between men and women. It is, however, the primacy given to the notion of power that is most important for the concerns expressed throughout the book. Whether it be the hierarchies established in media organizations, the bureaucratic modes of operation of the media, the cultural domination of the south, or the transnational control of global communication, all reflect essential relations of power. This is the heart of the matter.

Throughout recorded history, *peace* has generally been defined as an interval between wars. Even now, and even in the international peace movement itself, the emphasis has been primarily on military questions (disarmament) and interim agreements (peace treaties). But in our time—when so many nations have nuclear weapons, and with this, the capacity to destroy our globe—a new way of looking at both war and peace is needed.

Why has recorded history been so warlike? Why is war conventionally presented as both heroic and barbaric? Why do men seem so obsessed with violent conflict, with armed strength and weaponry? Are wars inevitable, inherent in the human condition? Or are they inherent in a particular type of social organization? Most important, is there a way of structuring human society so that peace is not merely a periodic event but a lasting system characteristic or state?

In my research and writing over the past two decades, these have been some of the guiding questions in the reexamination of Western culture. Employing what may be termed a *gender-holistic approach*, I have drawn from a data base that includes the whole of humanity—both its female and male halves. Moreover, I have also looked at the whole of Western cultural evolution—not only history but also prehistory.

My findings, which I will sketch in this chapter (and which are presented in more detail in my book, *The Chalice and The Blade*; see Eisler, 1987) indicate that a more peaceful social organization is possible. Specifically, they help to verify something that many of us have long intuited. This is that the status of women and the "feminine" in a social system not only shapes our personal life options as women and men but also profoundly affects the totality of a society's organization, having an impact on every one of its social institutions and its guiding system of values, and even more specifically, whether it is generally peaceful or warlike.

Moreover, these findings also suggest critical intervention points and strategies for the creation of a more peaceful (and with this, more ecologically and humanly balanced) future, some of which will be outlined in the concluding part of this chapter.

Reclaiming Our Past: The Partnership and Dominator Systems

The conventional view, which we are all familiar with as it is still presented as "truth" in most of our schools and mass media, is that

Western civilization begins with brutally male dominant and highly war-like societies. For example, we have been told that European civilization begins with the Indo-European invasions: with a way of structuring society in which women and anything associated with the feminine is held in contempt and relegated to a subordinate and subservient position.

We are also taught a number of overtly contradictory, but covertly congruent, versions of what came before. One version—conveyed to us through religious dogmas of "original sin" and sociobiological theories about "selfish genes"—is the view that male dominance and male violence are inevitable, either divinely or genetically ordained.[1] The other is that there was a time before patriarchy in our prehistory, but that it was so "primitive" and "undeveloped" as to be unworthy of serious attention; in short, that the course of "cultural evolution" inevitably leads to male dominance and war.[2]

But if we reexamine our past in terms of the conceptual framework I have proposed—taking into account the latest findings about our prehistory and drawing from a data base that includes both the female and male halves of humanity—a very different picture of our cultural evolution emerges.

The Ancient Roots of Peace: Old Clues and New Findings

A good entry point into this new, and more hopeful, picture of our cultural evolution is through a fresh look at the many familiar legends about an earlier, more harmonious and peaceful age. The Judaeo-Christian Bible tells of a garden where woman and man lived in harmony with each other and nature—a time before a male god decreed that woman henceforth be subservient to man. The Chinese *Tao Te Ching* describes a time when the yin, or feminine principle, was not yet ruled by the male principle, or yang, a more harmonious time when the wisdom of the mother was still honored and humanity lived in peace (see Blakney, 1955). The ancient writings of the Greek poet Hesiod tell of a "golden race" who tilled their fields in peaceful ease before a "lesser race" brought in their god of war (see Robinson, 1968, pp. 15-17).

While for many people these stories are only religious or poetic allegories, there is general agreement among scholars that in many respects they are based on prehistoric events.[3] However, until now, one key component—the allusion to a time when women and men lived in partnership—has generally been viewed as no more than fantasy.

But just as the early archaeological excavations of Heinrich Schliemann and Sophia Schliemann helped establish the reality of Homer's Troy, more recent archaeological studies indicate that the stories of a time when women were not dominated by men are also based on reality. For example, Mesopotamian and later biblical stories about a garden where woman and man lived in partnership may in part derive from folk memories of the first agrarian (or Neolithic) societies, which planted the first gardens on this earth. Similarly, the legend of how the glorious civilization of Atlantis sank into the sea appears to be a garbled recollection of the matrifocal Minoan civilization, a remarkably peaceful and uniquely creative culture now believed to have ended when Crete and some surrounding islands were massively damaged by earthquakes and enormous tidal waves.[4]

These new archaeological discoveries (coupled with reinterpretations of older digs using more modern scientific methods) reveal a long period of peace and prosperity when our social, technological, and cultural evolution moved upward; those many thousands of years when all the basic technologies on which civilization is built were developed in societies that were not male dominant, violent, and hierarchic. Most important, they show that although these early cradles of civilization—going back many thousands of years before Sumer—were not utopian societies in the sense of perfect societies, they were societies organized along very different lines from ours.

As Mellaart reports from his excavations of Catal Huyuk (the largest early agrarian or Neolithic site ever found), the characteristic social structure of these first cradles of civilization appears to have been generally equalitarian. He writes how the comparative size of houses, the nature of their contents, and the funerary gifts found in graves show that there were no extreme differences in status and wealth (Mellaart, 1967, 1975).[5]

Data from Catal Huyuk and other Neolithic sites also indicate that in these societies, where women were priestesses and craftspeople, the female was *not* subordinate to the male. Indeed, in sharp contrast to most present-day religions, the supreme deity was female rather than male: a great goddess who was the mother of both divine daughters and divine sons.[6]

Finally, contradicting the notion that war is "natural," these were societies that do not seem to have had wars. There is a general absence of fortifications as well as a general absence in their extensive and considerably advanced art of the scenes so ubiquitous in later art: of "noble warriors" killing one another in battles, of gods and men raping women, of "glorious conquerors" dragging back prisoners in chains (see e.g., Gimbutas, 1977, 1982).

Even more fascinating—and relevant to our time—is that this type of social organization seems to have continued well into the Bronze Age, culminating in the "high" civilization of Minoan Crete. As noted before, scholars have suggested that the destruction of this civilization—which seems to have occurred at a time of great earthquakes, tidal waves, and other natural disasters that sank large land masses into the sea—was in fact the basis for the legend of Atlantis. There is also increasing consensus that Minoan civilization profoundly influenced not only Mycenaean culture but also classical Greece, which incorporated many of its contributions (see, e.g., Platon, 1966; Hawques, 1968).

Noted Greek archaeologist Nicolas Platon (the former director of the Acropolis Museum and Superintendent of Antiquities in Crete, who excavated that island for more than 50 years) reports how this technologically developed civilization, with its viaducts, paved roads (the first in Europe), and advanced civic amenities, had a generally high standard of living. Even though there were differences in status and wealth, and probably a monarchic type of government, there is evidence of a large (and very unusual in comparison with other "high" civilizations of the time) emphasis on public welfare.

Here, as in the earlier Neolithic period, the subordination of women does not appear to have been the norm. Cretan art shows women as priestesses, as figures being paid homage, and even as captains of ships. As Platon (1966) writes, in Minoan Crete "the important part played by women is discernible in every sphere" (p. 161). And (as in the earlier Neolithic when images of female deities are ubiquitous) Platon (1966) reports how, in this last known matrifocal society, the "whole of life was pervaded by an ardent faith in the goddess Nature, the source of all creation and harmony" (p. 148). He further notes how this "led to a love of peace, a horror of tyranny, and a respect for the law" (p. 148).

These archeological findings indicate that, contrary to what we have been taught, the original direction in the mainstream of our cultural evolution was in this more peaceful and socially and ecologically balanced direction. But the archaeological record also shows that, following a period of chaos—of extreme systems disequilibrium or almost total cultural disruption—there occurred a fundamental *social shift*.

At this pivotal branching, the cultural evolution of agrarian societies that worshiped the life-generating and nurturing powers of the universe—in our time still symbolized by the ancient "feminine" chalice, or grail—was interrupted and radically transformed. There then appeared on the prehistoric horizon horde after horde of warlike pastoralist invaders from the more arid and barren peripheral areas of our globe who brought with them a social organization based on strong-man rule in both the family and the tribe.

In Europe these were Indo-European-language-speaking invaders—beginning around 4000 B.C. with a population that University of California archaeologist Marija Gimbutas calls the Kurgans and continuing with later waves such as the Achaeans and Dorians. It was these invaders who, as Hesiod writes, brought with them Ares, the Greek god of war, replacing an earlier "golden race" who "tilled their fields in peaceful ease" (quoted in Robinson, 1968, p. 4). Or as Gimbutas (1977) writes, these were people who literally worshiped "the lethal power of the blade" (p. 281)—the power to take rather than give life that is the ultimate power to establish and enforce human rankings.

Human Possibilities: Two Alternatives

Already in the 19th century, when archaeology was still in its infancy, evidence of societies that worshiped female deities was unearthed. But the scholars of that day concluded that if these were not societies in which men dominated women, they must have been societies in which women dominated men. In other words, if they were not patriarchies they must have been matriarchies.[7] Then when the evidence did not seem to support the conclusion that in these societies women dominated men, it again became customary to argue that human society always was—and always will be—dominated by males.

But if we objectively look at this conventional system of classification, we can see that matriarchy is *not* the opposite of patriarchy; rather, it is the other side of the coin of what we may call a *dominator* model of society. This is a way of structuring human relations for which—beginning with the *ranking* of one half of humanity over the other—the primary principle of social organization is ranking, be it men over women, men over men, race over race, or nation over nation. The real alternative to a patriarchal, or male-dominant, society is a very different way of organizing social relations. This is what I have termed the *partnership* model—where once again beginning with the most fundamental difference in our species between male and female—diversity is not equated with either inferiority or superiority and the primary principle of social organization is *linking* rather than *ranking*.[8]

Models of society are, of course, abstractions. But if we reexamine both prehistory and history using these models as analytic templates or tools, we see that societies that orient primarily to one or the other of these models do have characteristic configurations or patterns. And we also see that the reason these patterns were not generally seen in the past is that scholars were looking at a very incomplete and distorted picture—one that excluded no less than one half of the population: women.

For example, from the conventional perspective of focusing only on the activities and experiences of men, Hitler's Germany, Khomeini's Iran, the Japan of the Samurai, and the Aztecs of Mesoamerica would seem to represent completely different cultures. But once we also look at the situation of women in these societies, we are able to identify the social configuration characteristic of rigidly male dominated societies. We then see striking commonalities: all these otherwise widely divergent societies not only are rigidly male-dominant but also have a generally hierarchic and authoritarian social structure and a high degree of social violence, ranging from wife beating within the family to aggressive warfare on the larger tribal or national level.

Conversely, we can also see striking similarities between otherwise extremely diverse societies that are more sexually equalitarian, societies in which to be considered "real men" males do not have to be dominant. Characteristically, such societies tend to be not only much more peaceful but also much less hierarchic and authoritarian. This is evidenced by anthropological data (e.g., the BaMbuti and !Kung); by contemporary studies of trends in more sexually equalitarian modern societies (e.g., Sweden, Finland, and Norway), which are also generally more peaceful and equalitarian; and by the prehistoric data that have been briefly presented in this chapter.

Moreover, this configuration is also discernible if we reexamine the seemingly random times and places in recorded history when women and "soft" or "feminine" values reasserted themselves—periods I would characterize as times of partnership resurgence.

History, Women, and Peace: The Key Role of "Women's Issues"

The recorded history of Europe begins with ancient Greece. But in most conventional texts and courses the situation of women in Greek society is at best viewed as an ancillary issue. If it is noted at all, it is usually given just a few pages that focus on the custom of imprisoning women in separate women's quarters and other indicators of their low status in ancient Athens.

However, as classicist Eva Keuls (1985) points out, the extreme oppression of women in Athenian society was part of a larger picture that she calls *phallocracy*: a highly violent, militaristic and hierarchic society. In other words, although this is hardly what is stressed by most classicists, there are ample data to support the conclusion that, despite its fabled (and very limited) democracy, classical Athens was oriented primarily (though by no means exclusively) to what I have called a dominator model of society.

Nonetheless, Athenian culture also had a "softer," more creative, more "feminine" underside, which I believe may have been the remnant of what Gimbutas calls the earlier civilization of old Europe. Moreover, if we look at Athenian history in terms of the partnership and dominator models, we see that during the course of its history there appear to have been periods of partnership resurgence. Indeed, one of these seems to have occurred near the height of the classical period (in c. 415 B.C.E.) when, as Keuls (1985) notes, there are strong indications that the women of Athens rebelled against their oppression—and that this rebellion (caricatured in Aristophanes' play *Lysistrata*) was linked with something akin to our modern women's peace movement.

It could be argued that this linking of a thrust for peace and a public voice for women in both modern and ancient times is merely accidental. But if we reexamine other seemingly random times and places in recorded history when women and more "soft" or "feminine" values sought to reassert themselves from the perspective of cultural transformation theory, we begin to see that this connection is recurrent.

For instance, if we look at the movement religious scholars call "primitive Christianity" (which lasted for more than 100 years after Jesus died) we see that here, too, both women and so-called feminine values played leading roles. The teachings of Jesus—that we "do unto others as we would have them do unto us," that we "turn the other cheek"—clearly elevated "feminine" values such as caring and nonviolence to moral governance. Moreover, although this is rarely noted by most religious scholars, in many of the early Christian communities women and men lived as equals, with women taking the same leadership roles as men.

In fact, according to the Gnostic Gospels, Mary Magdalene was one of Jesus's main apostles; a major leader in the early church—and the only one who dared to stand up to Peter and reproach him for trying to set up the same kind of hierarchic religious structure Jesus had preached against. It is also notable that many of these early Christian communities, which both preached and practiced nonviolence and equality, saw the deity as female and male, in other words, as Holy Mother and Father.[9]

The Troubadours and Troubatrixes, who during the 12th century flourished in the courts of Eleanor of Aquitaine and her daughters Alix and Marie, likewise elevated woman and the feminine from their subservient and despised status. In doing this, they asserted that the feminine principle is integral to both women and men, arguing that masculinity should be a gentle thing—as in the term gentleman. It was the Troubadours who introduced what the church called mariology: the worship of a Divine Mother, in essence a reinstitution of the ancient worship of the Goddess.

In our conventional history books, the Troubadours and Troubatrixes have been mainly remembered for supposedly bringing the idea of romantic love into Western culture. But, as G. Rattray Taylor (1954) pointed out, they greatly humanized Western society. For it was they who spread the idea that a man's identity or "masculinity" does not have to be equated with domination and conquest. At the same time, they also challenged the dominator sexual stereotypes of male dominance and female subservience with the idea that women should be listened to rather than silenced—that in fact a truly "noble knight" takes directions from his lady.

As Taylor (1954) also points out, the Troubadours and Troubatrixes were hunted down as heretics by the orthodox church. Not coincidentally, here again we see a classic dominator configuration, as this male-dominant and highly hierarchic structure was also characterized by a high degree of institutionalized male violence. It was this church that in the name of Christian love systematically hunted down, imprisoned, tortured, and killed untold numbers of heretics. And again not coincidentally, this included millions of women who were branded "witches"—whose heresy it now appears was not only that many of them were wise women and healers who competed with the newly emerging doctors trained by the church but also that some of them still clung to the pagan worship of the Goddess and her horned-and-hoofed bull god son/consort (who in Christian iconography became the devil).

So what we see if we look at recorded history in terms of the tension between the partnership and dominator models is that what women did—and what was done to women—is not, as we have been led to believe, unimportant or peripheral. Quite the contrary, it is of critical importance, not only for women, but also for men.

Women as a Force in History: The Modern Feminist Movement

Perhaps the most striking case in point is the modern feminist movement. Once again, in our conventional histories, if it is mentioned at all, the 19th century Western feminist movement is described as a peripheral social phenomenon that eventually became the suffragist movement and won women the vote. But if we look at the elevation of women and so-called feminine values as the foundation for a partnership model of social organization, a very different picture emerges.

We can then see how the 19th century feminist movement helped to free women—half the population—from blatantly oppressive forms of male dominance, such as the "right" of a husband to control all his wife's property and even to beat her for disobeying his orders. Even beyond this, it greatly humanized the whole of society, because it made it possible for more women than ever before to bring what sociologist Jessie Bernard (1981) calls the feminine ethos of love and duty from the "private world" of the family to the so-called public world, or society at large.

It was through the influence of women (like Florence Nightingale and Jane Addams) that new professions like organized nursing and social work emerged. It was through the participation of women (like Sojourner Truth and Lucy Stone) that the abolitionist movement to free black slaves gained massive grass-roots support. It was through the unrelenting persistence of women (like Dorothea Dix) that the treatment of the insane and mentally deficient became more humane.

Moreover, it is not by accident but because this is characteristic of the social configuration in periods of partnership resurgence that the 19th century was also a time when major political and economic reforms were gaining ascendancy. For that was a time when, along with women, "feminine" values such as caring, nonviolence, and compassion were also struggling to regain some measure of social governance.

But as in earlier times of partnership resurgence, almost from the very moment that women and "feminine" values began to gain ascendancy, the dominator system's defenses began to mobilize.[10] As "divinely ordained" male dominance and male violence were challenged, Social Darwinists began to spread a new "scientific" gospel of naturally ordained male dominance and aggression. At the same time, as cultural historian Roszak notes, the idealization of "heroic" male violence along with an increase in male acts of violence against women presaged not only the "failure" of the first phase of modern feminism but ultimately the massive bloodbath of World War I (Roszak, 1969, pp. 87-106).

A similar pattern of partnership resurgence and dominator regression can be seen by using the conceptual prisms of cultural transformation theory to reexamine what took place in the United States during the 1960s. This was a time when the second phase of modern feminism gained unprecedented power as the women's liberation movement, when many women and men rejected the violence of war and the barbarity of racism, calling for a less unjust and oppressive economic and political system. But, once again, from the very beginning the partnership thrust was met with massive dominator resistance. And in the end the progressive 1960s and early 1970s were followed by the regressive 1980s.

As is characteristic of dominator regressions, the American fundamentalist alliance poured massive energy and resources into a drive to reverse women's gains. Their top priorities were to stop the Equal Rights Amendment (ERA); to again deprive women of reproductive freedom; and to return, as they openly proclaimed, women to their "traditional" (a code word for *subservient*) place. At the same time—in keeping with the dominator configuration of rigid male dominance, a high degree of institutionalized violence, and a generally hierarchic and authoritarian social structure—they pushed for increased militarization and opposed funding for social programs that would create a more equalitarian social structure. Instead, they successfully backed social and economic policies reversing many of the gains of women, poor people, blacks, and other minorities, thus again widening, rather than narrowing, the gap between those on the bottom and top.

Ironically, those seeking a return to the "good old days" when most men (and all women) still "knew their place"—and virulent sexism, racism, and anti-Semitism, along with rigid class stratifications and almost constant warfare were seen as "normal"—have throughout recorded history correctly seen so-called women's issues as central to their regressive agendas. But, even to this day many "progressives" from the middle to left view anything relating to women as a secondary matter—to be dealt with, if at all, only after the more "important issues" are addressed. And so—largely because during the centuries of recorded (or patriarchal) history vital matters profoundly affecting the problems, needs, and aspirations of no less than half of humanity have been generally viewed as "unimportant"—or as "just the way things are"—until now the dominator system has always violently reasserted its hold.

But now—when the lethal power of the blade, amplified a millionfold by megatons of nuclear warheads, threatens to put an end to all human

culture and man's "conquest of nature" threatens our very biosphere—
the dominator system may literally take us to an evolutionary dead end.
Now we are rapidly approaching another potentially decisive branching
point in our cultural evolution, a time of extreme, indeed increasingly
chaotic, social disequilibrium when we either move on to a partnership
future or we may have no future at all.

Revisioning Our Future: From Crisis to Opportunity

For many people, ours is a time of bewildering, often terrifying,
social disintegration and of mounting confusion, danger, and even
chaos; a time when the very survival of our species may be in issue. But
it is precisely because the problems impelling us to create new ways of
living are so urgent, that this is also a time of enormous opportunity.
Moreover, what we are now learning about how fundamental changes
in living systems occur—be they on the chemical or social level—indicates that it is precisely in periods of severe systems disequilibrium or
chaos that a fundamental systems shift can occur.

But social systems, like all living systems, seek to maintain themselves. Thus at the same time that we are seeing the unprecedentedly
powerful contemporary movement toward a partnership model of society, there is also massive dominator resistance.

What can we do to strengthen and accelerate the partnership movement? What can we learn about our present from the information we are
reclaiming about our past? And how can we use this information to
design for ourselves a more humane and sustainable future?

Cultural Transformation Theory: Toward a New Paradigm
for History and Society

In trying to find answers to these questions, I again and again found
the need to move beyond the conventional frames of reference. Gradually, I began to construct a new conceptual framework for the reexamination of both our past and the possibilities for our future. Using what
I have called the partnership and dominator models of social organization as analytical tools, this approach, which I have termed Cultural
Transformation Theory,[11] proposes the following:

1. If we look at our cultural history from a gender-holistic perspective, certain
   patterns or systems configurations that are otherwise not visible become
   apparent.

2. The contrasting systems configurations or patterns characteristic of the partnership and dominator models represent two basic alternatives for the organization of human society.

3. Largely due to what British archaeologist James Mellaart calls a veritable archaeological revolution, there are strong indications that for thousands of years Western cultural evolution was oriented primarily to a partnership model, but that during a period of great systems disequilibrium in our prehistory (approximately 5000 years ago) there was a major systems shift toward the dominator model.

4. Our time of increasing systems disequilibrium offers an unprecedented opportunity for another fundamental systems shift—this time from a dominator to a partnership model of society.

5. Recorded history can be better understood in terms of the tension between these two models and the degree to which a particular period orients to one or the other.

6. If we look at contemporary society using these two models of social organization, we can identify critical intervention points and strategies for the creation of a more peaceful future.

The Partnership and Dominator Models: Social Dynamics

A detailed discussion of cultural transformation theory and the partnership and dominator models is beyond the scope of this chapter.[12] But there are a number of points that I want to touch on because they are so important.

To begin with, I cannot stress enough that the social dynamics we are here dealing with are not matters of simple causes and effects, but of complex interactions.

As systems theorists like biologists Humberto Maturana (1975) and Vilmos Csanyi (1989) note, both biological and social organisms are self-organizing, self-maintaining systems composed of mutually reinforcing and supporting elements in continual interaction. Just as the body parts of a living organism (such as the stomach, brain, and skin) interact to maintain the whole system, so the various elements of social systems mutually reinforce and maintain one another. And just as the stomach, brain, and skin of different living organisms (e.g., lizards, cows, and humans) are not the same, the elements of societies orienting to a dominator or partnership model are also not the same.

Table 6.1 and Figure 6.1 show the interaction between three key elements that distinguish the dominator and partnership systems. As the two way arrows in Figure 6.1 show, these elements are mutually reinforcing and thus serve to maintain the particular roles, institutions, and values characteristic of each system.

TABLE 6.1   The Dominator and Partnership Models: Basic Configurations

Component	Dominator Model	Partnership Model
One: Gender Relations	The ranking of the male over the female, as well as the higher valuing of the traits and social values stereotypically associated with "masculinity" rather than "femininity."*	Equal valuing of the sexes as well as of "femininity" and "masculinity," or a sexually equalitarian social and ideological structure, where "feminine" values can gain operational primacy.
Two: Violence	A high degree of institutionalized social violence and abuse, ranging from wife- and child-beating, rape and warfare to psychological abuse by "superiors" in the family, the workplace, and society at large.	A low degree of social violence, with violence and abuse not structural components of the system.
Three: Social Structure	A predominently hierarchic** and authoritarian social organization, with the degree of authoritarianism and hierarchism roughly corresponding to the degree of male dominance.	A more generally equalitarian social structure with difference (be it based on sex, race, religion, or belief system) not automatically associated with superior or inferior social and/or economic status.

*Please note that the terms "femininity" and "masculinity" as used here correspond to the sexual stereotypes appropriate for a dominator society (where "masculinity" is equated with dominance and conquest) and *not* with any inherent female or male traits.

**As used here, the term hierarchic refers to what we may call a domination hierarchy, or the type of hierarchy inherent in a dominator model of social organization, based on fear and threat of force. Such hierarchies should be distinguished from a second type of hierarchy, which for clarity may be called an actualization hiearchy, for example, of molecules, cells, and organs in the body: a progression toward a higher and more complex level of function.

It is also important to note that, like all models, the dominator and partnership models of social organization are abstractions. No society conforms completely to either model. Thus even the most rigidly male dominated societies have to give some value to nurturing activities or they would not survive. But these societies characteristically relegate (and confine) nurturance to women inside a rigidly circumscribed male-controlled household. They also regard such "soft" behaviors as

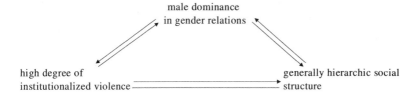

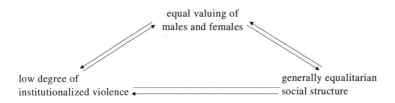

Figure 6.1. As these diagrams indicate, the relationship between the three major systems components is interactive, with all three mutually reinforcing one another.

unmanly or "effeminate"—and thus inappropriate for men (who make and carry out the social rules).

In other words, the differences between societies orienting primarily to a dominator or partnership model of society are matters of degree. But they are differences that profoundly affect everything about a society: its institutions, values, and technologies and whether it is generally peaceful or chronically warlike.

The closer a society orients to a dominator model, the more all relations (be they between women and men, tribes and tribes, nations and nations) are governed by fear of violence and punishment rather than by mutual understanding, respect, and trust. This is by no means to say that even in a society that orients very closely to the partnership model, we would never be afraid. Nor is it to say that we would never be mistrustful. The difference—and it is major—is that in a dominator society fear is systematically inculcated in us and trust (beginning with the trust between the female and male halves of humanity) is systematically undermined through dominator cultural myths and social institutions.

This leads to another important point I have stressed before: The partnership society is not a utopian or ideal society free of problems, conflicts, disappointments, or grief. Conflict is a natural aspect of life, as different organisms with different needs, purposes, and plans come together. Grief and disappointment are also inherent in life—if only because we must all die.

The difference—and again it is a major difference—lies in how we are taught to deal with these "givens." For example, in the dominator model, conflict is emphasized, but at the same time the violent suppression of conflict is institutionalized, and might is equated with right. By contrast, in the partnership model, conflict is openly recognized but, as pioneering psychiatrist Jean Baker Miller (1976) writes, it can be dealt with creatively in ways in which both parties learn and grow.

In short, some of the contrasts that may initially come to mind—such as that a partnership society has no conflicts or that competition is found only in dominator systems and cooperation is only found in partnership systems—are too simplistic and thus not helpful.

There is cooperation in the dominator model. A notable example is the cooperation of groups of men to conquer and/or suppress others, be they a modern army or the inquisitors of the Middle Ages. But it is a cooperation primarily founded on fear and aggression toward an "outgroup."

Also, contrary to what may first come to mind, there is competition in the partnership model. But in contrast to the dominator model, it is not the exploitive "dog-eat-dog" competition for which our natural human capacity for empathy has been insensitized by dominator socialization (as has particularly been the case in the upbringing of men). It is a different kind of competition: achievement rather than win-lose oriented that is modulated and regulated by feelings of empathy with others rather than by a drive to suppress and conquer others at any cost (as in the well-known adage "all's fair in love and war").

A final point relates to the tendency to confuse a partnership society with a leaderless or laissez-faire society. This, in my estimation, is one of the great fallacies that actually prevent the realization of a partnership future and will be discussed in more depth in the section that follows.

Strategies for Creating a Partnership World: Peace and Survival in the Nuclear Age

How can the patterns of violence, human and environmental exploitation, artificially created scarcities, and warfare be broken? In the first two sections of this chapter I have tried to lay out some of the theoretical and historical foundations for a new approach to our mounting global crises. In this final section, I will briefly outline a number of strategies that I believe can help to accelerate the urgently needed shift from a dominator to a partnership society.

All these strategies call for a systems approach, a recognition that the various parts of a social system are integrally interrelated. And all of them are based on a fundamental insight made possible by the study of society from a perspective that takes into account the whole of humanity (both women and men) and the whole of our history (including our prehistory): that so-called women's issues—such as reproductive freedom, development programs that fully integrate Third World women, and the education of men for peace and cooperation rather than conquest and domination—must be given top strategic priority.

This is by no means to imply that the issue is one of women versus men. The problems of male dominance and male violence are primarily social rather than biological. Clearly, throughout history not all men have been violent. And today many men are rejecting their identification with "hard," "masculine" attitudes and behaviors, for example, the men who are today redefining fathering in the more caring and nurturing way once stereotypically associated only with mothering.

The reason dominator societies are inherently warlike is not men as a sex.[13] It is rather the way male identity must be defined in male-dominant societies in which, by definition, "masculinity" is equated with domination and conquest, be it of women, other men, or nature.

From Sexual Stereotypes to Human Values:
The Feminization of Power

To maintain a male dominant society, boys must be systematically socialized for domination and therefore, for violence. Male violence has to be idealized, as we see in so much of our normative literature that celebrates violent "heroes" (for example, the biblical King David, the Homeric Odysseus, and modern "he-men" such as James Bond and Rambo). Indeed, in dominator societies violent behaviors are systematically taught to males from early childhood through toys like swords, violent video games, GI Joe dolls, guns, and missile sets, whereas only girls are systematically socialized for nurturance, compassion, and caring.

It is for these reasons that the massive contemporary questioning of stereotypical sexual roles—and with this the mass entry of women into the so-called "man's world" of politics and economics—is of such critical importance, not only for women but for men. But once again, here an important clarification is in order.

One of the lessons from our past is that what is needed is *not* merely an occasional or token woman at the top of a male-centered dominator hierarchy, but rather the mass entry of women into leadership positions. As history attests, women taking the stereotypical roles of men have had to bend over backward to constantly prove that they are not too soft or "feminine."

When women have to step into men's shoes through their relationship with a man (as in the case of empresses like Catherine the Great and presidents such as Corazon Aquino and Benazir Bhutto), what they do is still circumscribed by a "masculine" model of leadership and by an underlying dominator power structure. And even when a lone woman rises to the top of a male hierarchy (as in the case of prime ministers Golda Meir or Margaret Thatcher), she will still be under enormous pressure to display—indeed, excel in—stereotypical "tough" or "masculine" traits and behaviors.

What is needed is, therefore, not more token women leaders, but a more partnership-oriented society in which both women and men as policymakers can freely incorporate so-called "feminine" values. For, as evidenced by the greater emphasis on ecological balance and peace of women heads of state in nations such as Norway and Iceland, in societies in which women in politics are no longer an anomaly more "feminine" values also begin to make themselves felt.

Leadership is vital to any kind of society—be it one orienting to a dominator or a partnership model. But in the dominator model leadership is equated with *power over*, the power to dominate and control symbolized by the Blade. In the partnership model, leadership is equated with a very different kind of power, symbolized since remote antiquity by the Chalice or Holy Grail. This is the power to inspire, illuminate, and elicit from others their highest potentials. Or as feminist theorist Jean Baker Miller (1976) puts it, it is *power to* and *power with*; the power to enable us creatively to work together to attain mutually agreed on humanistic goals.

This more "feminine" exercise of power is in many ways still the ideal for women in mothering. This is, once again, why as a group (not as a token woman trying to fill male shoes in a male-dominant hierarchy) the leadership of women is so vital to the creation of a more just, ecologically balanced, and peaceful world.

But for women to exercise this kind of leadership, it is important that we recognize, and overcome, a number of deeply ingrained assumptions. One is the all too familiar notion that equates "real" leadership with strong-man rule, with "masculine" stereotypes of toughness and aggression. Another is the practice, ironically perpetuated by many women themselves, of labeling any woman who exhibits leadership qualities as "elitist" and tearing her down.

I stress this point because I have seen time and time again how, even in the women's movement, our patriarchal socialization to deny women leadership roles has worked against us, how the very women we must have to lead us have been prevented from being effective—thus in fact strengthening the very system that this movement is working to transform.

Only as women are equitably represented at all levels of leadership will the system itself be transformed. For it is to women that male-dominant societies have relegated the nondominating characteristics, attitudes, and behaviors that are here considered "effeminate" or inappropriate for men: caring and compassion, empathy and nonviolence. As long as women remain subordinate, so also do the human qualities that in our time may be survival requisites.This is why I believe the empowerment of women to assume leadership roles is a primary strategy for creating a more peaceful, balanced, and just world. And, not coincidentally, it is also why—be it on the right or left—most of those who still see war as a solution to global problems so adamantly insist that above all else the subordination of women is either divinely or naturally ordained.

The Remything Process: From Social Protest to Cultural Alternatives

I believe that another primary strategy for the creation of an ecologically balanced and peaceful future is what we might call the *remything process*: the interweaving of ancient and modern partnership stories and images to counter, and gradually to crowd out, the many dominator myths (both religious and secular) that idealize male dominance and male violence.

We are only now beginning to recognize that the way we think, feel, and act is profoundly affected by stories and images. We are also only now beginning fully to understand how many of our myths (such as the hero as killer) and images (such as the equation of sexual pleasure and brutal domination in pornography) have served to keep us trapped in dysfunctional and inhuman family and social patterns. But exposing or deconstructing such images is only the first step. The second, and far more important, step is to begin to provide alternatives. A great deal of contemporary art, particularly much of the highly fashionable deconstructionist art, mirrors—or more frequently parodies—contemporary consumer culture through what Jean Baudrillard calls "manipulatory play of signs without meaning"(Baudrillard, 1981). As Baudrillard and others openly state, this is an art born of despair, of a nihilistic conviction that all is hopeless and empty of meaning—and that we are unable to change it. According to this reasoning, the only appropriate response is to "deconstruct" reality, as any positive action is seen as doomed to be coopted into still further meaningless and empty mass culture forms.

Fortunately, as the artist and writer Suzi Gablik (1991) writes in her book *The Reenchantment of Art*, what is emerging today in art is not only deconstructive postmodernism but what she calls reconstructive postmodernism. "Reconstructive artists," she writes, "consider that art has the potential for radically reshaping the beliefs of society." Even more specifically, Gablik writes of the central role of reconstructionism in "accelerating the transformation from a dominator to a partnership society in all aspects of our lives" (Gablik, 1991, pp. 96-114).

I believe that the reexamination of art, music, literature, and our mass media using the prisms of the partnership and dominator models as conceptual tools can sensitize us to fundamental spiritual and intensely practical—indeed survival—questions. One such question is whether there is a distinction between innovativeness and creativity. For example, the Nazis were very innovative in finding new methods of causing pain and killing children, women, and men. But can we properly call this creativity? Or is it merely innovativeness in the service of the destructive Blade rather than the creative Chalice?

Another question is whether we should begin to make a distinction between self-expression and creativity. Particularly in a dominator system where we are chronically subjected to so much tension, frustration, and pain, self-expression very much focuses on negative images, which in turn serve to maintain dominator models of reality. This is not to say that we want to move toward any kind of censorship or that we want to inhibit our self-expression as a means for catharsis and possibly for raising other people's consciousness. But we may want to ask ourselves what kind of images we want to put out there.

We could also profit from examining in more depth some of the various strains of partnership-oriented images and stories now emerging. For example, many artists (both women and men) are creating Goddess images in various media. The chalice too is beginning to be a recurring theme (a dramatic example is Beth Ames Swartz's new *The Return of the Chalice* series [Beth Ames Swartz: A series of art works and paintings exhibited around the country during the 1980s], inspired by *The Chalice and the Blade,* Eisler, 1987.) Performance artists are providing us with rituals (very much like the shamans of old), such as a number of Mary Beth Edelson's projects and the *Re-membrance of the Goddess* rite performed by Virginia Sanchez in Mexico City, where hundreds of people symbolically put together the dismembered body of the Mexican Goddess with flowers.

Much of the creative ferment of the Renaissance and later the Enlightenment stemmed from what we may call the classical revival: the gradual reclamation of some of the lost knowledge of Greco-Roman civilization. But it now appears that some of the best aspects of classical antiquity derived from much more ancient or archaic civilizations, going back all the way to the Neolithic. I am convinced that what we are today rediscovering about prehistoric civilization could presage what we might call an archaic revival—and that this information is already changing some of our most familiar myths.

One of my favorite examples is Charlene Spretnak's (1978) version of Persephone's journey to the underworld. Rather than being abducted by a male god (which, as Mara Keller, n.d., points out is a later patriarchal story), here Demeter's daughter goes of her own free will. Although she is an immortal Goddess, she has compassion for us mortals and wants to find out firsthand about what we all inevitably face: death. In sharp contrast to the terrible fear of death instilled in us by dominator myths about a male deity who metes out eternal punishment in hell to those who do not believe in him, in this story the underworld is a realm from which there is a cyclical return, as symbolized by the seasonal return of Persephone every spring (see also Keller, 1988).

Recognizing the tremendous power of myths and images, we have through the Center for Partnership Studies circulated a concept paper (Eisler, 1989) proposing a new kind of project for the arts (or perhaps a series of projects) to be developed in cooperation with other organizations and individuals: the showing of works ranging from paintings and sculpture to computer-generated and performance art that exemplify the kinds of psychopoetic images and stories congruent with a partnership rather than a dominator model of society.

Another project, facilitated through the Center for Partnership Studies in cooperation with other organizations, was the first International Celebration of Partnership held in Crete in October 1992, organized by Margarita Papandreou, the former first lady of Greece and international coordinator of Women for Mutual Security. It is hoped that this event, which offered an opportunity to bring together social change agents from all over the world and attract media attention to the relationship between gender equity, ecological balance, and world peace, will take place biannually.

I write of these projects because I am intimately acquainted with them and because they illustrate how we can use conferences, cultural events, the arts and the media to begin laying the psychic foundations for a world of partnership and peace. I should add that the Center for Partnership Studies was established specifically to identify, strengthen, develop, and disseminate models of partnership in all aspects of our lives through research and education, and that I have personally devoted a great deal of time since 1987 to the Center, which has led to the formation of 21 Centers for Partnership Education in the USA, as well as one in the Seychelles Islands. But I also want to stress that there are obviously many other organizations that are working on various aspects of both formal and informal education to make it possible for people to accept, and function in, a social system structured primarily around partnership rather than domination.

The development in universities and colleges of women's and black studies as well as peace studies and gender studies (such as the University of Southern California's Program for the Study of Women and Men in Society) are important illustrations of what is being done in the area of formal or academic education. Each of these programs addresses a major component of partnership education. Perhaps a next step could be the integration of various elements from these programs into a Partnership Research and Education Program that could provide course guidelines for the general curriculum, thus serving as a catalyst for educational transformation.

Equally important are the many community-based conferences, workshops, and self-help groups (some of which I will touch on below) that have proliferated globally in the last decades. For these too are helping us reexamine what were not so long ago "givens" and, most important, are helping create more partnership-oriented alternatives.

Last, but certainly not least, are the mounting efforts to use our powerful contemporary media of mass communication to change people's consciousness. I would here include not only electronic mass media such as television but the plethora of small computers with such amazingly good software that individuals and small organizations can now produce the kind of copy that not so long ago required enormous staff and capital as well as the relatively low-cost fax and copying machines that today also make it possible for individuals and groups to communicate information in a matter of minutes to most parts of the globe. The ability to use these and other means of rapid information transfer are critical to the shift from a dominator- to a partnership-oriented world.

But it is the mass media that I believe hold the most promise and need our most urgent attention. For they not only are potentially the most important vehicle for social change but, unfortunately, are still by and large the most important vehicles for dominator systems maintenance, through their constant bombardment of our eyes, ears, and minds with messages that reinforce male-female dominator stereotypes, idealize warfare, present violence as "fun entertainment," and sell unsound products along with unsound values, such as the idea that more and more consumption is sustainable and will make us happy.

The recognition of the important role the mass media play in shaping our thoughts and actions is certainly not new. Research such as the study conducted by David Loye and Roderick Gorney in 1976 at the University of California, Los Angeles (UCLA), School of Medicine, has documented that what is shown on television affects the behavior of both children and adults in critical ways that are particularly pertinent to war or peace (Loye, Gorney, & Steele, 1977). For example, what this UCLA study showed is that men watching what the researchers termed programs high in "anti-social" behaviors (with a high violence content) tended to become more aggressive and less caring, whereas men watching more "prosocial" programs (modeling more helpful rather than hurtful behaviors) in turn became more helpful and considerate themselves.

There are other signs of a growing recognition that the contents of the mass media (as well as their organizational structures, which globally still largely exclude women from policymaking jobs) by and large still reflect, and reinforce, what I have here called a dominator rather than partnership model. For example, in *Unequal Opportunities: The Case of Women and the Media*, Margaret Gallagher (1981) extensively documented the gender bias of mass media worldwide, and numerous organizations ranging from Ann Simonton's *Women's Media Watch* in Santa Cruz, California, to the international Men Against Rape are working to bring wider attention to the objectification and dehumanization of women through all forms of mass media, from pornography to advertising.

There is also the call for a new world information and communication order (NWICO), previously backed by UNESCO, which not only supported third world demands for more cultural autonomy from the West, but also emphasized that the mass media have an important role to play in promoting a world of peace. Yet, ironically, as critical supporters of the NWICO process like Colleen Roach (1990) emphasized, the push for this supposed new world information and communication order is still controlled by male elites. In Roach's (1990) words, "the elitist nature of the NWICO has been most evident in the scarce attention it has paid to women's issues" (p. 298).

So once again we come back to the basics. No really new world order can be constructed as long as one half of humanity remains excluded. And if we are to construct a more peaceful world, we can no longer continue the socialization of men for domination and conquest and the relegation of women and so-called feminine values such as caring and nonviolence to a subservient place.

Because today the mass media are probably the most important shapers of people's values and perceptions worldwide, I believe that a concerted campaign to alter fundamentally the messages they deliver throughout our globe should be a top action priority. Because, more than any other single factor, such a campaign could help us lay the psychic foundations on which to reconstruct, not only our system of values but our social institutions.

Restructuring Society: Reintegrating the Personal and Political

At first glance, the restructuring of social institutions such as the family and our economic and political systems may seem an overwhelming, indeed impossible, task. But, in fact, there is already strong movement toward institutional restructuring in a number of key areas.

A notable example is the deliberate attempt to restructure family relations that millions of Americans today are actively working toward though a variety of means, all the way from family therapy to New Age workshops on better man-woman relations to self-help groups like Adult Children of Alcoholics. These efforts reflect the growing recognition that many of our most painful personal problems derive from patterns of behavior that have been systematically passed on from generation to generation in what are today commonly called "dysfunctional" families. Held together by fear and control, these families have also given rise to what are today described as addictive and codependent behaviors, which, by some estimates, affect over 90% of the population.

When millions of women and men suffer from the same problems, it should not be too difficult to convince people that these are not individual or idiosyncratic. And once these conditions are seen as what they are—social rather than purely personal—it should also be possible to show these millions of highly motivated, often desperate, people that to heal themselves they also have to heal society.

In her pioneering work in family therapy, psychologist Virginia Satir (1972) shifted the emphasis from individual healing to family systems healing. But what is increasingly recognized today is the need to take the next logical step; to look at both individual and family dysfunction in their larger context of social dysfunction.

In *Breaking Free of the Co-Dependency Trap*, psychologists Barry Weinhold and Janae Weinhold (1989) repeatedly make this point. Because they specifically equate the dysfunctional family with the dominator family and show the integral connection between family and social structure, this book is a useful tool for helping us accelerate the shift from a dominator to a partnership society. Weinhold and Weinhold write that "the dominator model creates a co-dependent society, and the partnership model creates an interdependent society in which people work cooperatively to support each other" (p. 28). Even more specifically, they stress that "any culture that ranks one sex over another, one religion over another or one race over another has organized a society that is bound to be codependent" (p. 32). Moreover, they point out that as "we begin to examine our basic patterns of relating in our intimate relationships, we can see that our patterns of relating must change at every level of the culture" (pp. 34-35).

To bring wider attention to the view of psychological and relational problems as not just familially but also socially rooted, I have been speaking at conferences of psychologists, family counselors, and other healing professionals. Moreover, to spread the awareness that a partnership family and society offer a viable alternative, I have together with my husband and partner, social psychologist and futurist David Loye, also completed the book, *The Partnership Way: New Tools for Living and Learning* (Eisler & Loye, 1990). Already in use by thousands of community, church, 12-Step, and other self-help groups as well as by colleges and corporations, *The Partnership Way* is designed to facilitate both dominator systems deconstruction and partnership systems reconstruction in all areas of our lives. Particularly relevant here is that it brings out not only the relationship between myths and reality but also the relationship between a dominator (control and fear-based) family and a world in which one nation (or tribe or race) dominates another through force or the threat of force.

I am convinced that the reintegration of the personal and the political orienting to a partnership rather than dominator model of society is the core of any effective education for peace. People who are brought up to see the domination of men over women and of parents over children as "natural" and "normal" are being socialized for a world in which one tribe, race, or nation dominates the other through force or the threat of force.

I am also convinced that to restructure our familial and political institutions requires a fundamental restructuring of our economic institutions. And once again this requires attention to hitherto ignored gender issues.

People brought up in societies in which "women's work" is held in contempt by men (as is the case of male-dominant societies) will fit well into an economic system in which respect and caring for others' needs is not truly valued. And this will be true whether the society is capitalist or socialist.

The retention of an underlying dominator structure in both the family and the state is an underlying reason why, despite its noble goals, the Soviet experiment with socialism evolved into yet another form of dominator economics and ultimately failed. This also helps explain why in the former Soviet Union the work of women, be it as homemakers or doctors, was not given equal value with work in occupations that were considered "men's work."

It is often said that a more peaceful world hinges on a new, more just and equitable economic order. I would like to suggest that such a new order cannot be created without what, building on the ideas of Hillary Rose (1983) and other feminist theorists, we might call the integration of caring labor. According to Marxist analysis, a key problem in the classical capitalist model is the alienation of labor. But what neither capitalist nor communist economic models have addressed is an even more fundamental problem: the alienation of caring labor.

Caring labor consists of the caring services without which society could not go on but that are generally left out of present economic calculations of "productivity" and are thus accorded very low reward in status and pay or no status or pay at all. Caring labor not only is the labor of women in giving birth and their work in caring for children, the ill, and the elderly (in dominator societies considered "unmanly" or fit only for women) but also is the work of the more creative men, the artists, philosophers, visionaries, and writers who through most of recorded history have also been considered "unmanly" or "effeminate."

Clearly caring labor is not a question of sex, as both men and women are capable of performing it. Moreover, its devaluation is not a matter of any inherent economic laws. As John Stewart Mill (1929) pointed out in *Principles of Political Economy*, the laws of economic distribution are man-made. And it is these man-made rules of the game that are still reflected and perpetuated by most current economic models. Examples are the virtual exclusion of caring labor from calculations of national gross product, the institutionalized devaluation of this type of labor in national and international calculations of "productive work" (such as the UN System of National Accounts) and the inflated economic value given instead to war-related and ecologically destructive practices.

Historically, the dominator model of economics—in which the traits, values, and work stereotypically associated with one half of humanity is given higher reward than that associated with the other half—shaped the construction and retention of these warped economic models.[14] For instance, when the unpaid services traditionally performed by women in the home were gradually professionalized as large numbers of women entered the public labor force—first as teachers and nurses in the 19th century and then as social workers, nutritionists, family therapists, and other caring counselors in the 20th century—they were unfailingly paid lower salaries than those accorded to stereotypically "male" professions. Moreover, as reflected in the well-known stereotypes of the "starving artist" or the "impractical do-gooder," the creative, nurturing, and life-enhancing work of both men and women has throughout recorded history been accorded little if any economic value.

Today, as we rapidly move to a postindustrial or service economy, the alienation of caring labor underlies the mounting debate over "comparable worth." I would, therefore, suggest that an important strategy for the construction of a more peaceful world is a major educational campaign around this "women's" issue. Even beyond that, I would suggest that a world of peace founded on a just economic order cannot be created without the elevation of women and so-called feminine values from the subservient place that they have occupied for most of recorded history.

I do not think it coincidental that women and men all over the world are today challenging some of our most basic assumptions—all the way from what it means to be a women or a man to what kind of familial, political, and economic institutions we can construct for ourselves. For at a certain level of technological development, the dominator model, with its emphasis on technologies of destruction and domination, quite literally goes into self-destruct, and we are rapidly approaching that point.

It is clear that the traditional approaches are not working, that we need to create new ways of living on this earth that make it possible for us to practice, and not just preach, nonviolence, caring, and cooperation— what sociologist Jessie Bernard (1981) calls a "female ethos of love/duty". But to say that fundamental change is necessary—and even as I have tried to show in this chapter—realistically feasible, is not to say that it must occur.

In the last analysis, it is we, every one of us, that is responsible for making the necessary changes. And, as I have also tried to show here, many of these changes revolve around a dual recognition that some of the most critical issues in our world today are the long neglected, so-called women's issues, and that peace and social and economic justice cannot just be grafted on to a social system based on the ranking of one half of humanity over the other.

Notes

1. For two important feminist works debunking the sociobiological dogma that male dominance and male violence are in our genes, see Tobach and Rosoff (1978) and Hubbard and Lowe (1979).

2. The view of social evolution as following a series of inevitable stages first gained popularity through the works of 19th-century thinkers such as Auguste Compte, Herbert Spencer, and Lewis Henry Morgan, whose thinking also greatly influenced Friedrich Engels, who based much of his *The origins of the family, private property and the state* (1972) on Morgan's ideas about stages of social evolution. Carrying on the tradition of Johann Gottfried Herder in his ideas for a philosophy of the history of humanity, German historian Breysig also developed a theory that history means stages of social and cultural evolution that are potentially humanitywide. For his first essay on the subject, see Breysig (1896); this thinking culminated in Breysig (1927).

3. See, for example, *The Dartmouth Bible*, annotated by R. Chamberlain and H. Herman, with the counsel of an advisory board of Biblical scholars (Chamberlain & Herman, 1950).

4. See Mellaart (1967, 1975). The first paper to advance the theory that Minoan civilization was destroyed by earthquakes and tidal waves was that of Marinatos (1939). Since then it appears more feasible that this is what so weakened Crete as to make possible the takeover by Achaean (Mycenaean) overlords, as there is no evidence that this takeover was through a full-scale armed invasion.

5. For other authors substantiating this position, see Gimbutas (1977, 1982), and Childe (1964).

6. This is substantiated in Mellaart (1967, 1975), Gimbutas (1977, 1982), Childe (1964) and Neumann (1955).

7. For a later proponent of this view, see Frazer (1969).

8. The partnership model is elaborated on in Eisler (1984, 1986, 1987) and Eisler and Loye (1983, 1986).

9. See Pagels (1979) for a fascinating account of some of the suppressed Christian gospels and the importance ascribed to the feminine as divine wisdom, or Sophia.

10. This dynamic lies, I believe, behind such historical disputes as that between Baird and Kelly-Gadol on whether women had a Renaissance. But they were looking at different aspects of the Renaissance. Baird was observing signs of partnership resurgence (e.g., the debates about granting women greater educational opportunities and not just relegating them to the domestic sphere). Kelly-Gadol was looking at the dominator resistance, and

ultimately regression (e.g., the primogeniture laws enacted precisely to prevent any real and lasting empowerment of women).

11. Cultural transformation theory is presented in more detail in Eisler (1987).

12. Much of the discussion that follows is taken from the partnership workbook written by Eisler and Loye (1990).

13. For some works on the complex interaction between biological and social factors, see Hinde (1974), Lewontin, Rose, and Kamin (1984), Lambert (1978), and Eisler and Csanyi (in press).

14. For excellent treatments of this subject, see Waring (1989), and Henderson (1981).

References

Baudrillard, J. (1981). *For a critique of the political economy of the sign.* St. Louis: Telos.

Bernard, J. (1981). *The female world.* New York: The Free Press.

Blakney, R. B. (Ed. & Trans.) (1955). *The way of life, Lao Tzu, Tao Te Ching.* New York: Mentor.

Breysig, K. (1896). Über Entwicklungsgeschichte (in 2 parts), In G. Seeliger (Ed.), *Deutsche Zeitschrift für Geisteswissenschaft, N.F.* (Monatsblaetter, pp. 161-174, 193-211).

Breysig, K. (1927). *Der Stufenbau und die Gesetze der Weltgeschichte.* Stuttgart: Cotta.

Childe, G. (1964). *The dawn of European civilization.* New York: Random House.

Csanyi, V. (1989). *Evolutionary systems and society: A general theory.* Raleigh, NC: Duke University Press.

Eisler, R. (1984). Violence and male dominance: The ticking time bomb. *Humanities in Society, 7*(1-2), 3-18.

Eisler, R. (1986, October 28-31). Woman, man, and the evolution of social structure. Paper presented at the Physis: Inhabiting the Earth Conference, Florence, Italy.

Eisler, R., (1987). *The chalice and the blade: Our history, our future.* San Francisco: Harper & Row.

Eisler, R. (1989). *Concept paper on partnership and the arts.* Pacific Grove, CA: Center for Partnership Studies.

Eisler, R., & Csanyi, V. (n.d.) *Human biology and social structure.* Unpublished manuscript.

Eisler, R., & Loye, D. (1983). The failure of liberalism: A reassessment of ideology from a new feminine-masculine perspective. *Political Psychology, 4*(2) 375-391.

Eisler, R., & Loye, D. (1986). Peace and feminist thought: New directions. In E. Laszlo & J. Y. Yoo (Eds.), *World Encyclopedia of Peace* (pp. 332-336). London: Pergamon Press.

Eisler, R., & Loye, D. (1990). *The partnership way: New tools for living and learning.* San Francisco: Harper & Row.

Engels, F. (1972). *The origins of the family, private property and the state.* New York: International Publishers.

Frazer, J. (1969).*The golden bough.* New York: McMillan.

Gablik, S. (1991). *The reenchantment of art.* London: Thames & Hudson.

Gallagher, M. (1981).*Unequal opportunities: The case of women and the media*. Paris: UNESCO.

Gimbutas, M. (1977). The first wave of Eurasian steppe pastoralists into copper age Europe. *The Journal of Indo-European Studies, 5*(4) 277-338.

Gimbutas, M. (1982). *The goddesses and gods of old Europe*. Berkeley: University of California Press.

Hawques, J. (1968). *Dawn of the gods: Minoan and Mycenaean origins of Greece*. New York: Random House.

Henderson, H. (1981). *The politics of the solar age*. New York: Anchor Books.

Hinde, R. (1974). *Biological bases of human social behaviour*. New York: McGraw-Hill.

Hubbard, R., & Lowe, M. (Eds.) (1979). *Genes and gender II*. Staten Island: Gordian Press.

Keller, M. (1988). The Eleusinian mysteries of Demeter and Persephone: Fertility, sexuality and rebirth. *Journal of Feminist Studies in Religion, 4*(1), 27-54.

Keller, M. (n.d.). *The Eleusinian mysteries*. Unpublished manuscript.

Keuls, E. (1985). *The reign of the phallus*. San Francisco: Harper & Row.

Lambert, H. (1978). Biology and equality: A perspective on sex differences. *Signs, 4*(1), 97-117.

Lewontin, R. C., Rose, S., & Kamin, L. (1984). *Not in our genes*. New York: Pantheon.

Loye, D., Gorney, R., & Steele, G. (1977). Effects of television: An experimental field study. *Journal of Communication, 27*(3), 206-216.

Marinatos, S. (1939). The volcanic destruction of Minoan Crete. *Antiquity, 13,* 425-439.

Maturana, H. (1975). The organization of the living: A theory of the living organization. *Journal of Man-Machine Studies, 7,* 313-332.

Mellaart, J. (1967). *Catal Huyuk*. New York: McGraw-Hill.

Mellaart, J. (1975). *The Neolithic of the Near East*. New York: Scribner's.

Mill, J. S. (1929). *Principles of political economy*. New York: Longman, Green.

Miller, J. B. (1976). *Toward a new psychology of women*. Boston: Beacon Press.

Neumann, E. (1955). *The great mother*. Princeton, NJ: Princeton University Press.

Pagels, E. (1979). *The gnostic gospel*. New York: Random House.

Platon, N. (1966). *Crete*. Geneva: Nagel Publishers.

Roach, C. (1990). The movement for a New World Information and Communication Order: A second wave? *Media, Culture and Society, 12*(3), 283-307.

Robinson, J. M. (1968). *An introduction to early Greek philosophy*. Boston: Houghton Mifflin.

Rose, H. (1983). Hand, brain, and heart: A feminist epistemology for the natural sciences. *Signs, 9*(1), 73-90.

Roszak, T. (1969). The hard and the soft: The force of feminism in modern times. In B. Roszak & T. Roszak (Eds.), *Masculine/feminine* (pp. 87-106). New York: Harper.

Satir, V. (1972). *Peoplemaking*. Palo Alto, CA: Science and Behavior Books.

Spretnak, C. (1978). *Lost goddesses of early Greece*. Berkeley: Moon Books.

Taylor, G. R. (1954). *Sex in history*. New York: Ballantine.

Tobach, E., & Rosoff, B. (Eds). (1978). *Genes and gender*. Staten Island: Gordian Press.

Waring, M. (1989) *If women counted*. San Francisco: Harper & Row.

Weinhold, B. K., & Weinhold, J. B. (1989). *Breaking free of the co-dependency trap*. Walpole, NH : Stillpoint.

7

Feminist Peace Researchers, Culture, and Communication

COLLEEN ROACH

Roach's chapter also adopts a feminist perspective on peace that shares many of the ideas put forth by Eisler and Collins. This chapter highlights the importance of *language* as one of the primary carriers of culture, and notes that the dehumanizing aspects of the military vernacular have been criticized by a number of feminist writers. Thus when General Powell referred to the Iraqi Army as *it,* he was embodying a long-standing tradition of military culture.

Roach's concept of culture used in this chapter is slightly different than that of the two previous chapters in that she focuses more on *mass culture* products such as movies and books. The central connection between militarism and sexism referred to by Roach in her text is accepted by most feminist peace researchers such as Eisler: The widespread violence toward women sanctioned by most societies serves as a primal paradigm for the wholesale violence of war. Mass culture mirrors this connection, because, as this chapter notes, the period of the Persian Gulf War also witnessed particularly gruesome acts of violence toward women in mass culture. Pornography—a very contentious topic even among feminists—also played a role in preparing soldiers to do battle against the people of Iraq.

In reflecting on what is to be done, this chapter is not overly optimistic about the potential of progressive media, some of which continue to privilege male writers. Roach ends her chapter by echoing her coauthors' call for solidarity with the south. As Gloria Steinem has noted, "Women are a Third World wherever we are" (Steinem, 1988, p. xix).

AUTHOR'S NOTE: An earlier version of this chapter was published in 1991 in *Media Development, 38*(2) pp. 3-6.

First we're going to cut it off and then we're going to kill it.

General Colin L. Powell, Chairman of the U.S. Joint Chiefs of Staff
(New York Times, February, 17, 1991)

The opening quote to this chapter was made in February 1991, shortly before the launching of the ground phase of the Persian Gulf War. However chilling General Powell's explanation of U.S. strategy for dealing with the Iraqi Army may have been, many people outside of military circles undoubtedly understood it as only a metaphor and not an actual course of action. As we now know, reality proved otherwise. The U.S.-led Western coalition engaged in what has been described as one of the most devastating aerial bombardments in history. We may never know exactly how many Iraqi soldiers died during this phase of the war (estimates of total Iraqi soldiers killed range from 35,000 to 150,000) but we do know one thing: General Powell's words were not a metaphor. All the men and women killed in the Gulf War—be they American, Kuwaiti, British, Israeli, or Iraqi—are to be mourned. But the senseless slaughter of the thousands of Iraqi soldiers departing Kuwait will certainly be remembered for years to come as one of the most barbaric military actions of our era. That our species has indeed descended to some new level of dehumanization was evident in the interviews in the popular press with American pilots returning from their mission accomplished. Many of them—according to papers such as the *New York Post*—referred to their successful sorties as "turkey shoots." They gave very little evidence of any concern at the loss of human life.

The scale of calculated brutality in this war obliges us to probe more deeply into the phenomena of war and peace. In this probing, we would do well to look at an important but generally unacknowledged body of feminist literature that has been quietly produced over the last decade. It may not only shed some new light on the age-old question of why we go to war against another country but also help us to understand how this question is connected to another: why we are at war with ourselves.

The Literature of Feminism

Defining feminism is no easy task. Cagan (1983), an American feminist and social activist, offers one definition that is to my liking:

> Feminism is a political perspective that demands an end to the oppression of people because of their gender, and an end to the institutional and individual structures that define men as more valuable than women. Feminism rests on a belief that we can live in a world without hierarchies of control and domination, that people can exercise control over their own lives and live in harmony with others, and that women can share equality of opportunity and freedom. (p. 94)

Hooks's (1981) usage of the term adds elements that are of particular relevance for a perspective built on solidarity with the third world:

> Feminism is a commitment to eradicating the ideology of domination that permeates Western culture on various levels—sex, race, and class . . . and a commitment to reorganizing society so that the self-development of people can take precedence over imperialism, economic expansion and material desires. (pp. 194-195)

There are at least three types of feminist literature that are of relevance to war, peace, and culture. First of all, there is a very interesting body of work by feminist peace researchers whose writings are directly linked to the study of war and peace. Here, some of the names that come to mind are Reardon (1985), Eisler (1987), Brock-Utne (1985, 1989), and Boulding (1988a, 1988b); there are many others who have written on women and peace, such as Cagan and Ehrenreich.[1]

My own introduction to feminism in fact took place through the literature of feminist peace researchers. I think that many women (and perhaps men) who are social activists but are put off by the academic jargon of some feminist writing on communication and culture will be pleasantly surprised with what they will find in these writers. Many feminist peace researchers have incorporated both hard and soft issues into their work. There is a real concern, for example, in the writings of Brock-Utne and Reardon with the political economy of oppression and the effects of militarism in the third world. Yet they are not afraid to also talk about the need for relying on new strategies for peace that depend more on the intuitive and nurturing sides of human nature to build a new peace process.

Second, there is a body of feminist literature not directly related to peace but that has been used by women peace researchers because of its relevance to their work. Here, I am referring, for example, to the work of Gilligan (1982), the Harvard educator whose book *In a Different Voice* became a touchstone for many peace researchers who have argued that the different moral development of women makes them more prone to peace than men.[2] Another example would be the work of feminist theoreticians of language (e.g., Kramarae, 1980; Thorne, Kramarae, & Henley, 1983), which has also fed into feminist critiques of the dominant male discourse of the military establishment.

An increasing number of feminist peace researchers believe that deciphering the forces of militarism must ultimately lead to a critique of Western scientific rationality and, in particular, technology. For this reason, a third type of literature has been integrated into their writings: the work of feminist scientists and science philosophers such as Harding (1986) and Fox-Keller (1985). Finally, it should also be mentioned that although much of it does not have an explicitly feminist orientation, the work being done on women's representation and role in the media and popular culture can offer support for a feminist approach to peace.

Culture and Language

Psychologists and anthropologists for many years looked to Freud and the biological determinists to explain why human beings go to war. Freud posited that there is an innate instinct of man toward aggression, usually linked to the frustration of impulses. Biological determinists reach a similar conclusion by holding to the assumption that the roots of war and collective violence lie somewhere in the biological mechanisms that men and other animals have in common.

However, in recent years there has been a growing number of anthropologists and psychologists interested in peace research who are essentially concluding that war is above all a *cultural* phenomenon (see *The Seville Statement on Violence*). Anthropologist Greenhouse (1987), while acknowledging that the literature in anthropology is highly diverse, nonetheless writes,

> Is human aggression innate? Are the causes of war in nature or in culture? . . . The orientation of the literature strongly suggests that war is a cultural phenomenon, that is, that its roots are in the human mind, and not in the genes. (p. 32)

Holt (1987), a psychologist engaged in peace research, agrees that "the overwhelming consensus of behavioral scientists rejects the notion that something in human nature makes war inevitable" (p. 9). Holt's central argument, like that of Greenhouse, is that war is primarily part of a vast cultural complex composed of value systems, ideology and mythology, all of which are conveyed by the mass media, mass culture, and education (Holt, 1987, pp. 53-60).

Greenhouse's (1987) conclusion points in a direction followed by certain feminist peace researchers—the power of the imagination:

> We do know that war is an aspect of many cultural ideologies, but we also know that ideologies . . . are flexible idioms that express selectively the cultural propositions that are capable of life in human minds. This is cause for hope, since cultural analysis suggests that the causes of war lie not in the land, nor in some implacable demand for blood or honor, nor in human genes, but in imaginations that tolerate both the image and the reality of wholesale violence, at least for the moment. (p. 44)

All feminist peace researchers would not necessarily agree that the causes of war are to be found in our minds, because such thinking could obfuscate the political and economic factors underlying organized violence against a nation.[3] But many feminist writers do seem to show greater willingness than their male counterparts to look at the cultural aspects of war, especially when culture is defined in the way of researchers like Greenhouse and Holt to include values, ideology, mythology, and imagination.

One of the primary conveyors of culture is the medium of language. For this reason, it is an increasingly important area of inquiry for feminist writers. General Powell's statement referring to the Iraqi Army as *it* obviously is much more than words; *it* translates a military mindset that has converted the enemy not only into an Other but into a nonhuman Other. This is not the only example of how language was used—or rather misused—in the Gulf War to prevent public opinion from thinking in terms of the loss of human life. Sanitized phrases heard throughout the war such as "collateral damage," "saturation strikes," and "carpet bombing" all meant one thing: killing.

One of the most well-known analyses of military language circulating in feminist peace circles was written by Cohn (1987) at Harvard University's Center for Psychological Studies in the Nuclear Age. Cohn spent a year with all male members of the defense establishment and was struck by their use of language. Death, destruction, and war were all reduced to an ice cold, rational discourse with a definite sexual subtext (i.e., constant references to "penetration aids," and nuclear weapons that give you "more bang for your buck"). Emphasizing that this language does not originate in individuals but in a broader cultural context, Cohn (1987, p. 708) found that the only way to engage in dialogue with the defense teams was to adopt their own language.

In an article in the feminist magazine *Ms.*, Cohn wrote that "the Gulf War has apparently inspired military briefers to new heights of obfuscation." Instead of death and destruction, we hear of "flying sorties," "engaging the Iraqi Army," "taking out Iraqi assets," and "softening up the Republican Guard." Cohn's (1991) conclusion is that language is designed to hide one central fact: "war is a contest between states, in which the fundamental activity is destroying human creations, and injuring and killing human beings" (p. 88).

Gregory (1989), examined military writings on weaponry and concluded that the process of linguistic reification used by the authors had a number of untoward effects:

> The linguistic reification distracts us readers, and thereby leads us to think through the issue incompletely. Images of weapons racing each other draw our inner eye to pictures of aerial combat and mechanical armies in the sky. So engaged, we're unlikely to think about people making and implementing decisions in scientific research labs or government offices down on earth. . . .
>
> The reifications have another effect. While making human beings and their activities invisible, they raise into the foreground a fictional world of smart, fast machines. These machines are not merely the ones we know in the real world. Through the magic of metaphor, these war machines acquire consciousness and will. They engage in battles, run races and act intelligently without human agency. . . . In our mind's eye, they have been anthropomorphically transformed. (pp. 13-14)

Galtung (1989) has not only written on language and war per se but has also extended the metaphor of cultural violence[4] to sexist language:

> Certain languages—those with a Latin base such as Italian, Spanish, French and English, but not those with a Germanic base such as German and Norwegian—make women invisible by using the same word for the male as for the entire human species. The important movement for non-sexist writing is a good example of deliberate cultural transformation away from cultural violence. (p. 22)

The Tie That Binds: Violence

But it is the actual violence of war, according to feminist writers on peace, that is profoundly connected to the violence against women.

Many feminists such as Reardon and Cagan find that the essential connection between sexism and the war system is that both rely on the prevalence of violence. Their argument is as follows: Because widespread violence toward women is socially sanctioned by prevailing cultural norms—with the mass media and mass culture playing a very important role—it serves as a sort of primal paradigm for violent warfare against other peoples. In short, because violence toward the Other, represented by women, is commonplace in almost all societies and cultures, it makes sense that violence toward other races and countries is widely accepted.

This connection was made explicit in a statement made on January 10, 1991, to the press by a delegation from the Woman's International League for Peace and Freedom in Baghdad:

> We are against the use of force in settling conflict situations. When people develop the attitude that differences can be settled through violent means, then we perpetuate a mentality that brings violence into all human relations, and right into the home, where women and children are the primary victims. (quoted on Peacenet, January 16, 1991)

There are several subarguments made on the issue of violence. Cagan (1983), who states that "violence against women stands as a cornerstone of the oppression of women"(Cagan, 1983, p. 95), draws a parallel between women and weaker nations preyed on by larger forces:

> The ever-present possibility of rape parallels the threat of military intervention strong nations use against weaker ones. Stay in line or you will get hurt. Play by the rules or the most brutal force will bear down upon you. In both cases a broader and more subtle system of ever-present inequality lies behind and is defended by the more overt form of coercion. (p. 95)

Eisler's (1987) work summarizes a common finding of many anthropologists and sociologists: The more highly militarized a culture is, the more likely it is to have a high degree of violence toward women. Reardon (1985), who drew extensive parallels between militarism and sexism in her book *Sexism and the War System,* makes another observation common to many feminists: Women are not just victims of physical violence but are also much more oppressed than any other social group by the structural violence exacerbated in highly militarized societies.

But it is actual physical violence toward women that provides a particularly striking illustration of how militarism relates to violence toward women. In December 1989, Canada experienced the worst mass murder in its history. A lone gunman, Marc Lepine, went to the University of Montreal's engineering school, and, separating the men from the women, systematically slaughtered 14 females with a high-powered hunting rifle. Before killing himself, Lepine had ranted and raved about the women being "a bunch of feminists." This massacre of women, which has received very little attention by the U.S. media, has been widely explored in the Canadian press. Two journalists for the *Toronto Star* (Weston & Aubry, 1990) did an extensive background study of the killer. On the one hand, the journalists' in-depth story offers few surprises: Lepine was a loner, with a history of bad professional and personal relations, particularly with women, whom he felt had ruined his life. Buried in the article, however, are other indications that Lepine had been profoundly influenced by the war culture. In his room, the journalists looked through his library and found that "he had a lot of war books." They also found that he had taped many movies from television—"Lots about war in those." The journalists interviewed his landlord, who reported that he had told him that he was "going off to join the armed forces." As reported, Lepine's suicide note bemoaned the fact that he was "rejected by the army" for antisocial behavior. Last, the *Toronto Star*'s description of the Montreal massacre[5] is more appropriate for a battle zone:

> There is mayhem in the main corridor outside Room 230. The 50 men who left the room as ordered are screaming at others to run away. Inside the classroom 6 women are dead. . . . He is out in the main corridor again, down at the other end of the photocopier, moving with the methodical precision of a trained soldier. He keeps his back to the wall. He wheels. Fires. Wheels and fires again. The wounded are moaning for help. (Weston & Aubry, 1990, p. A18)

One of the best analyses linking the violence of war to violence against women has been produced by a Canadian peace group called Act for Disarmament (see the Appendix). A brochure describing one of their 1992 projects, *Violence Against Women: The War All Around Us,* begins with a grim list of the high statistics on the number of women in Canada and elsewhere who are sexually abused, physically abused, or killed every year by men. It then states quite simply: "This is a war."

"If we saw these figures for any other group of people, we would recognize it as a war" (ACT for Disarmament, 1992). Other connections made by this group of activists are also of relevance:

> We also see violence against women in Canada and around the world as part of a larger culture of violence. We realize that the same culture that makes it possible for men to abuse women with impunity makes it possible for nations to go to war with each other, and for large, rich countries to exploit, invade, or colonize smaller countries. . . . Our aim is to create a culture of peace. (ACT for Disarmament, 1992)

In discussions about women and violence at an EXPRO meeting, Liane Norman, director of the Pittsburgh Peace Institute, told an interesting story. She had been on a trip to Nicaragua during the war, and her group—made up of both men and women—was being escorted through a rather dangerous military zone. They were afraid, but one of the men noted that many of the men seemed more afraid than the women. He asked her why, and she realized that it was because women are used to being afraid all the time.

Is it any wonder that *Ms.* magazine's editorial against the war in the Persian Gulf noted that "for most women, daily life is a combat zone"? (Morgan, 1991).

Mass Culture and Violence

The role of mass culture in war has been a fruitful area of exploration for several years. Writers have looked at many different aspects of mass culture that promote machismo and militarism, such as the ever-popular *Rambo* movies of the 1980s, the video war games, and even the military garb worn by civilians.[6] And anyone having lived through events in the United States during the Persian Gulf war certainly knows that both mass culture and the mass media played no small role in promoting prowar sentiment against Iraq. Here, I am referring not only to television's high-tech glorification of the war, but also to the racist anti-Iraq and anti-Hussein T-shirts that could be bought at any local gas station as well as the yellow ribbons and flags that festooned homes and automobiles.[7]

However, there is another very disturbing aspect of American mass culture, which relates to the connection between the violence of war and the violence against women mentioned above. Precisely during the months of the buildup to the war and the war itself (December 1990 to February 1991) there was an enormous media hype to promote the movie *Silence of the Lambs*. One of the stars of the movie (Jodie Foster) was ubiquitous on the little screen, appearing in innumerable interviews, talk shows, and so on. Late-night news and the print media rivaled each other in their ample references to this new thriller, billed as outdoing *Psycho* and other murder classics of the silver screen. By April 1991, it had set a near record in the United States, heading the box-office returns for five consecutive weekends. When released in England in June 1991, it did set a record, with its initial showing, bringing in more money than any first-run movie in the industry's history. The film was subsequently showered with the highest acclaim from the motion picture industry and movie critics, receiving both the New York Film Critics Circle Award and several Oscars.

Silence of the Lambs and its storyline are truly gruesome: An imprisoned psychopathic genius killer, who is apt to eat his victims, is called on by a young FBI agent to help find another serial killer on the loose. This particular serial killer has the habit of not just killing and torturing young women, but starving and skinning them (both of which are depicted on the screen).

If this sounds in bad taste, it was apparently outdone in another product of American mass culture that unlike *Silence of the Lambs* did generate extreme controversy. Precisely during the period of the Gulf War, heated debates took place over the novel *American Psycho* by Ellis (1991). Ellis's work offered such graphic descriptions of the dismemberment and torture of women that the National Organization of Women (NOW) launched a boycott, even establishing a hot line with taped excerpts from the book so readers could judge for themselves. The controversy became so intense that the book's original publisher even backed out of its contract, forfeiting a considerable advance to the author.

Influenced by this backlash, Beatty, a senior editor at *Atlantic Monthly,* took a similar stand. He refused to publish a favorable review of a novel by West on mass murderers of women called *The Women of Whitechapel and Jack the Ripper* (West, 1991). According to the *New York Times* Beatty stated that he could not praise the artistic merit of a work that is morally deplorable (cited in Cohen, 1991). Beatty's letter to the rejected reviewer is worth quoting:

> Writers have to concern themselves with the moral consequences of their
> art, it seems to me, and magazines must be socially responsible: they

cannot, we cannot, publish something that asks us to admire the literary merit of a book about chopping women up. Not when so many of them are being chopped up all over this terrible anarchy we are living in. (cited in Cohen, 1991)

Violence in American mass culture has reached such a feverish pitch that even some of the mainstream mass media have sounded an alarm. *Newsweek* magazine, in a cover story of April 1, 1991, titled "Violence in our Culture," asked a rhetorical question: "As America binges on make-believe gore, you have to ask: what are we doing to ourselves?"(Plagen, Miller, Foote, & Yoffe, 1991, p. 46). Noting numerous examples of recent bloodletting directed against women in song lyrics, movies, television, and books, including both *American Psycho* and *Silence of the Lambs, Newsweek* observed: "In all of pop culture (as in most of society) women are the victims of choice. . . . An awful lot of hostility against women is being played out in popular culture these days and it's not pretty"(Plagen, Miller, Foote, & Yoffe, 1991, p. 46).

Perhaps the most striking connection between mass culture's degradation of women and militarism was also provided during the Gulf War. Several writers, commenting on the war, noted that the American pilots on the aircraft carriers were shown pornographic movies before they took off on their bombing missions over Iraq (Weisstein, 1991, p. 131).

Noting that "the sexual dimension of warfare can be downright scary," Gottlieb (1991) added,

In the Persian Gulf, navy pilots on the "U.S.S. Kennedy" told an Associated Press reporter they had been watching pornographic movies before flying bombing runs. The *Washington Post* reported that the military censored the story, claiming it would be "too embarrassing." (p. 39)

The above examples suggest that we should learn to "make connections" (a feminist slogan) and take note of the synchroneity of massive violence inflicted on a country and the violence against women that is part and parcel of our mass culture.[8]

The Silencing of Women on Peace

For decades women have played very important roles in peace movements both as activists and organizers. They have taken leadership positions in countries such as Israel, northern Ireland, and Argentina.

Yet when issues of war and peace are discussed in mainstream media, women's voices are heard about as often as they are in the corridors of military power. And in spite of the important work being done by some of the feminists cited in this chapter, peace research is still, as Reardon (1985) reminds us, very much "another male preserve" (p. 71).

While the silencing of women in the mainstream media is not surprising, one might have hoped that progressive information channels more open to the peace movement would seek out women's voices. In the United States, unlike many countries in Western Europe, there are only a handful of progressive media. One such publication, with a long history of progressive politics, is *The Nation* magazine. In September 1990, *The Nation* launched a new "peace forum." Within two months, it had published four contributions, all from men. I wrote an unpublished letter to the editor pointing out that whereas it had started the series by stating that it was asking several *people* to comment on the peace movement, it would have been more accurate if it had written that it was asking several *men* to comment. I also pointed out that *The Nation*'s record put it in the same ranks as the *New York Times*, which published an article surveying progressive voices on the Gulf Crisis in November 1990, which referred to no less than 12 men with not even a token woman. *The Nation* ended the series with two additional authors, both men. In 1991, *The Nation* also published a forum titled "How to End the War." Again, we find four male experts.[9]

Another important alternative publication in the United States is *The Progressive*. Its editor, Knoll, was one of the few left-of-center commentators to be interviewed on the war by the public television system. Although its promotional literature promised a more feminist agenda than *The Nation*, this does not seem to be the case. In March 1991, it published an issue entirely devoted to peace. There were nine authors with one woman. The fact that the few established alternative media in the United States seem to be no less open to airing the opinions of women than the establishment media confirms what both Eisler and Reardon concluded: Conservative political movements have been much more successful in gender politics than progressive political formations.

Hope on the Horizon?

In January 1991, as the U.S. Congress debated on whether or not to go to war, there were some small signs that feminist discourse had filtered through to the corridors of power. As reported in a front-page *New York Times* article, during the congressional war debates in early January 1991, Representative Andrew Jacobs of Indiana stated, "Must we all believe that we're playing Rambo, that we're playing war games here? It's forever. It's total war for the kid who gets blown away"(Clymer, 1991, p. A1). Congressman Joseph Kennedy II of Massachusetts also made an impassioned speech from the floor of the House, stating that "There's a misguided machismo mentality in America now, a John Wayne attitude, that says some how or another, this is the way we should conduct foreign policy. We ought to be the bully boy"(Kennedy, 1991, p. 2).

Jacobs's and Kennedy's sentiments were not seconded by many of their cohorts, leading one to the conclusion that women cannot expect to find much pacifist support from those representing the state. But an essential question needs to be posed: Is there any basis for believing that women do, in fact, believe more strongly in peace than men? Although American women seem to have supported the war in the Gulf when it actually began, before its onset in early December, the gap between women and men favoring U.S. intervention was a full 25 points, leading Harris, of polling fame, to refer not to a gender gap but to a gender *gulf* (Harris, 1991).

Another hopeful sign on the horizon is the creativity shown by many feminists promoting peace through new actions. In this regard, Eisler's work is very innovative. In her book *The Chalice and the Blade,* Eisler (1987) examined a wide range of archaeological and anthropological evidence that indicated a recurrent pattern of what she calls "partnership resurgence and domination regression." In sum, Eisler finds that since prehistoric times, there have been repeated attempts to create peaceful, loving cultures in which women and men worked together as partners. However, each resurgence of these societies has been met by a cycle of resistance by militarized male dominator societies. Eisler believes that the cultural transformation necessary for peace will only be brought about by promoting partnership models of human relations and is now conducting workshops on this theme around the country.

Conclusion: Women and the Third World

This chapter began by referring to events of 1991 in the Persian Gulf. Although the political-economic factors of war are not to be neglected, I have argued that the pervasive war culture of our societies has also contributed substantially to both sexism and militarism. If the Gulf War was only a prelude to increased military actions in the third world—and there is every indication that this is the most likely scenario—women will be very much affected by the new wave of rising militarism. Since the 1970s, an important strain of feminist literature has called for solidarity between women everywhere and the peoples of the Arab world, Asia, Africa, and Latin America.[10] This may be an idea whose time has come.

Notes

1. Recent works on women and war include Diedrich and Fischer-Hornung (1990), Elshtain (1987), Gioseffi (1988), Hunter (1991), MacDonald, Holden, and Ardener (1988), and Norman (1990). Caldicott's (1986) classic book, *Missile Envy*, also deals with women's perspectives on war.

2. The debate on differences (genes vs. gender, nature vs. nurture, etc.) is one of the most long-standing and as yet unresolved issues in feminist writing. For a recent treatment of this question, see Hunter (1991).

3. The common thinking on war as a result of political and economic inequalities is reflected in an article examining conflicts in the third world. The author directly responds to the idea of wars beginning in our imaginations: "It is often assumed that there is more than a correlation between poverty, inequality, and the resort to arms, that there is a causal relationship between them. This is an axiom, intuitively supported, that wars begin not just in the 'minds of men' but in the misery of poverty and inequality as much as in an anarchic international system" (Chubin, 1991, p. 153).

4. *Cultural violence* is defined by Galtung (1989) as "those aspects of culture, the symbolic sphere of our existence—exemplified by religion and ideology, language and art, empirical science and formal science (logic, mathematics)—that can be used to justify, legitimize direct or structural violence" (p. 2).

5. *The Montreal Massacre* is the title of a book of letters and poems by Quebec feminists expressing their anguish over this event, and linking the massacre to society's hatred of women (Malette & Chalouh, 1991). For an analysis of the media coverage of the Montreal massacre, see Raboy (1992).

6. For one of the most complete compilations of research relating war to culture, see Luckham (1984).

7. Yellow ribbons became a symbol of hope for the American hostages taken by Iran during the 1970s. In the Gulf War, although there was some sparring over symbols between prowar and antiwar activists (with the latter attempting in some cases to appropriate the flag and yellow ribbons) the ribbons were widely interpreted by politicians as a sign of support for the U.S. military action.

8. With specific reference to *American Psycho, Silence of the Lambs,* and other recent offerings of mass culture, Robbins's (1991) research notes the connection between the war in the Persian Gulf and the unleashing of fictionalized serial killers on the American public. He points out,

There are those (following Jean Baudrillard) who like to tell us that the screen has now eclipsed reality; that we are now living in a world of image, simulation and spectacle. There is, indeed, something suggestive in this observation. But before we become too seduced by this post-modernist scenario, we should remember the *real* men and women who were *really* slaughtered beyond the screening of the Gulf War. We should consider the implications of the fact that there is a symbiotic relationship between fictional serial killers and *real* ones, who *really* slaughter. (pp. 11-12)

9. According to a survey by the editor of the *Socialist Review*, in 1990 the percentage of women contributors to *The Nation* was 18%—lower than any other progressive publication except *Monthly Review*.

10. In the 1970s, writers such as Steinem and Sontag popularized the idea that women are a third world wherever they are (see e.g., Sontag, 1973). In a more recent article, Brock-Utne (1991) fleshes out this connection.

References

ACT for Disarmament. (1992). *Violence against women: The war all around us* (brochure). Toronto: ACT for Disarmament.

Boulding, E. (1988a). Warriors and saints: Dilemmas in the history of war. In E. Isakkson (Ed.), *Women and militarism*. London: Harvester Wheatsheaf.

Boulding, E. (1988b). *Building a global civic culture: Education for an interdependent world*. New York: Columbia University Teacher's College Press.

Brock-Utne, B. (1985). *Educating for peace*. New York: Pergamon Press.

Brock-Utne, B. (1989). *Feminist perspectives on peace and peace education*. New York: Pergamon Press.

Brock-Utne, B. (1991). Underdevelopment and the oppression of women: A feminist perspective. In E. Boulding, C. Brigagao, & K. Clements (Eds.), *Peace, culture & society* (pp. 212-228). Boulder, CO: Westview Press.

Cagan, L. (1983). Feminism and militarism. In M. Albert & D. Dellinger (Eds.), *Beyond survival: New directions for the disarmament movement* (pp. 81-118). Boston: South End Press.

Caldicott, H. (1986). *Missile envy*. New York: Bantam.

Chubin, S. (1991, February). Third world conflicts: Trends and prospects. *International Social Science Journal*, XLIII(127), 147-161.

Clymer, A. (1991, January 12). Baker warns of fast strike if Kuwait deadline passes; Support in congress is seen. *New York Times*, pp. A1, A7.

Cohen, R. (1991, July 3). Book notes. *New York Times*.

Cohn, C. (1987). Sex and death in the rational world of defense intellectuals. *Signs, 12*(4), 687-718.

Cohn, C. (1991). Decoding military newspeak. *Ms., 1*(5), 88.

Diedrich, M., & Fischer-Hornung, D. (1990). *Women and war: The changing status of American women from the 1930s to the 1940s*. Providence, RI: Berg.

Eisler, R. (1987). *The chalice and the blade*. New York: Harper & Row.

Ellis, B. E. (1991). *American psycho*. New York: Random House.

Elshtain, J. B. (1987). *Women and war.* New York: Basic.

Fox-Keller, E. (1985). *Reflections on gender and science.* New Haven, CT: Yale University Press.

Galtung, J. (1989, August). *Cultural violence.* Unpublished manuscript, University of Hawaii, Manoa.

Gilligan, C. (1982). *In a different voice.* Cambridge, MA: Harvard University Press.

Gioseffi, D. (1988). *Women and war.* New York: Touchstone.

Gottlieb, J. (1991, April). The sexual connection. *The Progressive, 55*(4), 39.

Greenhouse, C. (1987). Cultural perspectives on war. In R. Varynen (Ed.), *The quest for peace: Transcending collective violence and war among societies, cultures and states* (pp. 32-47). London: Sage.

Gregory, D. V. (1989). The dictator's furnace. *Peace Review, 1*(1), 12-16.

Harding, S. (1986). *The science question in feminism.* Ithaca, NY: Cornell University Press.

Harris, L. (1990, December 1). The gender gulf. *New York Times.*

Holt, R. (1987, May). *Converting the war system to a peace system: Some contributions from psychology and other social sciences.* Paper presented at EXPRO Conference, Cohasset, MA.

Hooks, B. (1981). *Ain't I a woman? Black women and feminism.* Boston: South End Press.

Hunter, A. E. (1991). *On peace, war and gender: A challenge to genetic explanations* (Genes and Gender VI). New York: The Feminist Press at the City University of New York.

Kennedy II, J. P. (1991). Statement on the floor of the House of Representatives regarding the Persian Gulf crisis (Press Release). Washington, DC: Office of Hon. Joseph P. Kennedy II.

Kramarae, C. (Ed.). (1980). The voices and words of women and men [Special issue]. *Women's Studies International Quarterly, 3*(2-3).

Luckham, R. (1984). Arms and culture. *Current Research on Peace and Violence,* (Tampere Peace Research Institute) *7*(1), 1-64.

MacDonald, S., Holden, P., & Ardener, S. (Eds.). (1988). *Images of women in peace and war.* Madison: University of Wisconsin Press.

Malette, L., & Chalouh, M. (Eds.). (1991). *The Montreal Massacre.* Charlottetown, Prince Edward Island: Gynergy Books.

Morgan, R. (1991). Digressions [Editorial]. *Ms., 1*(5).

Norman, E. (1990). *Women at war: The story of fifty million nurses who served in Vietnam.* Philadelphia: University of Pennsylvania Press.

Plagen, P., Miller, M., Foote, D., & Yoffe, E. (1991, April 1). Violence in our culture. *Newsweek.* pp. 46-52.

Raboy, M. (1992). Media and the invisible crises of everyday life. In M. Raboy & B. Dagenais (Eds.), *Media, crisis, and democracy* (pp. 133-143). London: Sage.

Reardon, B. (1985). *Sexism and the war system.* New York: Columbia University Teachers College Press.

Robbins, K. (1991, June 20). Screening Violence. Paper presented at Conference on the Media and the Gulf War, Istanbul, sponsored by the IAMCR (International Association of Mass Communication Research) and ILAD (Turkish Mass Communication Research Association.)

Sontag, S. (1973). The third world of women. *Partisan Review, 60*(2), 180-206.

Steinem, G. (1988). Introduction. In M. Waring (Ed.), *If women counted: A new feminist economics* (pp. xvii-xx). New York: Harper & Row.

The Seville Statement on Violence. (1991). In A. E. Hunter (Ed.), *Genes and gender VI: On peace, war, and gender* (Appendix, pp. 168-171). New York: The Feminist Press at the City University of New York.

Thorne, B., Kramare, C., & Henley, N. (Eds.). (1983). *Language, gender and society.* Rawley, MA: Newbury Publishing House.

Weisstein, N. (1991, July 15-22). Response to "What is patriotism?" *The Nation,* p. 131.

West, P. (1991). *The women of Whitechapel and Jack the Ripper.* Woodstock, NY: The Overlook Press.

Weston, G., & Aubry, G. (1990, February 8). Lepine's own failures fed hatred of women. *Toronto Star,* pp. A1, A18.

8

Ethnic Discourse and the New World Dysorder:
A Communitarian Perspective

MAJID TEHRANIAN

The end of the Cold War has not given birth to peace. Tehranian's chapter takes as its starting point that the north's new world order is actually a *dysorder* (as in *dysfunctional*). In the midst of great confusion and chaos, Tehranian signals five global megatrends affecting both the north and the south: globalism, regionalism, nationalism, localism, and spiritualism. Each of these trends is played out within a context of continuing modernization, in which communication technology and new cultural forces are essential features.

This chapter's timeliness in exposing some of the deep cultural roots of current ethnic conflicts is apparent. Although offering a cogent analysis of the inner tensions and contradictions of these conflicts, the author clearly takes sides on which tendencies may lead us out of the morass: a global vision based on communitarian principles and not hegemony, an inclusionary not exclusionary view of regionalism, a democratic-benign nationalism and not its totalitarian variant, a liberal and not parochial localism, and a spiritualism that is ecumenical rather than fundamentalist.

Tehranian's contribution, like the other chapters in the book, integrates mass communication issues into his analysis. But it is primarily in the realm of culture—what Galtung (this volume) signaled as the most important force—where this chapter joins hands with the other authors. Like them, he also calls for a genuine multiculturalism, which could be an antidote to the rising racism in the United States (our own version of ethnic conflict). Perhaps the most interesting aspect of this chapter is its combination of hard and soft issues: The political economy of communication and culture is in harmony with discussion of values and spirituality.

AUTHOR'S NOTE: Ethnic discourse is employed here in its most general sense, suggesting an increasing prevalence of ethnic conflict since the end of the Cold War and the rise of ethnic issues in the public discourse of politicians, the media, and other representations of world events. Note also that it is dysorder as in dysfunctional. I wish to thank Christine Kris for her suggestions of *dysorder* and Colleen Roach for her helpful comments and suggestions on the original draft of this chapter.

When the forms of an old culture are dying, the new culture is created by
a few people who are not afraid to be insecure.

Rudolf Bahro

The rise of ethnicity as a central problem of our time has a dual origin.
The most immediate cause is, of course, the end of the Cold War. From
Yalta in 1945 to Malta in 1989, the world was dominated by the tidal
rivalries between the East and West with a rising undercurrent of
north-south conflicts and contentions.[1] The universalist ideological
pretensions of communism and liberalism left little room for the claims
of ethnic and national loyalties except in the third world where national
liberation movements attempted to chart a third way under the rubrics of
national self-determination and nonalignment. While these attempts succeeded in gaining national independence for many Asian and African
countries, they failed to give adequate recognition to the enormous racial,
ethnic, and tribal diversity of the newly independent nations themselves.
Ethnicity and ethnic discourse thus remained repressed under the weight
of a world order characterized by bipolarity and nation-state rivalries.

The end of the Cold War, however, has unleashed the centrifugal, ethnic,
and tribal forces within nation-states. (For a map of current world conflict
spots, mostly of ethnic origin, see Figure 8.1. For a sample of ethnic
conflict on American campuses, see Tehranian, 1991c.) It has led to the
breakup of the former Soviet Union, the world's last multinational empire,
the breakdown of multiethnic patchworks such as Yugoslavia and Iraq, has
threatened the breakup of other nation-states such as Canada and India and
unleashed racial and ethnic violence in the United States, Israel, South
Africa, and other multiracial and multiethnic societies. If we pair these
events with other developments such as the rise of religious fundamentalism, we may argue that the rise of primordial identities as opposed to civic
and status identities has profound historical roots in the processes of
modernization itself. Modernization as a process of universal leveling of
societies into relatively homogeneous entities has encountered four great
reactions in modern history, which may be labeled as *countermodernization, hypermodernization, demodernization,* and *postmodernization.*

The universalist, rationalist, scientific, and technological discourse
of modernity, so well articulated in the ideologies of liberalism and
Marxism, had for long camouflaged a hegemonic project by a new modern,
technocratic, internationalist elite. This elite has largely imposed its will

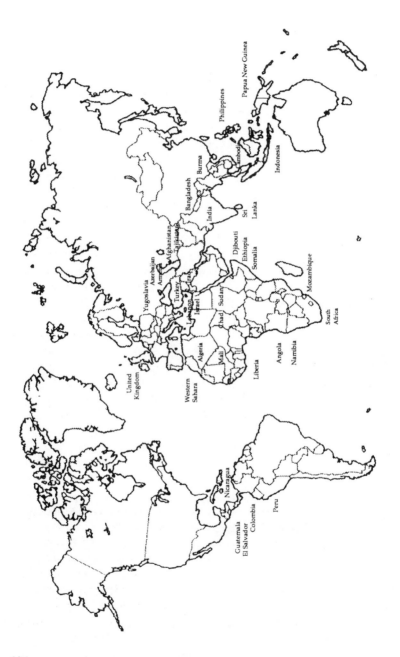

Papua New Guinea
Philippines
Burma
Bangladesh
Indonesia
Cambodia
India
Sri Lanka
Afghanistan
Tajikistan
Azerbaijan
Armenia
Djibouti
Ethiopia
Somalia
Yugoslavia
Turkey
Iraq
Iran
Mozambique
Lebanon
Israel
Sudan
Chad
South Africa
Algeria
Mali
Angola
Namibia
United Kingdom
Liberia
Western Sahara

Nicaragua
Guatemala
El Salvador
Colombia
Peru

194

LEGEND

CW = civil war
X = war of secession or independence
10 = conflict lasting more than 10 years
F = foreign involvement
P = new peace
UN = UN peacekeeping involvement

Latin America	CW	X	10	I	F	P	UN
Colombia			10	I			
El Salvador						P	UN
Guatemala				I		P	UN
Nicaragua						P	UN
Peru				I			

Africa	CW	X	10	I	F	P	UN
Algeria	CW						
Angola	CW		10		F	P	UN
Chad			10	I			
Djibouti				I	F		
Ethiopia		X	10	I		P	
Liberia	CW			I	F		
Mali				I			
Mozambique	CW		10	I		P	
Namibia			10	I		P	UN
Somalia	CW	X		I			
South Africa	CW		10				
Sudan	CW	X	10				
Western Sahara		X	10		F	P	UN

Europe	CW	X	10	I	F	P	UN
Armenia		X					
Azerbaijan		X					
Tajikistan	CW						
Turkey				I			
United Kingdom			10	I			
Yugoslavia	CW	X					

Asia	CW	X	10	I	F	P	UN
Afghanistan	CW		10	I		P	UN
Bangladesh			10	I			
Burma			10	I			
Cambodia	CW		10	I	F	P	UN
India		X	10	I			
Indonesia		X	10	I			
Iraq	CW			I			
Israel				I		P	
Lebanon	CW		10		F		
Papua New Guinea		X	10				
Philippines			10	I			
Sri Lanka		X	10	I			

Figure 8.1. World Conflict Zones-July 1992.

SOURCE: Tehranian & Tehranian, 1992. Reprinted with permission of Hampton Press.

195

on the rest of a multiethnic, multiracial, multireligious, and traditional-ist world. With the demise of the Cold War, the fraternal bonds of capitalist and socialist-technocratic elites have been further strength-ened. The world centers of wealth and power now speak the language of a new internationalism, a new world order. The world peripheries are left with no universalist ideologies except the universalism of human suffering and religious hopes. National and parochial cultures as op-posed to universalist and cosmopolitan cultures have thus gained a new lease on life in the peripheries. Countermodernization in the name of neotraditionalist religious ideologies (Judaism, Christianity, Islam, Bud-dhism, and Hinduism) is challenging the authority of the modern, secular state in many parts of the world. In the past, hypermodernization as the ideology of rapid transition to an industrial society has historically worked through nationalism, fascism, and communism to mobilize natural and human resources in the cause of state power; it will continue to be the reaction of some of the late-comers to industrialization such as China. Demodernization in the name of environmentalist, feminist, and spiritualist ideologies is taking issue with the modernist ideas of progress as exploitation of nature and engineering of society. Postmod-ernization is going even further in its critique of modernity by calling into question the absolutist claims of positivist science (scientism) and by simultaneously proposing its own absolutisms of nihilism and rela-tivism. In the face of these challenges, the continuing projects of modernization have no other option but to co-opt elements of the emerging ideologies.

The world is clearly in a state of transition from an old to a new, yet undefined order torn between contradictory potentials. Hoffman (1990) captured the essential feature of this uncertainly by using the metaphor of a bus to characterize the world situation: "The world is like a bus whose driver—the global economy—is not in full control of the engine and is himself out of control, in which children—the people—are tempted to step on either the brake or the gas pedal, and the adults—the states—are worried passengers. A league of passengers may not be enough to keep the bus on the road, but there is no better solution yet" (p. 122). Although Hoffman's characterization of states as adults and people as children reveals an unabashed elitist bias, his implicit point about the need for cooperation is well taken. The futile wars of the past few decades (from Korea to Vietnam and the Middle East) brought no conclusive victories except untold death and destruction on all sides. The Cold War was won by no side except, perhaps, Germany and Japan. The presumed victor, the United States, is in a state of economic disarray while the presumed vanquished, the ex-Soviet Union, presents the world's communist imperial system in a state of dissolution and reorganization. As Kennedy (1987) argued, both superpowers extended their military grasp beyond their economic reach and are now facing the dire consequences.

In the midst of these contradictions, however, five global megatrends seem to stand out, each characterized by inner tensions between two distinctly different tendencies and discourses. These trends may be defined as globalism, regionalism, nationalism, localism, and spiritualism. Accelerating processes of world communication through travel and tourism, the print media, global broadcasting, telephone and satellite networks, transborder data flows, as well as the global dissemination of the miniaturized media such as telephones, modems, copying and fax machines, personal computers, audiocassette and videocassette recorders, and connectivity among them—have all immensely contributed to what might be called *an acceleration of history.* While it took two world wars in this century to dissolve the Ottoman, Austro-Hungarian, British, French, Dutch, Belgian, Spanish, and Portuguese empires, the Soviet empire dissolved within a few years through glasnost and the rapid exposure of the Soviet society to the world media, videocassette recorders, fax machines, and computer networks. This is not to claim for technology an exclusive or even decisive role in revolutionary changes but to suggest that technology always augments the social forces already present and pressing for social change. How does world communication contribute to the contradictory potentials and choices in the five global trends suggested above? In what way does the international public discourse reflect these trends and frame the policy choices?

Globalism: Hegemonic Versus Communitarian

Globalism is perhaps the most apparent of all five trends. It is particularly visible to the eyes of international travelers at world airports, hotel chains, fast-food restaurants, and those ubiquitous signs of modern civilization—the Big Mac, Coca-Cola, Madonna, and Michael Jackson. The Big Mac has conquered the Old World (London, Paris,

Moscow, Beijing) for the new. The Coca-Colonization of the world has reached the remotest villages around the globe. *Striking a Pose*[2] and breakdancing may be edging out proletarian solidarity, national fervor, and religious devotion.

The engine of globalism is modern capitalism, dating back to the 16th century, tearing down the traditional barriers of feudal, tribal, racial, ethnic, and even national loyalties in favor of the internationalism of the world marketplace of ideas and commodities. Its carriers are the global corporations typically operating in more than 100 countries, locating wherever government interference is the least and profit opportunities the most. Its chief technologies are energy, transportation, and telecommunication, the three successive technological breakthroughs leading to three successive long waves of global economic growth. The latest wave, the third industrial revolution, is characterized by the application of computing technologies to all facets of life in manufacturing (Computer Assisted Design-Computer Assisted Manufacturing; CAD-CAM), administration, education, travel, and entertainment. Without telecommunication, transborder data flows, and electronic fund transfers, the global economy and corporation would have been inconceivable. Globalism's strategies of conquest are horizontal, vertical, and spatial integration[3] of the key world industries from oil to transportation and telecommunication. Its lubricants are the transfers of capital from the centers to the peripheries orchestrated by the World Bank and International Monetary Fund, mobilizing world capital, allocating it globally, and reducing the risk for private investors.

Globalism, however, has produced both majestic successes and grand failures. It has brought modern industrial civilization to the remotest regions of the world, but it has also created growing gaps and antagonisms between the rich and poor, humans and nature, and centers and peripheries. Capitalism and communism as the twin faces of globalism, both originating in the Enlightenment project, have also imposed on the world a secular, scientific, and technological worldview that considers human progress in primarily material terms. This ideology of *developmentalism* is now worldwide. In the peripheries, where the processes of development have taken place piecemeal and unevenly, the social system is often torn between a modernizing elite and a traditional mass. Frequently, the two sectors of the population live in separate quarters, sometimes as if in separate countries and centuries. As bits and watts (indicators of information and energy consumption) increase in mass production and consumption, life is diminished under a system of modernized poverty. Whereas poverty in traditional societies is made tolerable by relative equality, the ethics of self-denial and mutual obligation, and the bonds of community, modernized poverty is driven to despair in a prevailing environment of relentless acquisition, conspicuous consumption, and unabashed greed in the larger society. Modernized poverty thus breeds atomistic mobility, status anxiety, social envy, rising expectations, frustrations, regression, and aggression. The negative internalities of dualistic modernity (such as time-consuming acceleration, sick-making health care, stupefying education, countercommunicative mass communication, and information-void news) thus outpace the positive externalities of growth and development. This process used to be primarily characteristic of third world societies, but increasingly the inner cities of the first and second worlds of development also are plagued by class, racial, and ethnic dualisms. Witness the race riots of the United States in 1965 and 1992.

Globalism as a megatrend is, however, torn between two hegemonic and counterhegemonic discourses. There are those who argue for the worldwide triumph of liberal capitalism, the "end of history" as Fukuyama (1989) called it, suggesting that only the boring details are left yet to be worked out, that the great Hegelian battle of ideas in history has come to a conclusive end, that there is little need for a public discourse on the fundamental goals of development. This view is also resonating in American academic circles in a debate between the declinists, led by Kennedy's (1987) *The Rise and Fall of the Great Powers* and the revivalists, led by Nye's (1990) *Bound to Lead*. While Kennedy argues that all modern great powers, including the United States, have gone through a cycle of economic expansion, military overreach, and a consequent economic and political decline, Nye suggests that a unique combination of resource endowments, democratic power, and cultural appeal bounds[4] the United States to continue as the lone superpower and world leader. The Pentagon has joined this debate by the preparation of leaked documents setting out the blueprint of a proposed strategy for continued U.S. world hegemony (*New York Times,* May 26, 1992). That hegemony, the Pentagon argues, can be guaranteed only through continued U.S. military preparedness while limiting the autonomy of other potential centers of military power such as Japan, Germany, Russia, and others. In the U.S. presidential elections of 1992 a related debate also took place: The globalists, led by President Bush, saw America's future in its continued active role in making the world safe for the global corporations, whereas their Democratic and independent critics proposed to refocus on America's domestic problems.

In contrast to the hegemonic, globalist perspectives, there are others who also claim a globalist perspective but with an accent on the local. Think Globally, Act Locally is their motto (Feather, 1980). The notions of Spaceship Earth (Fuller, 1978), Gaia hypothesis (Lockwood, 1988), common security, sustainable development, soft and appropriate technology, Think Globally, *Dial* Locally all suggest a commonality of human destiny and a need for greater equality that requires devolution of power and communication. In a follow-up to their seminal study of *Limits to Growth* (Meadows & Meadows, 1972), conducted twenty years later, Meadows and Meadows (1991) recapitulated their earlier conclusions as follows:

1. Human use of many essential resources and generation of many kinds of pollutants have already surpassed rates that are physically sustainable. Without significant reductions in material and energy flows, there will be in the coming decades an uncontrolled decline in per capita food output, energy use, and industrial production.

2. This decline is not inevitable. To avoid it two changes are necessary. The first is comprehensive revision of policies and practices that perpetuate growth in material consumption and in population. The second is a rapid, drastic increase in the efficiency with which materials and energy are used.

3. A sustainable society is still technically and economically possible. It could be much more desirable than a society that tries to solve its problems by constant expansion. The transition to a sustainable society requires a careful balance between long-term and short-term goals and an emphasis on sufficiency, equity, and quality of life rather than on quantity of output. It requires more than productivity and more than technology; it also requires maturity, compassion, and wisdom. (pp. xv-xvi)

The publication of the earlier version of *Limits to Growth* was followed by a heightened public discourse on the ecological problems. The new edition is coming out at a time in which the memories of the Three Mile Island, Chernobyl, Exxon-Valdez, Bhopal, and the Persian Gulf War ecological disasters are still fresh in people's minds. There is also a worldwide movement for sustainable development as pronounced in the Rio Declaration of the Earth Summit of June 1992. The green movement and parties have found in the color green a symbol for their central concern with the preservation of the environment in the face of the onslaught of relentless growth. But destruction of nature is not the only problem. Destroying the delicate bonds of community is the other equally significant cost of rapid and despotic modernization. The traditions of civility and mutual obligation have eroded under the onslaught of acquisitive individualism and its fetishes of commodity and identity. There is a need, therefore, for a new balance between liberty, equality, and community, the three axial principles of modern democracies. Since this balance has been undermined in capitalist societies by a relentless pursuit of individual greed and in communist societies by a bureaucratic devotion to state goals, a revival of civil society and its epistemic communities through devolutions of power is called for.[5] I have called this approach to social change *communitarian* (Tehranian, 1990a, 1990b, 1991b). Under the leadership of Etzioni, a new movement bearing the same name has recently emerged in the United States with its own programs and publications (including a new periodical, *The Responsive Community*).

A communitarian perspective on the new world order differs sharply from coercive or hegemonic perspectives. It would call for nonviolence, ecologically sensitive and socially responsible sustainable development, protection of human rights, the upholding of human responsibility toward all layers of human community from local to global, and a celebration of cultural diversity. Three elements seem essential to the construction of an effective world community: common interests, norms, and laws. Two factors have strengthened global common interests: threats to human survival through ecological disasters and mass violence, and opportunities in a global economy based on peaceful trade and cooperation. An emerging consensus on international norms recognizes the global political, economic, and ecological interdependence. These norms emphasize the need for the global protection of the environment, use of technology, trade, and development policies to overcome the gaps between the rich and the poor, a universal application of the Universal Declaration of Human Rights, and a collective denunciation of the use of violence in national and international conflicts. The world community ultimately depends on a fragile moral community. Without solidifying these norms, it will be torn apart. But norms without laws and laws without sanctions will have little effect. The world community must be, therefore, a community of interests, norms, laws, and sanctions.

Regionalism: Exclusionary Versus Inclusionary

Given the enormous heterogeneity of the world, however, a global community is best achieved through an interlocking system of smaller and more homogeneous communities. Regionalism is one such trend. This may be called an Age of Regions. Regional formations such as the European Economic Community (EEC), the Association of South East Asian Nations (ASEAN), the North American Free Trade Area (NAFTA), and others represent efforts by groups of relatively close countries to establish effective communities of interests, norms, laws, and sanctions. There is a risk, of course, that these budding regional blocs could turn into intense economic competition and possible political confrontation rather than cooperation. Fortress Europe versus Fortress America versus Fortress East Asia is not an unlikely scenario. Regionalism can be, therefore, exclusionary or inclusionary. It can foster a new type of regional chauvinism or it can provide a protective shield for its members against the global hegemonic projects while opening up to the rest of the world for mutual cooperation and benefit.

Regional formations, however, reflect the present dualistic structures of the world system divided between centers and peripheries. First, at the apex of this hierarchy stands North America with its peripheries in South and Central America. NAFTA is the regional expression of this center. Second, catching up and occasionally surpassing North America in per capita income is Western Europe with its old colonial peripheries in Asia and Africa and its new potential peripheries in Central and Eastern Europe. The EEC and the European Union thus represent a broadening regional organization, including Western and Eastern European countries. Third, aspiring to the top position is Japan together with its peripheries in East Asia, some of which are out-Japanizing the Japanese by remarkable rates of economic growth driven by export development strategies. These include South Korea, Taiwan, Hong Kong, and Singapore trailed by Malaysia, Indonesia, and Thailand. Although the Pacific Economic Cooperation Conferences (PECC) and the Asia Pacific Economic Cooperation (APEC) are broader in membership, the East Asian countries play a critical role in these regional formations. Fourth, Russia in the new Commonwealth of Independent States (CIS) presents a new periphery for Western, Japanese, and North American investment while acting as a center in relation to its own Asian peripheries. Fifth, China plays a similar role for Japanese transfers of technology and capital while acting as a center in relation to its less developed regions such as Mongolia, Tibet, and Sinkiang. Sixth, itself similarly vulnerable to Western penetration, India is acting as a center for its multilingual empire as well as the smaller nations of South Asia. This regional formation is represented by the South Asian Association for Regional Cooperation (SAARC). Seventh, the ASEAN region stands out as a unique combination of countries united in common efforts to attain economic growth and avoid periphery status through regional cooperation. In addition to Indonesia, Malaysia, Singapore, Thailand, the Philippines, and Brunei, the ASEAN countries may soon admit Cambodia, Burma, and Vietnam to their ranks. Eighth, despite a unity of language and culture, the Arab world presents a less successful regionalist project. A strategic military location, the possession of oil resources by some and not others, and traditional national and tribal rivalries have divided and weakened the Arabs in their efforts toward such unity. The beleagued Arab League is the main regional expression of Arab unity. Ninth, Latin America with its wealth of population and resources presents yet another periphery united by a common Hispanic-Portuguese culture, divided by different types of political regimes, promising of regional collaboration for development. The Organization of American States (OAS) is its main expression with some subregional organizations. Tenth, a new regional formation under the name of Economic Cooperation Organization (ECO), consisting of Pakistan, Iran, Turkey, and the former Muslim Soviet republics of Azerbaijan, Kazakistan, Turkemenistan, Uzbakestan, Tajikistan, and Kirghistan was formed in February 1992. The new Islamic Republic of Afghanistan might join ECO later. Eleventh, and finally, stands the vast continent of black Africa south of the Sahara with its dark history of white exploitation, famines, tribal conflicts, sluggish growth, and current awakening to a new need for regional cooperation.

Regionalism is driven by a complex of forces to detour past hostilities; to achieve regional security; to obtain economies of scale, scope, and status; to strengthen common cultural ties; and to protect against global or regional hegemonic projects. Culture and communication thus play a central role in regional formations. A common cultural heritage as in Europe and Latin America, a common language as in the Arab world, common economic and security problems as in the ASEAN region, and close cultural backgrounds and aspirations as in the newly formed ECO, each have played a role. But regional integration is easier said than done. It requires economic complementarity, political trust, and cultural affinity. Even Europe, which has been in the forefront of regional integration is now having second thoughts on the pace of its movement toward monetary and political unification. Little and cosmopolitan Denmark, for instance, in mid-1992 showed signs of doubt on trading the luxury of a unique identity for a European grand design. While smallness might be a handicap, big is not necessarily beautiful.

Nationalism: Totalitarian-Aggressive
Versus Democratic-Benign

It is easier to achieve national rather than regional integration. The entire history of nationalism is an effort to mold a state in the image of a single nation with a common language, culture, economy, and political system. Nationalism has proved a relatively successful method of political organization in the modern world precisely because it is a step closer to the realities of human diversity than imperial systems. States that are multinational, with the possible exception of Switzerland, face problems of internal security. Witness the former Soviet Union, Yugoslavia, India, Iraq, Iran, Afghanistan, Sri Lanka, Canada, and the United States.

During the Cold War, the death of nationalism was slightly exaggerated. The end of the Cold War has witnessed a new surge of ethnic consciousness and nationalism around the world. With the decline of the universalist ideological pretensions of liberalism and communism, primordial identities have resurfaced as the most potent force in domestic and international politics. We now have about 178 countries in the United Nations, increasing as the new states in the former Soviet Union and Yugoslavia become members. There are, however, more than 5,000 nations spread around these countries, many of them restive and clamoring for independence and statehood. Witness the Kurds, the Palestinians, the Québécois. Of the 120 violent conflicts currently waged around the world, 72% are ethnic wars. There are currently some 15 million refugees in the world and over 150 million displaced people. Most of these dislocations are the result of protracted ethnic conflicts erupting into violence. There are some 4,522 living languages in the world, of which 138 languages have more than 1 million speakers. Many languages have, unfortunately, died out. The number of languages in the United States before the coming of Columbus in 1492 was over 1000. Today it is only 200 (Shah, 1992). Every language represents human creativity at its noblest, the voice of gods breathing life into a dead world. "In the beginning was the Word." We must preserve those languages that live and resurrect those that have died.

A kind of alternative United Nations, called the Unrepresented Nations and Peoples Organization (UNPO), was formed on February 11,

1991, to assist the world's disenfranchised minorities toward national self-determination. A total of 14 nations and peoples made up UNPO's original roll. The organization had nearly doubled its membership to 26 by 1992, representing nearly 350 million people. Along with its 26 full members, UNPO also welcomes "observer" nations such as the native American groups. In August 1991, 10 observer nations participated in the UNPO General Assembly. The largest member nation is Kurdistan with a population of 25 million in the Middle East; the smallest is probably Belau, a tiny U.S. island trusteeship territory in the Pacific with a population of 14,000. What unites these peoples is a common sense of frustration over the denial of their elementary individual and collective human rights. In Turkey, for instance, the Kurds have not even been acknowledged as Kurds; they are referred to as "mountain Turks." The people of Belau have voted repeatedly in the past few years to refuse nuclear weapons on their shores, but they are being pressured by the U.S. government to accept nuclear warships to achieve an independent status. Tibet has been occupied by China since 1950 and the Uyghur people of Sinkiang have been subdued by the central authorities in Beijing. A condition for membership in UNPO is, however, the renunciation of violence as a means of achieving self-determination (see *Los Angeles Times,* April 23, 1992, pp. E1-6, and the UNPO Covenant published at the UNPO headquarters in The Hague).

To defend and celebrate the cultural diversity that the emergence of such forgotten peoples represents, is a great challenge. The forces of globalism and regionalism often tend to homogenize and destroy cultural diversity, much to the impoverishment of the world. However, nationalism also has often been used as the hegemonic project of a dominant ethnic group to repress the weaker ethnic groups. Nationalism can be, therefore, democratic and benign or totalitarian and malignant, externally aggressive and internally repressive. Swiss nationalism, for instance, is an example of the former. Nazi German and Fascist Italian nationalisms provide examples of the latter. More recently, the nationalism of the colonized peoples has demonstrated how this ideology can be a liberating force in history, whereas the nationalism of the colonizers shows how exploitation and repression of the subjected peoples can be justified under the noblest of moral claims such as the white man's burden or Manifest Destiny. Nationalism has achieved much in art and culture, economic progress, and political unity. But it has also produced untold misery and genocides such as the near extermination of the native Americans and native Hawaiians in the United States (Stannard,

1989), the Jewish Holocaust in Europe, and the repression of the Palestinians in Israel.

The trouble with cultural and national identity is that it is often presented as nonnegotiable. Much of the violence of the modern world can be traced back to religious, national, or racial ideologies camouflaging material, economic and political conflicts of interests. The Gulf War, for instance, was fought in the name of superior Western standards of moral conduct. What if Kuwait's main product were broccoli? Would President Bush have sent nearly 1 million U.S. troops to the Gulf War? Contrast Iraq's invasion of Kuwait with Serbia's invasion of Bosnia, which has been largely left to its own devices. The moral standards invoked in the Gulf War were similarly circumvented in Los Angeles when trial by a jury of peers in the African-American Rodney King case threatened to bring a guilty verdict on the white policemen who had beaten him nearly to death. The trial was transferred to a white suburb of Los Angeles where the jury was expected to and did, in fact, deliver a not-guilty verdict. These examples of moral obtuseness may seem worlds apart, but they point to a single problem in the modern world. Class, ethnicity, race, and nationality are so intimately intertwined in a hierarchy of wealth, income, and status that it is often easy to pour conflicting economic interests into racial, ethnic, or national passions and violence. While economic conflicts are negotiable, however, ethnic, racial and national conflicts tend to be treated as nonnegotiable. That is why racism so often provides a convenient ideological vehicle for class interests.

Through interactive public discourse rather than hegemonic one-way communication, the media can contribute to peace and mutual understanding in domestic as well as international affairs. However, much of the world media is controlled either by government or commercial interests motivated primarily by propaganda or profit motives. In social and political conflicts, therefore, the tendency is toward a threefold process of simplification of issues, that is, dichotomizing, personalizing, and trivializing public issues toward a construction of media reality considerably at odds with the existential realities of social life. Broadcasting particularly lends itself to these excesses. The visual impact of television is especially suited to an appeal to the right brain, to one-dimensional, singular constructions of reality rather than plurality of meanings. Witness the Gulf War and its portrayal of that conflict as a sanitized, high-tech, visual game with a minimum of human casualties and suffering. No one has yet carefully assessed the real casualties of that war. But the postwar reports indicate over 150,000 dead; 100,000 maimed; and the creation of 1 million Kurdish, Shi'ite, and Palestinian refugees followed by epidemics, vendettas, and high infant mortality rates that resulted from breakdown of basic utilities in Iraq and Kuwait. Approximately 80% of the American public receives its news through television, and 80% of the same public was reported to have supported the war. Is there any correlation between these two statistics?

The global village has been historically dominated by broadcasting networks in the service of subtle and not-so-subtle nationalist propaganda. Although between 1965 and 1990, world radio and television sets have dramatically increased in numbers and distribution in favor of the less developed countries (LDCs), the major transmitting networks continue to be dominated by Western media organizations. World radio sets increased from 530 million in 1965 to 2.1 billion sets in 1990.[6] The share of LDCs increased from 21% to 44% of the total. World television sets increased from 180 million in 1965 to 1 billion in 1990. The share of LDCs increased from 17% to 45%. World radio broadcasting is clearly dominated by the United States, the UK, Germany, France, China; a declining Russia; and an ascending Taiwan, South Korea, Egypt, India, and Iran—and most of it in pursuit of each country's own partisan politics. World television broadcasting is currently dominated by CNN and Visnews as well as Worldnet (distributing television programs that "enhance U.S. diplomacy abroad"), the BBC commercial World Television News, Deutschland TV, and Canal France International, most of which have entered the arena with generous government subsidies. However, the pioneer in the field is purely commercial. Turner's Cable News Network was established in 1980 and is now available on satellite or cable in 137 countries. Its rival is BBC World Service Television, set up in 1991 as a commercial venture after the BBC tried and failed to win government support.

Localism: Parochial Versus Liberal

While nationalism has clearly been a prevailing historical force for the past two centuries, localism is a relatively novel trend pointing to a deepening of the democratic forces. The processes of decolonization and democratization that started with the American Revolution in 1776 have now penetrated everywhere. The continuing world democratic revolution has gone through four long waves. From 1776 to 1848, this revolution was primarily aimed at the overthrow of monarchies and independence for the colonies in Europe and the Americas. World War I (1914-1918) led to the breakdown of the Russian, Austrio-Hungarian, and Ottoman empires and the weakening of European control over their colonies in the Middle East and North Africa. World War II (1940-1945) led to the final breakdown of the British, French, Belgian, Dutch, Portuguese, and Spanish empires in Africa and Asia. The end of the Cold War in 1989 and the breakdown of the Soviet Union may be considered as the fourth wave in a continuing revolution.

The new democratic revolution, however, is focused on local empowerment. Localism is the ideological expression of this trend, emphasizing local knowledge, local initiative, local technologies, and local organization. The torch of leadership has similarly passed from the ideologues of the great revolutionary movements of the 19th and 20th centuries to the technologues of 20th-century technocracies in government and business and to the communologues of the grass-root, localist movements that speak in the vernacular of local knowledge and epistemic communities. As the slogan Think Globally, *Dial* Locally also suggests, the global communication network has brought to the local communities the power to link with communities of affinity throughout the world. The local initiatives for nuclear-weapons-free zones (NWFZs) has increased from 250 in 1982 to 5,000 in 1991 (Boulding, 1991). There are already 24 countries that have unilaterally declared themselves as NWFZs. There are also five formal NWFZ treaties signed among governments. A global idea thus depends for its implementation on local movements and organizations (Boulding, 1991; Tehranian, 1991a). The formation of municipal foreign policy organizations in many cities in the United States is another manifestation of how local communities are no longer willing to allow the U.S. Department of State to be their sole representative in matters of grave international concern.

However, localism also is caught in a tension—between parochialism and liberalism. Parochial localism tends to be narrow minded, bigoted, and persecutionary. The phenomenon of David Duke in Louisiana politics may be considered as an archetype of such trends. Unabashed racism coupled with local prejudices and organizations such as the Ku Klux Klan has proved a powerful tonic at times of dwindling resources and diminishing expectations. The Rodney King case in Los Angeles also demonstrates the parochial power of localism. In 1992, the jurors in Simi Valley were acting in perfect harmony with their own local views of white policemen as protectors of law and order when they handed down a verdict of not guilty, despite overwhelming evidence to the contrary. When localism combines with a national trend toward racism as demonstrated by the Republican party's willingness to use race as an issue in elections (witness the Willie Horton television ads in the 1988 presidential elections), the outcome can be tragic as demonstrated in the Los Angeles riots of 1992. The Rodney King case also demonstrated both the power and impotence of television in the face of local prejudices. Powerful visual portrayals of a helpless black man beaten to the ground by a group of four white policemen brought about a national outcry for racial justice, but it could not bring a guilty verdict from a jury of 12 who were deeply entrapped by their own localist worldview. Powerful images of looting and beating of the whites in Los Angeles by black rioters has created a backlash for what Vice President Dan Quayle has called "law and order" against the "poverty of values."

The hierarchies of inequality within nations in which women, minorities, and immigrants are often trapped at the bottom of the social structures of injustice and violence, ultimately cannot be corrected except through grass-root initiatives and actions. No matter how powerful the global, regional, and national forces, it is local conditions and power configurations that shape the routinized structures of violence, as seen in the inner-city ghettos. The communities in the U.S. South did not change the scourge of segregation for more than 100 years; when the South was industrialized, the institutional structures were changed at the local level. The same can be said of the dismantling of apartheid in South Africa. The new segregation in urban America relegates 20% of the population to the conditions of an underclass whose chances for upward mobility are nearly nil. The postindustrial information society of high technology and fully automated factories (e.g., CAD-CAM) has created conditions of structural unemployment and unemployability for this population. The male unemployment rate among the black population of U.S. inner cities is about 50%. Such conditions cannot change until remedies take into account not only state and national forces but also the local level.

The United States presents only one of the most advanced and violent cases of what is unfolding in a post-urban world. Only 12% of Americans now live in big cities. More than 50% of Americans now live in small towns and suburbs. But cities are defined in a peculiar way. As *The Economist* (May 9, 1992) points out, Beverly Hills is a city completely surrounded by Los Angeles with its own mayor, government, police force, and tax structure. Compton, too, has complete autonomy. But the two cities could not be further apart in their respective mis/fortune. One is the home of Hollywood glitter; the other is a black slum close to south central Los Angeles. Beverly Hills has lavish municipal services; Compton has almost none. If the maps could be redrawn to mix rich and poor neighborhoods, the two sides of the track could share burdens with greater peace and security for both.

Transportation and telecommunication are making it increasingly possible, in part via *telework,* to live and work in small towns or what continues to be inappropriately called suburbs. These "edge cities," as Garreau (1991) calls them, are where the new high-tech industries, commercial services, and shopping malls locate. The city of Los Angeles is a patchwork of such autonomous suburbs, connected with the world's most sophisticated freeway system, enabling their residents to bypass the undesirable neighborhoods while having easy access to urban beaches, theaters, museums, and other desirable facilities. While the business districts in the big city and the small edge cities experience revival and expansion, the inner cities decline. Philadelphia, America's 5th largest city, encapsulates this paradox. In the past decade, Philadelphia's skyline in the business districts has been transformed by architecturally exciting new skyscrapers while the ghetto areas have gone into a downward spin. The city's population is down to around 1.5 million, compared with 2 million in 1970—but its suburbs are ever more populous. Average suburbanites do not see much benefit to burden sharing. Many of them have escaped the cities to avoid high taxes and soaring crime. It would be difficult if not impossible to convince them that it is in their own interest to give some of their local taxes to the cities from which they have escaped. In the meantime, the inner cities in the United States and many other parts of the world burn both actually and metaphorically.

Spiritualism: Fundamentalist Versus Ecumenical

The world is thus desperately in need of a new ethics of social responsibility. The acquisitive society of the modern world has unleashed boundless human energies and dazzling technologies for production but it has failed to provide fairness or a sense of community. As gaps grow among and within nations, modernity also will increasingly fail to provide security not only for the poor but also for the rich and the middle class. The response to this moral and political crisis has been the rise of a new spiritualist movement in many parts of the world.

The movement has, however, assumed two contradictory faces—fundamentalist and ecumenical.

During the past decade, countries as wide apart in geography, history, social structure, and culture as the United States, India, Iran, Israel, and Guatemala have come under the political impact of fundamentalist religious movements.[7] The presidential elections of the late 1970s and 1980s in the United States were profoundly influenced by the rise of the new fundamentalist Christian movement, particularly in the Bible Belt. Presidents Carter, Reagan, and Bush each in their own unique style campaigned on a political platform pleasing to the fundamentalists on such social issues as prayer at schools, restrictions on abortion, and ban on pornography as well as a general bemoaning of the decadence of a liberal and permissive society. India's last election in 1991 was marked by the spectacular successes of a fundamentalist Hindu party in a country constitutionally dedicated to a secular regime. Similarly, in the 1980s, the Jewish fundamentalist parties in Israel profoundly affected the balance between the Labor and Likud parties in favor of the latter. And in Guatemala, where only 30% of the population is Protestant, a fundamentalist was elected to the presidency in 1990.

Fundamentalism appears primarily as a reactive phenomenon—to the unsettling effects of rapid social change (hypermodernization in developing countries, postmodernization in the developed), to marginalization (of the ethnic majorities as in the cases of the Malay in Malaysia and the Hindus in India), to relative material or psychological deprivation (among the urban ghetto or yuppie fundamentalists), and to commodity fetishism as an antithesis to its own identity fetishism. It may or may not be a passing social phenomenon as it seizes power (as in Iran) or is frustrated by the superior power of the state (as in Egypt, Syria, Iraq, or Algeria), as it is gradually integrated into the mainstream of cultural life (as in the case of the Moral Majority in the United States), or as it is allied with the ruling elites in preserving the status quo (as in the United States, Guatemala, and Saudi Arabia). Its alternative strategies thus consist of revolutionary militancy (for total power), withdrawal (from mainstream society), accommodation (with the rest of society), or a relentless conservation of traditional religious values and norms. One of its unintended consequences might be to pave the way for greater epistemological tolerance between religious and secular worldviews as each one softens its monopolistic truth claims. Alternatively, it may take over and rule with an iron fist until it too is chastened by the human facts of diversity and need for tolerance.

But the rise of fundamentalism signals a deeper yearning for a spiritual home in a cold and callous modern world characterized by ceaseless wants and anxieties. In this world, individuals are torn away from the ties of community and atomized by those routinized and anonymous technocracies of modernity that reward them with commodities while robbing them of their souls. The secular ideologies of progress, nationalism, liberalism, and communism, were thought for a while to provide a new, effective sense of community and social responsibility. However, the secular ideologies never addressed, let alone resolved, the human conditions of finitude, fragility, and morality. Primordial identities (religion, race, ethnicity, and gender)—which were thought by such great social pundits as Marx, Freud, and Weber to be withering away in the modern world—have come back to the political arena with vengeance. Culture as the last repository of collective defense against the onslaught of modernity and its alien and alienating consequences has assumed a new force and vitality.

Accelerating physical, social, and psychic mobility, facilitated by the technologies of transportation and telecommunication, is producing multiple and syncretic identities and cultures for most peoples of the world. What appeared to be nonnegotiable, one's body (race, gender, age), time (historical home), and space (geographic home) is becoming increasingly negotiable. Veiled Muslim women can watch *Death of a Princess* (the BBC-WGBH-produced saga of a Saudi princess stoned to death in Saudi Arabia with her lover for adultery) via smuggled videotapes and draw their own conclusions about how they wish to redefine themselves. Michael Jackson's breakdancing has penetrated the hardest bastions of cultural protectionism in third world societies. Wherever press and broadcasting are muzzled, audiocassettes and videocassettes have provided an alternative channel for alternative news and views (Iyer, 1988). In 1979, a cassette revolution helped to overthrow the shah of Iran. In 1988, at the beginnings of glasnost in the former Soviet Union, the video production and sale of alternative newscasts in videocassette rentals became a growth industry. In 1989, the use of fax machines in China undermined the efforts of the government to control the news of the Tiananmen Square massacre. In 1990-1991, in a relatively liberal and media-saturated country such as the United States, the managed media's portrayal of the Gulf War was so powerfully challenged by events and alternative channels of communication (computer networking, video documentaries of the aftermath of the war) that the war "victory" lost much of its legitimacy a year later.[8] Political and cultural pluralism is thus not only desirable but also possible and perhaps inevitable. We must not only tolerate and respect differences but also celebrate them through multiculturalism and a revitalization of the public sphere of discourse (Habermas, 1983).

However, we need to forge a unity out of this human plurality, to orchestrate a harmony out of the dissonance of voices. This unity cannot come but out of the oneness of the human spirit. The world is discovering a new sense of oneness. The continuing possibility of a nuclear holocaust, augmented by the proliferation of nuclear weapons, the risks of a deteriorating environmental crisis, the rise of state and anomic terrorism against innocent bystanders—all seem to bring the more socially sensitive and responsible world citizens closer together into a new solidarity, a new tribe, a new spirit. The new spiritualism has no name, no rituals, no pope, no ayatollah, and no creed. But it is certainly in the air. It finds its inspiration in the totality of the spiritual heritage of humankind—in all religions great and small, in all philosophies secular or religious. It may be termed *philosophia perennia* in that the message has been perennially preached, in *Tao Te Ching,* the *Upanishads,* the Old and New Testaments of the Bible, the Koran, and in the Sufi songs. It calls for the unity of all races, nationalities, ethnic and religious groups in the struggle to navigate the blue Spaceship Earth safely through these turbulent times.

Notes

1. Yalta was the site of the Allied Conference that attempted but failed to shape the post-World War II world around U.S.-Soviet cooperation, starting a Cold War between the two countries. Malta was the site of a conference between presidents Bush and Gorbachev that put an effective end to the Cold War.

2. This is the title of a Madonna video.

3. Horizontal integration is control of a single industry over a large territory. Vertical integration is control of different stages of production in a complex of interrelated industries such as production of crude oil, refining, transport, and distribution in the petroleum industry or publishing, broadcasting, cable, computing, and musical and video retailing in the media industries. Spatial integration is control of a conglomerate of industries over a vast expanse of territory. In all cases, control of one segment reinforces control of others.

4. Nye is using *bound* in a double sense, predicting a future and suggesting a constraining duty—notes from a lecture entitled *Bound to lead: The changing nature of American power* at Harvard by Joseph Nye, Jr., (July 24, 1990).

5. An *epistemic community* may be defined as a community of meaning, rooted in a common cosmology, language, art, culture, and education.

6. The figures in this paragraph are drawn from *The Economist,* May 2, 1992, pp. 21-22.

7. Like most other overused terms, *fundamentalism* may be a word beyond salvation. It may have become a term to cover up our ignorance about a very complex phenomenon. Although there is a general tendency toward an inordinate attachment to religious dogmas, *fundamentalism* as a term may not be an appropriate label for all of these movements. Moreover, the term has now become so pejorative that it might have lost much of its analytical value. The term is more appropriate, of course, with respect to the Protestant movements that wore it as a badge of honor by claiming to return to the fundamentals of the Bible. Of late, some former Protestant fundamentalist leaders prefer the terms *Pentecostal* and *Evangelical*. In the case of Jewish, Islamic, or Hindu fundamentalism, it might be even more accurate to call them religious nationalism. On these points, see Juergensmeyer (1992a, 1992b) and Tehranian (in press).

8. The foregoing examples were observed by the author.

References

Boulding, E. (1991, January 14-16). *The zone of peace concept in current practice: Review and evaluation.* Paper presented at the Inaugural Conference of the Centre for Peace Studies, Curtin University and University of Western Australia.

Feather, F. (Ed.). (1980). *Through the 80s: Thinking globally, acting locally.* Washington, DC: World Future Society.

Fukuyama, F. (1989). The end of history. *National Interest, 16,* 3-18.

Fuller, R. B. (1978). *Operating manual for spaceship earth.* New York: Dutton.

Gareau, J. (1991). *Edge city: Life on the new frontier.* New York: Doubleday.

Habermas, J. (1983). *A theory of communicative action* (3 vols.). Boston: Beacon Press.

Hoffman, S. (1990). A new world and its troubles. *Foreign Affairs, 69*(4), 115-122.

Iyer, P. (1988). *Video night in Kathmandu: And other reports from the not-so-far-East.* New York: Knopf.

Juergensmeyer, M. (1992a, June 1-3). *Ethnic nationalism in Mongolia.* Paper presented at an International Conference on Restructuring for Ethnic Peace, University of Hawaii, Manoa.

Juergensmeyer, M. (1992b, June 1-3). *The rise of Hindu nationalism.* Paper presented at an International Conference on Restructuring for Ethnic Peace, University of Hawaii, Manoa.

Kennedy, P. M. (1987). *The rise and fall of the great powers: Economic change and military conflict.* New York: Random House.

Lockwood, J. (1988). *The ages of Gaia: A biography of our living earth.* New York: Norton.

Meadows, D. H., & Meadows, D. L. (1972). *Limits to growth.* New York: Universe Books.

Meadows, D. H., Meadows, D. L., & Randers, J. (1991). *Beyond the limits.* Post Mills, VT: Chelsea Green.

Nye, J., Jr. (1990). *Bound to lead: The changing nature of American power.* New York: Basic Books.

Shah, S. (1992, Spring). The roots of ethnic conflict. *Nuclear Times,* 9-15.

Stannard, D. E. (1989). *Before the horror: The population of Hawaii on the eve of Western contact.* Honolulu: Social Science Research Institute, University of Hawaii.

Tehranian, M. (1990a). *Technologies of power: Information machines and democratic prospects.* Norwood, NJ: Ablex.

Tehranian, M. (1990b). Communication, peace, and development: A communitarian perspective. In F. Korzenny & S. Ting-Toomey (Eds.), *Communicating for peace.* Newbury Park, CA: Sage.

Tehranian, M. (1991a, October 24-26). *Creating spaces for peace: A comparative overview of zones of peace.* Paper presented at an International Conference on Peace and Security in the Asia-Pacific Region, Cheju, South Korea.

Tehranian, M. (1991b). Communication and theories of social change: A communitarian perspective. *Asian Journal of Communication, 2*(1), 1-30.

Tehranian, M. (Ed.). (1991c). *Restructuring for ethnic peace: A public debate at the University of Hawaii.* Honolulu: Spark M. Matsunaga Institute for Peace.

Tehranian, K., & Tehranian, M. (Eds.). (1992). *Restructuring for world peace: On the threshold of the 21st century.* Cresskill, NJ: Hampton Press.

Tehranian, M. (in press). Fundamentalisms, education, and the media: An introduction. In M. Marty & S. Appleby (Eds.), *Fundamentalism and society.* Chicago: Chicago University Press.

Tehranian, M. (in press). Islamic fundamentalism in Iran and the discourse of development. In M. Marty & S. Appleby (Eds.), *Fundamentalism and society.* Chicago: Chicago University Press.

9

Communication, Peace, and International Law

HOWARD FREDERICK

The entirety of Frederick's chapter is, in a sense, an answer to the various problems raised by his coauthors. This chapter shows us that there exists, on the books, so to speak, a vast body of international law relating communication to peace, in both its negative and positive aspects. Most of this international law on communication, culture and peace was elaborated at the United Nations, which is all the more reason why this international body should return to its original mission of promoting peace for all peoples.

From Frederick's overview of the basic principles of global communication law, one thing is clear: communication media may not be used to promote war. On the surface, this assertion seems disarmingly simple, since it is evident that war propaganda played an essential role in the Persian Gulf confrontation. But international law is not like national law. Even if states have ratified or signed the conventions, declarations, and resolutions making up this body of international law—which is often not the case—there is, in Frederick's words, "no global enforcer."

Nonetheless, if Western civilization is truly at an impasse, as suggested by several of the authors in this book, the new emerging paradigms of governance can make use of the inherent idealism in this body of law. Opponents of racism and sexism may be surprised, for example, to learn of the existence of specific conventions and declarations outlawing racism in the media and stereotyping of women that leads to discrimination. Although the present conjuncture is not favorable to their interests, the countries of the south may take some small measure of comfort in the fact that information sovereignty is promoted in international communication law.

Many of his coauthors emphasize that Western culture has suffered tremendously from individualism and competition, which are, in turn, reflected in our mass communication processes. Frederick's support for the rights of peoples suggests that this notion of international law may help reestablish the sense of community that has been lost in modern societies. Support for this principle may also lead to a much-needed democratization of international organizations. Lest we forget, the United Nations's constitution begins with "We the people . . . ."

Information is the oxygen of the modern age. Breezes of electronic beams flow through the Iron Curtain as if it were lace. Trying to control the flow of information is a hopeless desperate cause. The Goliath of totalitarian control will rapidly be brought down by the David of the microchip.

Ronald Reagan

Between the strong and the weak it is freedom which oppresses and law which liberates.

Jean Baptiste Lacordaire

Introduction

For centuries, communication has played a powerful role in exacerbating tensions among nations. From the Peloponnesian war to the Nicaraguan war, nations have used communication channels to manipulate domestic public opinion and to disinform opposing populations (Frederick, 1993, chap. 2).

Mass communication media also have the potential to bring about peace, build confidence among nations and strengthen international understanding. In the last 45 years, the world has witnessed an increased role for the media in international relations, an intensification of ideological struggle, and a tremendous explosion of global information technologies. These facts challenge the international law of communication and information to keep apace.

Ronald Reagan's statement (quoted above) is typical of the cavalier attitude that many Americans have about the role of communication and information in international relations. Beginning after World War II, the United States and its allies have pressed a global campaign to guarantee the free flow of information (Blanchard, 1986). But by the end of the 20th century, as former Finnish President Kekkonen said,

The flow of information between states—not least the material pumped out by television—is to a very great extent a one-way unbalanced traffic, and in no way possesses the depth and range which the principle of freedom of speech requires. (quoted in Stover, 1984, p. 31)

How can we even the playing field between the info-powerful and the info-weak? In a world of increasing disparities between the rich and poor, Lacordaire's approach is attracting increasing support. Vulnerable countries are calling on international communication and information law to protect their interests. Dominant countries are resisting international law because the unrestricted free flow of information and communication benefits them in profit and influence. Fortunately, the founding of the United Nations and the subsequent growth in international law has led to a great enrichment and codification of international communication and information law.

Historical Development

Nations have respected the international law of communication and information for more than a century.[1] In fact, we can say that this is one of the oldest bodies of continuously respected international law in the world. So it is no surprise that some of the oldest specialized agencies of the United Nations deal primarily with communication and information: the International Telecommunications Union (ITU), founded in 1865; the Universal Postal Union (UPU), 1874; and the World Intellectual Property Organization (WIPO), 1883.

The reason for this is that by the second half of the 19th century, information flows had already become a factor in international relations. National political leaders found themselves needing to persuade their own population as well as their opponents. Late-19th-century battles for international public opinion led to regulatory approaches through the law of neutrality. The 1907 *Convention Respecting the Rights and Duties of Neutral Powers and Persons* (U.S. = SRE) included several provisions limiting or controlling propaganda activities (Bowman & Harris, 1984, T37). For example, article 3 of this convention forbade belligerents from establishing a telegraph station on the territory of neutral countries or using an existing station on neutral territory for military purposes. Article 9 required any restrictions or prohibitions taken by a neutral power to be applied uniformly to both belligerents.

Of course, World War I and the Russian Revolution ideologized international relations in general and gave a powerful role to the media of international political communication. The League of Nations dealt with this development very early on. Meeting for the first time just six days after the Treaty of Versailles came into force, league delegates wanted to break with the past by replacing power politics and secret diplomacy with international cooperation, collective security and open diplomacy. League delegates envisioned a new role for the press. In a 1925 resolution titled the *Collaboration of the Press in the Organization of Peace,* the league stated, "The Press constitutes the most effective means of guiding public opinion towards moral disarmament, which is a concomitant condition of material disarmament" (Nordenstreng, Gonzales Manet, & Kleinwächter, 1986, p. 105).

Throughout the history of international relations, every time a new innovation in communication technology appears, sooner or later international law arises to regulate it. Gutenberg's invention of the printing press led Milton to call for a "right to freedom of expression." Morse's discovery of the telegraph led to the creation of the International Telegraph Convention. The development of wireless radio led to the International Radio Telegraph Convention. The great radio propaganda wars of the 1930s led to the famous *International Convention Concerning the Use of Broadcasting in the Cause of Peace* (U.S. = NS), the first multilateral effort to regulate peacetime propaganda (Bowman & Harris, 1984, T158; Nordenstreng et al., 1986, pp. 106-108; Ploman, 1982, p. 169). Although this convention was ignored during World War II, this binding international treaty still has more than two dozen adherents.

Definitions

International law traditionally was defined as the body of rules governing relations between sovereign states (meaning "national governments"). In the past, the subjects of international law were states, which in turn applied that law to the so-called objects of international law, namely citizens (natural persons) and to private firms (now considered juridical persons).

But in the present age, other international actors have challenged the supremacy of the state. International organizations, nongovernmental organizations, and private firms can now be the subjects of international law. The most significant change, however, is the increasing role of individuals in international law. The 1945 United Nations Charter acknowledges individual human beings as personalities in international law. The 1948 Universal Declaration of Human Rights outlines the rights and duties of individuals, and the 1966 Human Rights Covenants enshrine those rights in binding law. As the Nuremberg judges ruled concerning Nazi war criminals, "individuals have international duties which transcend the national obligations of obedience imposed by the individual state" (Kaufman, 1968, p. 15).

Modern international law is concerned with such individual human rights, racial prejudice and gender discrimination. So the definition of international law now includes all the institutions and processes governing matters of international concern and the norms or rules they produce. This definition allows for the law-creating part played by international organizations, multinational corporations, political parties, pressure groups, liberation organizations, and individuals. Extending this definition to the subject of this chapter, international communication and information law comprises those legal institutions, instruments and processes that govern communication among and between individuals, peoples, cultures, nations and technologies.

Can international law be applied to private media firms and individual communicators? (see Downey, 1984, p. 342). States themselves are, of course, the subjects of international law. Thus state-controlled or -financed mass media (e.g., government broadcasting stations) are necessarily included here. But must a State restrain private citizens who, for example, might be broadcasting destabilizing propaganda to other countries?

It is true that private media were traditionally not subjects of international law. But from Article 26 of the 1969 *Vienna Convention on the Law of Treaties* (U.S. = S) (Bowman & Harris, 1984, T538), we can deduce that states today have general obligations in the sphere of international law that they cannot evade by pointing to domestic laws. Furthermore, the modern definition of international law definitively includes individuals as subjects. The manner in which international law is enforced on private media is a matter of a state's sovereign prerogative. The point is that these measures must be promulgated. Private media must comply with laws of the state in which they operate. If international law prohibits propaganda for war or racism, the state has an obligation to regulate the private media in this regard.

In the history of international communication and information law, one startling incident stands out regarding the accountability of individual communicators. Nazi propagandist Julius Streicher, editor of the anti-Semitic newspaper *Der Stürmer* was accused of crimes against humanity under the 1945 *Charter of the International Military Tribunal* (U.S. = SRE), the so-called Nuremberg Tribunal, which had the power to try and punish Axis soldiers who committed crimes against peace, war crimes, and crimes against humanity. The judges interpreted crimes against humanity to include propaganda and incitement to genocide and determined that for more than 25 years Streicher had engaged in writing and preaching anti-Semitism and had called for the extermination of the Jewish people in 1938. Based on a content analysis of articles from *Der Stürmer*, the judges further determined that Streicher had aroused the German people to active persecution of the Jewish people. The International Military Tribunal found Streicher guilty and condemned him to death by hanging.

Principles of International Law

All international law is based on the seven fundamental principles specified in the 1945 United Nations Charter (Nordenstreng et al., 1986, pp. 111-112) and in the 1970 Declaration on Principles of International Law Concerning Friendly Relations and Cooperation Among States in Accordance with the Charter of the United Nations (Nordenstreng et al., 1986, p. 155). Members of the United Nations are required to guide their actions in accordance with these principles and to compel all natural and juridical persons under their jurisdiction to act in agreement with them. We will return to these later when we summarize the fundamental principles of international communication and information law.

Non-Use of Force. States may not threaten or use force against the territory or independence of another state or against the rights to self-determination, freedom, and independence of peoples. A war of aggression constitutes a crime against peace. States may not organize mercenary forces or civil strife in another states nor may they occupy another state through military force or recognize that occupation as legal.

Peaceful Settlement of Disputes. States must settle their international disputes by peaceful means in a way that does not endanger international peace and security. States in dispute must seek negotiation, mediation, and settlement and, short of a resolution, must not aggravate the situation.

Nonintervention. No state has the right to intervene directly or indirectly in the internal or external affairs of another state. This includes not only armed intervention but also any form of economic or political coercion against the political, economic, or cultural integrity of another state. Every state has the inalienable right to choose its own political, economic, social, and cultural system without outside interference.

International Cooperation. Whatever their differences may be, states have the duty to cooperate with one another, to maintain peace and security, and to promote economic stability and progress. This means conducting international relations according to the principles of equality and nonintervention and promoting respect for and observance of human rights and elimination of racial discrimination and religious intolerance.

Equal Rights and Self-Determination of Peoples. All peoples have the right freely to determine their political status and to pursue their economic, social, and cultural development without external interference. States must promote friendly relations, end colonialism, and guarantee respect for and observance of human rights. States must refrain from any threat or use of force that deprives their own or any other people of self-determination, freedom, and independence.

Sovereign Equality of States. The United Nations Charter is based on the sovereign equality of all states, notwithstanding differences of an economic, social, political, or other nature. This means that states are equal before the law and enjoy the full rights of sovereignty and territorial integrity. All states must respect the political, social, economic, and cultural systems of other states and live in peace with all states.

Good Faith Obligations. States must fulfill in good faith their obligations under recognized international law. States must be aware of such obligations; commitments to the United Nations Charter always take precedence over any other international agreement.

Sources of International Law

At the international level, a complex and sometimes chaotic constituitive process has developed involving state elites, international officials of public and private organizations, and even ordinary citizens who establish and maintain the basic structures for making key international decisions. As a result, a bewildering assortment of covenants, conventions, treaties, resolutions, declarations, protocols, and acts make up what we call international law. Article 38 of the Statute of the International Court of Justice (Bowman & Harris, 1984, T181) has classified three primary sources of international law (in order of precedence).

1. International Conventions. International conventions are called treaties in U.S. parlance and include "international conventions, whether general or particular, establishing rules expressly recognized by the contesting States."(Bowman & Harris, 1984, T181). Conventional law includes both multilateral and bilateral agreements. In formal terms, treaties bind only states signatories. But when a very large number of states adhere to a treaty or accept its terms without becoming signatories, a treaty becomes an independent source of international law. This includes such universally respected (but not universally ratified) instruments as the *1949 Geneva Conventions* (U.S. = SRE) (Bowman & Harris, 1984, T238-241), the 1948 Convention on the Prevention and Punishment of the Crime of Genocide (U.S. = SRE) (Bowman & Harris, 1984, T225; Nordenstreng et al., 1986, p. 119; Ploman, 1982, p. 29), and the 1969 *Vienna Convention on Law of Treaties* (U.S. = S) (Bowman & Harris, 1984, T538).

There is a continuum of universality among international conventions. At one pole are the constituent documents, especially charters and constitutions, of modern international intergovernmental organizations, to which most, if not all, states belong. Next come multilateral agreements laying down legal norms to which most or a large number of states adhere. Then there are multilateral treaties to which a small number of states, perhaps only the states in a particular region, adhere. Finally there are the bilateral agreements, which in fact make up the greatest number of binding international agreements. In international communication and information law, the bulk of agreements are bilateral. For the United States alone, they range from dozens of bilateral agreements on amateur radio reception to a score of agreements on U.S.-Mexican radio interference.

2. International Custom. A second primary source of international law is referred to as customary law, consisting of principles that are derived from actual behavior of states rather than from formal legislation. The

International Court of Justice defines customary law as "a general practice accepted as law" (Bowman & Harris, 1984, T181). Custom is an outgrowth of state practice. These practices are reflected in such promulgations as official governmental statements and proclamations, international conferences, diplomatic exchanges, national court decisions, and national legislation. Customary law arises out of international norms, the lawfulness of which depends on the concrete behavior of states over a long period of time.

In modern international relations, there are innumerable customary practices that have become international law. Customary law operates in such areas as sovereignty, diplomatic recognition, consent to sanctions, good faith obligations, freedom of the seas, and numerous other international responsibilities. The problem of showing that a particular practice is customary law arises primarily in ideological disputes and technological matters.

3. General Principles of International Law. The third primary source are the so-called general principles of international law. When international law emerged, "the general principles of law recognized by civilized nations" (Bowman & Harris, 1984, T181) were the only norms that could be generalized from the national to the international level. But today there is less reliance on general principles, because many have already become customary law. Although some principles have been widely recognized, such as *pacta sunt servanda* ("agreements are to be honored"), they provide a basis for judicial decisions only when no rules of customary law or conventional law apply.

These, then, are the three primary sources of international law, but there is another area of international-law-in-creation that merits our particular attention: the so-called secondary sources of international law (Bowman & Harris, 1984, T181). They include the judicial decisions and teachings of legal scholars, decisions of the World Court and international tribunals, and publications of the International Law Commission of the United Nations.

Another important secondary source are the innumerable declarations, resolutions, and recommendations by intergovernmental organizations. With the exception of Security Council resolutions and some International Civil Aviation Organization (ICAO) measures, they are as a rule not legally binding. But they do have a legal function. Some have led to binding conventions. For example, the 1963 *Declaration of Legal Principles Governing the Activities of States in the Exploration and the*

Use of Outer Space (Ploman, 1982, p. 272) led 4 years later to the *Treaty on Principles Governing the Activities of States in the Exploration and Use of Outer Space, including the Moon and other Celestial Bodies* (U.S. = SRE) (Bowman & Harris, 1984, T500; Nordenstreng et al. 1986, p. 149; Ploman, 1982, p. 268). Similarly, the nonbinding Universal Declaration of Human Rights led ultimately to the binding 1966 Human Rights Covenants.

Enforcement of International Law

The rights and duties of a state under international law are superior to any obligations and rights that state may have under domestic law. According to Articles 27 and 46 of the 1969 Vienna Convention on Law of Treaties, when a state has agreed to the terms of a valid and binding treaty, it cannot excuse its nonadherence because the treaty was declared unconstitutional by its supreme court. States incorporate international legal standards into domestic law in a variety of ways. The route usually leads from signing a convention, to ratification, to implementation in domestic law, and finally to enforcement of those provisions (Jankovic, 1984, pp. 287-302; Sieghart, 1985, pp. 50-58). National legislation provides the legal basis for enforcing international law.

Difficulties arise when some states neither ratify nor pass any enacting legislation to implement the conventions under discussion. Furthermore, even if a state does ratify a treaty, current international legal procedure allows a state to make reservations to a treaty, that is, to exclude or modify the legal effect of certain provisions of the treaty in their application to that state. Reservations to treaties must receive the consent of other signatories. In contrast, statements of interpretation— deriving from the principle that contracting states should themselves interpret the convention that they conclude with another—do not require such consent (Jankovic, 1984, pp. 299-302).

Unfortunately, the political behavior of states is the product of many variables. States can and do violate international law for political ends. Unlike in domestic law, in international law there is no "global enforcer" to punish violators. Governmental leaders sometimes uphold international law only when doing so will yield short-term gains. These commitments are often fragile and may be abandoned when they no longer seem to serve national interests. What is worse, with the important exception of the Optional Protocol to the 1966 International Covenant on

Civil and Human Rights, international law does not give individuals or organizations a means of directly enforcing its provisions.

Yet before we despair of the effectiveness of international law, we must note that there are countless areas of international relations where international law is respected and observed. There are numerous international legal instruments that regulate areas as diverse as trade and finance, transportation, and diplomatic affairs, just to name a few. Within the field of global communication there is a great measure of respect and adherence. From coordination of international radio frequencies to prohibitions on transport of obscene publications, from guarantees on the privacy of diplomatic communication to enforcement of copyright provisions, from assignment of geostationary orbit positions to the universality of postal communication: Most fundamental principles of international communication and information law are widely recognized and honored throughout the world.

International law is most effective when states have a common interest in its maintaining order. The law of diplomacy, for example, has been one of the most successful and durable fields of international law. For centuries, national leaders have depended on it for the security of their envoys. Similarly, the law of boundaries and territorial acquisition has enjoyed wide support among nations. For more than 300 years, the basic principles of the law of the seas have been widely accepted and enforced. Similarly, it is in the interests of all global media to ensure orderly, interference-free information flows.

The International Court of Justice—known as the World Court—is the principal judicial organ of the United Nations. States may submit disputes to the court, but the court does not automatically have jurisdiction over a dispute. The parties to the dispute must accept the jurisdiction of the court before the case can proceed. Many disputes cannot be resolved because one party refuses the jurisdiction of the court. Even when the parties do not accept World Court jurisdiction, there are many other avenues of dispute resolution that otherwise follow international law. These include the United Nations itself, regional organizations, diplomatic conferences, and multilateral commissions, where international law plays a great role, together with other factors, in resolving disputes.

The problems of World Court jurisdiction and enforcement are clearly seen in the case of *Nicaragua v. United States*. During the early years of the Reagan presidency, the United States spent millions of dollars to arm the Nicaraguan Contras, ex-Somocista National Guards fighting to overthrow the Nicaraguan government from Honduras and Costa Rica. In addition, the United States itself mined Nicaragua's harbors in early 1984 and published a CIA manual for guerrilla warfare that encouraged acts contrary to the general principles of international law.

In April 1984, the Nicaraguan government filed suit in the World Court charging that the United States had intervened and used military force. Nicaragua maintained that this aggression violated the United Nations Charter, the Charter of the Organization of American States as well as general and customary international law. The United States immediately announced that it would not accept the court's jurisdiction in Central America for two years.

In 1984, the court accepted contentious (compulsory) jurisdiction that results in a decision that is binding on the parties and is theoretically enforceable, if necessary, through the UN Security Council. The court issued an interim ruling stating that the United States should immediately stop mining Nicaraguan harbors. It rejected the U.S. argument denying jurisdiction. In 1985 the United States announced that it would neither present a defense nor abide by the court's decision. In 1986 the court ruled that U.S. activities were not justified as self-defense; that U.S. training, financing, and arming of the Contras as well as U.S. mining of Nicaraguan harbors were in violation of customary international law; and that the U.S. embargo on trade with Nicaragua was a treaty violation. It ordered the United States to cease all such activities immediately. The United States vetoed the UN Security Council's enforcement resolution.

As Representative Weiss said,

> The Reagan Administration's decision to withdraw from the World Court's compulsory jurisdiction violated a solid policy of support for the court over the last four decades. This country was founded on a respect for domestic and international law. By continuing to reject the jurisdiction of the World Court, the administration has betrayed our American traditions and acted contrary to our own long-term interests. (quoted in Ginger, 1989b, pp. 223-226)

Human Rights Law and Communication

I will now survey those major international legal instruments that establish regulatory principles for international communication and information.[2] I begin with three of the four documents that make up the so-called International Bill of Human Rights.[3]

The first, written in the crucible of a post-Fascist Europe dominated by Western liberalism, is the 1948 *Universal Declaration of Human Rights.* Its famous Article 19 declares:

> Everyone has the right to freedom of opinion and expression; this right includes freedom to hold opinions without interference and to seek, receive and impart information and ideas through any media and regardless of frontiers. (Nordenstreng et al., 1986, p. 123; Ploman, 1982, p. 12)

The declaration does not guarantee *absolute* freedom of opinion or expression. Article 19's provisions, like all other human rights safeguarded by the declaration, are qualified by Article 29, which declares:

> 1. Everyone has duties to the community in which alone the free and full development of his personality is possible.
> 2. In the exercise of his rights and freedoms, everyone shall be subject only to such limitations as are determined by law solely for the purpose of securing due recognition and respect for the rights and freedoms of others and of meeting the just requirements of morality, public order and general welfare in a democratic society.
> 3. These rights and freedoms may in no case be exercised contrary to the purposes and principles of the United Nations. (Nordenstreng et al., 1986, p. 125; Ploman, 1982, p. 12)

The other documents of the International Bill of Human Rights are the 1966 *Human Rights Covenants,* which make the principles set forth in the Universal Declaration legally binding. For all the emphasis the United States places on human rights, it is disappointing that it has not ratified any of these important instruments of international law.

The 1966 *International Covenant on Civil and Political Rights* (U.S. = S) restates the famous formulation of the Universal Declaration in its own Article 19:

> 1. Everyone shall have the right to hold opinions without interference.
> 2. Everyone shall have the right to freedom of expression; this right shall include the freedom to seek, receive and impart information and ideas of all kinds, regardless of frontiers, either orally, in writing or in print, in the form of art, or through any other media of his choice. (Nordenstreng et al., 1986, p. 142; Ploman, 1982, p. 27)

Here too the exercise of these rights is not absolute:

3. The exercise of the rights provided for in paragraph 2 of this article carries with it special duties and responsibilities. It may therefore be subject to certain restrictions, but these shall only be such as are provided by law and are necessary: (a) for respect of the rights or reputations of others; (b) for the protection of national security or of public order, or of public health or morals.

We see that each of these documents presents a two-edged sword in regard to freedom of expression. Freedom brings with it both rights and duties. Here we see the essence of what had become the American and the former Soviet positions. One view would give states the right freely to disseminate information throughout the world without restrictions. The other would give states the right to stop communication threatening national security, public order or morality. That is why the State Department declared a reservation, should the covenant ever be ratified by Congress, "that States party to the Covenant should wherever possible refrain from imposing any restrictions or limitations on the exercise of the rights recognized and protected by the Covenant, even when such restrictions and limitations are permissible under the terms of the Covenant" ("Editorial," 1991, p. 6).

It is important to note that the International Covenant on Civil and Political Rights goes beyond the Universal Declaration of Human Rights in one significant respect. While the Universal Declaration only prescribes, the Covenant on Civil and Political Rights also proscribes; it actually prohibits certain content. Article 20 states unequivocally:

1. Any propaganda for war shall be prohibited by law.
2. Any advocacy of national, racial or religious hatred that constitutes incitement to discrimination, hostility or violence shall be prohibited by law. (Bowman & Harris, 1984, T498; Nordenstreng et al., 1986, p. 142; Ploman, 1982, p. 21)

Finally, there is the *Optional Protocol to the 1966 International Covenant on Civil and Human Rights* (U.S. = NS), now ratified by more than 40 governments. This document is significant in that it allows individual citizens who have experienced violation of their human rights to petition directly to the United Nations Human Rights Commission for redress of grievances (this is called individual communication) (Bowman & Harris, 1984, T499; see also Ghandhi, 1986).

Beyond the International Bill of Human Rights there are two other human rights documents that treat communication and information

aspects of racism. The 1966 *International Convention on the Elimination of All Forms of Racial Discrimination* (U.S. = S):

> condemn[s] all propaganda and all organizations which are based on ideas
> or theories of superiority of one race or group of persons of one color or
> ethnic origin, or which attempt to justify or promote racial hatred, discrim-
> ination in any form.

It forbids certain information activities. It prohibits

> all dissemination of ideas based on racial superiority or hatred, incitement
> to racial discrimination, as well as all acts of violence or incitement to such
> acts against any race or group of persons of another color or ethnic origin,
> and also the provisions of any assistance to racist activities, including the
> financing thereof;
>   [And forbids] organizations, and also organized and all other propa-
> ganda activities, which promote and incite racial discrimination, and shall
> recognize participation in such organizations or activities as an offense
> punishable by law. (Bowman & Harris, 1984, T490; Nordenstreng et al.,
> 1986, p. 136; Ploman, 1982, p. 30)

Similarly, the 1973 *International Convention on the Suppression and
Punishment of the Crime of Apartheid* (U.S. = NS) declares apartheid
to be a crime against humanity and makes individuals as well as
institutions and organizations criminally liable. It goes on to make it
criminally illegal to:

> (a) Commit, participate in, directly incite or conspire in the commission of
> [the crime of apartheid];
>   (b) Directly abet, encourage or cooperate in the commission of the crime of
> apartheid. (Bowman & Harris, 1984, T638; Nordenstreng et al., 1986, p. 164)

The one human rights instrument that the United States finally signed,
ratified, and implemented in 1988 is the 1948 *Convention on the Prevention and Punishment of the Crime of Genocide* (U.S. = SRE). The
Genocide Convention prohibits certain communication activities. It
makes punishable "direct and public incitement to commit genocide,"
defined as the "intent to destroy in whole or in part, a national, ethnical,
racial or religious group" (Bowman & Harris, 1984, T225; Nordenstreng
et al., 1986, p. 119; Ploman, 1982, p. 29; see also Ginger, 1989a).

Finally let us have a look at human right documents treating discrimination against women. The 1979 *Convention on the Elimination of All Forms of Discrimination Against Women* (U.S. = S) commits its signatories to take steps in all areas of life, including information and communication,

> to modify or abolish existing laws, regulations, customs and practices which constitute discrimination against women [toward] the elimination of prejudices and customary and all other practices which are based on the idea of the inferiority or the superiority of either of the sexes or on stereotyped roles for men and women; [and] to eliminate any stereotyped concept of roles of men and women. (Bowman & Harris, 1984, T769)

Many declarations and resolutions apply human rights standards to communication and information. Picking up again with women's rights, the 1975 Mexico City Conference during International Women's Year makes explicit reference to communication in the 1975 *Declaration of Mexico on the Equality of Women and Their Contribution to Development and Peace:*

> All means of communication and information as well as all cultural media should regard as a high priority their responsibility for helping to remove the attitudinal and cultural factors that still inhibit the development of women and for projecting in positive terms the value to society of the assumption by women of changing and expanding roles (*International Human Rights Instruments,* 1983, p. 127).

The *Nairobi Forward-Looking Strategies for the Advancement of Women* specifies that

> all existing impediments to the achievement by women of equality with men should be removed. To this end, efforts should be intensified at all levels to overcome prejudices [and] stereotyped thinking. (Ginger, 1989b, p. 246)

Unlike prohibitions against racist and genocidal propaganda, international law does not unequivocally prohibit information content that stereotypes and discriminates against women. On the whole, international law does not impose a duty on governments to eliminate sexist propaganda.

Security, Peace, and Communication

We have already seen that human rights treaties forbid war propaganda and racial hatred. But many other documents on security and disarmament include provisions addressing the content of communication.

In the 1947 declaration on *Measures to be Taken Against Propaganda and Inciters of a New War,* the General Assembly:

> condemns all forms of propaganda, in whatsoever country conducted, which is either designed or likely to provoke, or encourage any threat to the peace, breach of the peace or act of aggression. (Nordenstreng et al., 1986, p. 113; Ploman, 1982, p. 47)

The 1970 *Declaration on the Strengthening of International Security* prohibits states from "any attempt aimed at the partial or total disruption of the national unity" and "organizing, instigating, assisting or participating in acts of civil strife" against another state (Ploman, 1982, p. 48). The 1978 *Final Document of the Tenth Special Session of the General Assembly on Disarmament* encourages states to

> ensure a better flow of information with regard to the various aspects of disarmament, to avoid dissemination of false and tendentious information concerning armaments, and to concentrate on the danger of escalation of the armaments race and on the need for general and complete disarmament under effective international control. (Nordenstreng et al., 1986, p. 179; Ploman, 1982, p. 49)

The 1981 *Declaration on the Inadmissibility of Intervention and Interference in the Internal Affairs of States* details the relationship of communication and information activities to national security. Noninterference means the following:

> The right of States and peoples to have free access to information and to develop fully, without interference, their system of information and mass media and to use their information media in order to promote their political, social, economic and cultural interests and aspirations. . . .
>
> The duty of a State to refrain from the promotion, encouragement or support, direct or indirect, of rebellious or secessionist activities within other States. . . .

The duty of a State to abstain from any defamatory campaign, vilification or hostile propaganda for the purpose of intervening or interfering in the internal affairs of other States. (Nordenstreng et al., 1986, pp. 187-188)

The 1983 *Declaration on the Condemnation of Nuclear War* specifically

condemns the formulation, propounding, dissemination and propaganda of political and military doctrines and concepts intended to provide "legitimacy" for the first use of nuclear weapons and in general to justify the "admissibility" of unleashing nuclear war. (Nordenstreng et al., 1986, p. 193)

Complementing these instruments on security and disarmament is international law treating peace and international understanding. Best illustrative of this category are the many declarations and resolutions that call on states to encourage media to work in the service of peace, international understanding, and confidence-building among the peoples of the world.

The 1965 *Declaration on the Promotion Among Youth of the Ideals of Peace, Mutual Respect and Understanding Between Peoples* proclaims, "All means of education . . . instruction and information intended for the young should foster among them the ideals of peace, humanity, liberty and international solidarity" (Nordenstreng et al., 1986, p. 134; Ploman, 1982, p. 52).

The 1978 *Declaration on the Preparation of Societies for Life in Peace* "recognize[s] the essential role of . . . the mass media . . . in promoting the cause of peace and understanding among nations," declares that states have the duty to "refrain from propaganda for wars of aggression," and calls on states to ensure that "media information activities incorporate contents compatible with the task of the preparation for life in peace of entire societies and, in particular, the young generations" (Nordenstreng et al., 1986, p. 181; Ploman, 1982, p. 54).

The 1984 *Declaration on the Right of Peoples to Peace* "declares that the preservation of the right of peoples to peace and the promotion of its implementation constitute a fundamental obligation of each State" (Nordenstreng et al., 1986, p. 194).

UNESCO's 1978 *Mass Media Declaration,* officially known as the *Declaration on the Fundamental Principles Concerning the Contribution of the Mass Media to Strengthening Peace and International Understanding, to the Promotion of Human Rights and to Countering*

Racialism, Apartheid and Incitement to War emphasizes the positive roles that mass media channels should play:

> Mass media have an important contribution to make in the strengthening of peace and international understanding and in countering racialism, apartheid and incitement to war [and in] eliminat[ing] ignorance and misunderstanding between peoples, mak[ing] nationals of a country sensitive to the needs and desires of others, [and] ensur[ing] the respect of the rights and dignity of all nations. . . .
>
> The mass media contribute effectively to the strengthening of peace and international understanding, to the promotion of human rights, and to the establishment of a more just and equitable international economic order. (Nordenstreng et al., 1986, pp. 227-228; Ploman, 1982, p. 172)

Outside the General Assembly

UN specialized agencies and other intergovernmental organizations have contributed a great deal to international communication and information law. The most active has been UNESCO.

Although the *C* in UNESCO stands for *culture,* it could easily also stand for communication. For decades UNESCO has fought to improve communication systems around the world. Indeed, many of the underlying premises of the *Constitution of UNESCO* (U.S. = withdrawn) are based on a communication analysis of peace and war. In the constitution's preamble we read:

> [S]ince wars begin in the minds of men, it is in the minds of men that the defenses of peace must be constructed;
>
> [I]gnorance of each other's ways and lives has been a common cause, throughout the history of mankind, of that suspicion and mistrust between the peoples of the world through which their differences have all too often broken into war. . . .
>
> States Parties . . . are agreed and determined to develop and to increase the means of communication between their peoples and to employ these means for the purposes of mutual understanding and a truer and more perfect knowledge of each other's lives.

UNESCO's fundamental purposes and functions include to:

> collaborate in the work of advancing the mutual knowledge and understanding of peoples, through all means of mass communication and to that

end recommend such international agreements as may be necessary to promote the free flow of ideas by word and image. (Bowman & Harris, 1984, T184; Nordenstreng et al., 1986, p. 211; Ploman, 1982, p. 71)

Let us look at how UNESCO has dealt with communication and information issues in relation to peace and human rights. The 1974 statement on *UNESCO's Contribution to Peace and Its Tasks With Respect to the Promotion of Human Rights and the Elimination of Colonialism and Racialism* calls for strengthening the role of

Member States to make wider use of the information media and organs for reaching the general public to intensify the struggle against racialism and apartheid and other violations human rights and fundamental freedoms . . . [and] to inform the public on the abominable practices of racial segregation. (Ploman, 1982, p. 77)

The 1978 *Declaration on Race and Racial Prejudice* is very concrete about the role of the media:

The mass media and those who control or serve them . . . are urged . . . to promote understanding, tolerance, and friendship among individuals and groups and to contribute to the eradication of racism, racial discrimination and racial prejudice, in particular by refraining from presenting a stereotyped, partial, unilateral or tendentious picture of individuals and of various human groups. (Nordenstreng et al., 1986, p. 230; Ploman, 1982, p. 79)

Outside of the UN system there are numerous regional and transregional organizations and conferences that supplement the work of the United Nations and its specialized organizations. Some of these organizations have constitutions or other constituitive documents with general statements that have great relevance for communication and information issues. All have adopted resolutions or declaration that either deal with communication and information specifically or treat related topics, such as disarmament or human rights.

The *Non-Aligned Movement,* made up of 99 nations and two independence movements, has no constitution, but the periodic summit meetings have treated communication and information extensively. A 1976 *Political Declaration* notes with concern

the vast and ever growing gap between communication capacities in non-aligned countries and in the advanced countries, which is a legacy of their

colonial past. . . . The emancipation and development of national information media is an integral part of the over-all struggle for political, economic
and social independence. (Nordenstreng et al., 1986, p. 288; Ploman, 1982,
p. 119)

The 1979 *Political Declaration* recognizes that "non-aligned and
other developing countries have made notable progress along the path
of emancipation and development of national information media" and
"considers that the building up of national information media and mass
communication systems . . . are essential preconditions . . . for a multi-
dimensional flow of information" (Nordenstreng et al., 1986, p. 296;
Ploman, 1982, p. 116).

Another important international forum for information issues is the
Conference on Security and Cooperation in Europe (CSCE), composed of
35 European countries, the United States, and Canada. Meeting first in
Helsinki, Finland, in 1975, the *Final Act* of these Helsinki Accords has a
huge section on communication and information. It calls on signatories to

make it their aim to facilitate the freer and wider dissemination of information of all kinds . . . and to improve the conditions under which journalists . . . exercise their profession. (Nordenstreng et al., 1986, pp. 333-334;
Ploman, 1982, p. 118).

Periodic follow-up meetings of the Helsinki signatories have moni-
tored compliance of the information section of "Basket Three," which
deals with respect for human rights and the movement of people and
information (Nordenstreng et al., 1986, p. 337).

Turning to regional organizations, the 1950 *Convention for the Protection of Human Rights and Fundamental Freedoms,* ratified by all
member states of the Council of Europe, asserts that

Everyone has the right to freedom of expression. This right shall include
freedom to hold opinions and to receive and import information and ideas
without interference by public authority and regardless of frontiers.

But this important document of the European Community provides a
comprehensive list of limitations to free expression:

The exercise of these freedoms, since it carries with it duties and responsibilities, may be subject to such formalities, conditions, restrictions or
penalties as are prescribed by law and are necessary in a democratic society,

in the interests of national security, territorial integrity or public safety, for the prevention of disorder or crime, for the protection of health or morals, for the protection of the reputation or rights of others, for preventing the disclosure of information received in confidence, or for maintaining the authority and impartiality of the judiciary. (Bowman & Harris, 1984, T256; Nordenstreng et al., 1986, p. 341).

In the Americas, the 1969 *American Convention on Human Rights* (U.S. = S), to which 20 governments in the Western Hemisphere are parties, guarantees in Article 13 that:

everyone shall have the right to freedom of thought and expression [which] shall not be subject to prior censorship but shall be subject to . . . (a) respect for the rights or reputation of others; or (b) the protection of national security, public order, or public health or morals. . . . Any propaganda for war and any advocacy of national, racial or religious hatred that constitute incitements to lawless violence or to any other similar illegal action against any person or group of persons on any grounds including those of race, color, religion, language, or national origin shall be considered as offenses punishable by law.

In Article 14 these American countries pledge that:

anyone injured by inaccurate or offensive statements or ideas disseminated to the public in general by a legally regulated medium of communication has the right to reply or make a correction using the same communications outlet, under such conditions as the law may establish. (Bowman & Harris, 1984, T547; Nordenstreng et al., 1986, p. 342; Ploman, 1982, p. 106)

This right to reply is reminiscent of the 1952 *Convention on the International Right of Correction* (U.S. = NS) which requires news correspondents and agencies:

To report facts without discrimination and in their proper context and thereby to promote respect for human rights and fundamental freedoms, to further international understanding and cooperation and to contribute to the maintenance of international peace and security. . . .

In cases where a Contracting State contends that a news dispatch capable of injuring its relations with other States or its national prestige or dignity . . . is false or distorted, it may submit its version of the facts . . . to correct the news dispatch in question. (Bowman & Harris, 1984, T291; Nordenstreng et al., 1986, p. 127)

In 1987, Burkina Faso became the 12th party (and the first in 20 years) to join the Right to Correction Convention. The other 11 adherents are Cuba, Cyprus, Egypt, El Salvador, Ethiopia, France, Guatemala, Jamaica, Sierra Leone, Uruguay, and Yugoslavia.

Basic Principles of International Communication and Information Law

What fundamental principles about media practice and performance surface from this analysis of international communication and information law? Here I present basic principles in international communication and information law.

Communication media may not be used for war and aggression. The universally respected principle that prohibits the threat or use of force by one state against another forbids not only wars of aggression but also propaganda for wars of aggression. This means that propaganda glorifying the threat or use of force in international relations is prohibited by law. States are forbidden from spreading warmongering content themselves, for example, through government-owned and -operated international radio stations. They are also obligated to stop any war propaganda emanating from their territory on the part of private groups.

Communication media shall not be used to intervene in the internal affairs of another state. The principle of nonintervention forbids all forms of interference or attempted threats against a state or against its political, economic, and cultural elements. This includes organizing, assisting, fomenting, financing, inciting, or tolerating subversive information activities directed toward the overthrow of another state, or interfering in civil strife in another state. It also bans systemically undermining public support to disintegrate the opponent's inner cohesion, gradually putting its state leadership in a condition of uncertainly and discouragement, diminishing its ability to act under the pressure of a national public opinion undergoing a process of reorientation. This principle prohibits subversive foreign broadcasts that attempt to change another country's governing system or that try to foment discontent and incite unrest.

All dissemination of ideas based on racial superiority or hatred, incitement to racial discrimination is punishable by law. The information activities of all organizations that are based on ideas or theories of superiority of one race or group of persons of one color or ethnic origin or that attempt to justify or promote racial hatred or discrimination in any form are prohibited. International law prohibits all dissemination of these ideas as well as all organizations that promote and incite racial discrimination. It is a crime against humanity directly to abet, encourage, or cooperate in the commission of racial discrimination.

The direct and public incitement to destroy a national, ethnic, racial, or religious group is punishable by international law. Incitement includes using the media to encourage another person to destroy in whole or in part, a national, ethnic, racial, or religious group. It also includes propaganda and incitement to commit murder, extermination, enslavement, deportation, and other inhuman acts performed against any civilian population before or during war.

States are obligated to modify the social and cultural practices, including information and communication activities, that are based on the inferiority or the superiority of either of the sexes and to eliminate any stereotyped concept of roles of men and women. States may be obligated to change media practices that advocate discrimination against women.

Media should play a positive role in educating and enlightening the public toward peace. Throughout international law, media are repeatedly called on to promote a better knowledge of the conditions of life and the organization of peace. Media activities should incorporate contents compatible with the task of the preparation for life in peace. The mass media must contribute effectively to the strengthening of peace and international understanding and to the promotion of human rights.

People enjoy equal rights and self-determination in communication and information. All peoples have the right freely to pursue their chosen system of economic, social, and cultural development. This includes the right to develop local information and communication infrastructures without the interference of external parties, to establish communication policies for the benefit of the people, and to participate in international information relations without discrimination.

States enjoy sovereign equality in communication and information infrastructures. Every state has an inalienable right to choose its political, social, economic, and cultural systems without interference in any form by another state. States enjoy the full rights of sovereignty and territorial integrity in the area of communication and information. From this we derive the principle of information sovereignty, which includes the right to a locally controlled communication infrastructure, the right to an indigenous communication policy, the right to participate as an equal in international information relations, the right to transmit non-belligerent foreign propaganda, the right to conclude bilateral or multilateral agreements in the area of communication and information, and the obligation to respect the information sovereignty of other states. Every national communication system has juridical expression through an information authority, especially in its constitutional, penal, civil, press, copyright, post, and telecommunications laws.

Disputes about communication and information must be settled peacefully. The principle that governments must settle their disputes by peaceful means applies to the processes of international communication and information. Many international communication activities require advance coordination and, if conflict arises, peaceful resolution through negotiation. This principle implies that conflicts such as unwanted direct satellite broadcasting must be settled by negotiation. If a nation is aggrieved in an area of international information relations, it may call on the violating nation to settle the dispute in a way that does not endanger international peace and security. This duty also implies that states must refrain from and prevent hostile and subversive ideological campaigns.

Communication and information demand international cooperation. Despite their differences, states have a built-in incentive to cooperate in the field of international communication. International broadcasters need to coordinate their frequencies to avoid interference. New technologies such as global computer networks and international satellite television cannot succeed technically without the willingness of states to work cooperatively toward mutually beneficial solutions. Future technologies cannot prosper without international cooperation in setting technical standards. Cooperation guarantees technical success and assures the sovereign equality of states.

Good faith obligations require states to uphold international communication and information law. States must fulfill in good faith their obligations under recognized international law. States must be aware of such obligations and obligations to the United Nations Charter and cannot refrain from upholding them by pointing to national law. This applies in all areas of international law, including international communication and information law.

Certain kinds of international information content are prohibited. There is an absolute ban on war propaganda. In addition, there are prohibitions on communication content advocating hatred, acts of violence, or hostility among peoples and races. Media may not advocate colonialism, nor may they be used in propaganda against international treaties. This includes all communication activities that attempt to prohibit or impede the fulfillment of in-force treaty obligations among states. In addition, the circulation of obscene publications is forbidden under binding international law.

The free and unrestricted flow of information is encouraged. Everyone has the right to freedom of opinion and expression; this right includes freedom to hold opinions without interference and to seek, receive, and impart information and ideas through any media and regardless of frontiers. Although this right is often abused by powerful countries and transnational corporations, it is important to remember that this is one of the fundamental goals of international communication and information law.

The Evolving Right to Communicate

International law is constantly evolving. Two new concepts that have attracted considerable attention are the rights of peoples and the right to communicate.

International law in its modern form deals with the rights of states (national governments) as well as with the rights of individuals. Another emerging concept is the rights of peoples, and this has sparked a debate about where the locus of rights lies.

Two conflicting approaches have dominated this debate. According to one, largely Western, approach, only the rights of individuals could be seen as human rights. Rights vested in larger entities such as churches, trade unions, states, and corporations were desirable, but they could not be *human* rights. International law, in this view, did not support such rights as freedom of expression as collective rights. Individuals could exercise their human rights in association with other humans. But rights belonged to the individual.

Another approach held that rights belonged collectively to society and not to individuals. Under this view the state was supreme and was the guarantor of rights and freedoms to individuals (Fisher, 1982, p. 24). While the first approach emphasized personal liberties such as freedom of expression, association, and travel, the second approach stressed freedoms such as the right to quality health care, employment, shelter, and education—rights and freedoms guaranteed to society as a whole. This approach was dominant in the former socialist countries of Eastern Europe.

A third approach, representing a growing third world position, lies between the two dominant positions. The concept of peoples' rights has a long history and a dynamic present. As early as 1790, the French National Constituent Assembly made reference to both the rights of man [*sic*] and the rights of peoples. The term has appeared often in post-World War II human rights instruments and UN resolutions. The United Nations Charter itself was adopted in the name of "We the Peoples" and it recognizes the self-determination of peoples. Both of the great 1966 covenants in their first articles assert, "All peoples have the right of self-determination."

There are two fundamental differences between the concept of people and the individual. The crux of the difference lies in cultural differences in the role of the individual in society. In Africa, for example, as in many cultures around the world, a person is not an isolated individual but rather a member of a larger social group. This contrasts with the Western view of the individual wherein a person is perceived as having a unique identity and a group is merely a collection of individuals (Cathcart & Cathcart, 1988, p. 186). The other distinction is that a people is different from the state, which often cannot be counted on to protect the basic rights of peoples.

Sohn (1982) summarizes the rights of peoples this way:

> One of the main characteristics of humanity is that human beings are social creatures. Consequently, most individuals belong to various units, groups, and communities; they are simultaneously members of such units as a family, religious community, social club, trade union, professional association, racial group, people, nation, and state. It is not surprising, therefore,

that international law not only recognizes inalienable rights of individuals, but also recognizes certain collective rights that are exercised jointly by individuals grouped into larger communities, including peoples and nations. (p. 48)

Sohn (1982) details such peoples' rights as the right to self-determination, the right to development, and the right to peace. He also mentions the rights to obtaining food, to benefit from or share in the common heritage of humanity, to satisfy basic needs, to achieve disarmament, and to communicate (p. 48).

The African Charter on Human and Peoples' Rights best illustrates how contemporary law now accepts the right of peoples (Bowman & Harris, 1984, T806; Nordenstreng et al., 1986, p. 344). With cultural differences that deemphasize individuality, this basic African human rights document treats peoples as much as it treats individuals. Kiwanuka (1988) summarizes: "The main attributes of peoplehood are . . . commonality of interests, group identity, distinctiveness and a territorial link" (pp. 87-88).

Applying the concept of peoples' rights to communication, we find that groups such as political parties and trade unions generate and promote ideas independent of individuals or the state. Larger aggregates such as social communities and peoples are held together by communication networks, on which they rely to promote and develop their identities both within themselves and vis-à-vis others. As the MacBride commission of UNESCO stated, "Freedom of speech, of the press, of information and of assembly are vital for the realization of human rights. Extension of these communication freedoms to a broader individual and collective right to communicate is an evolving principle in the democratization process" (International Commission, 1980, p. 265).

One of these evolving peoples' rights is the right to communicate (see especially Fisher, 1982, as well as Anawalt, 1984). As we have seen above, Article 19 of the Universal Declaration of Human Rights includes the freedom to "seek, receive and impart information." But the Universal Declaration does not guarantee the right to communicate. It includes a passive right simply to "receive and impart" information, while the right to communicate is a dedication to the interactive spirit of liberty and democracy. The most diverse segments of the population must have access to international communication channels.

Toward the end of the 1970s, spurred on by the information debates in the Non-Aligned Movement and UNESCO, human rights advocates began to call for an active right to communicate for individuals and groups who had no access to the large transnational media channels. The father of the right to communicate is widely acknowledged to be the Frenchman d'Arcy, who stated first in 1969:

> The time will come when the Universal Declaration of Human Rights will have to encompass a more extensive right than man's right to information. . . . This is the right of man to communicate.

The concept was buoyed especially by the MacBride commission, which ordered no less than seven separate studies on the right to communicate (see Cocca, 1980; d'Arcy, 1980; El-Oteifi, 1980; Fisher, 1980; Harms, 1980; Pastecka, 1980; Richstad, 1980; many are contained in Fisher & Harms, 1983). The MacBride commission's final report recommended the following:

> Communication needs in a democratic society should be met by the extension of specific rights such as the right to be informed, the right to inform, the right to privacy, the right to participate in public communication—all elements of a new concept, the right to communicate. (International Commission, p. 265)

How should this new right be defined? One Canadian report described the essential components of the right to communicate as "the rights to hear and be heard, to inform and to be informed" (Canada, 1971, p. 3). Hindley (1977) lists the following constituents of a general right to communicate: the rights to speak and be heard, to a reply and to make a reply, to listen, to see and to be seen, to express oneself in writing or in print, to express oneself in the form of art, and to be selective.

Harms (1980) proposed the following language:

> Everyone has the right to communicate. The Components of this comprehensive human right include but are not limited to the following communication rights:
> —a right to assemble, a right to participate, and related *association* rights;
> —a right to inform, a right to be informed, and related *information* rights;
> —a right to privacy, a right to language and related *cultural evolution* rights.
> Within the world communication order, the achievement of a right to communicate requires that communication resources be available for the satisfaction of human communication needs.

Active participation in the communication process is the "core of the right to communicate." The right to communicate is partially protected by existing instruments, but according to a UNESCO (1982) consultation of experts, it is also essential

> that adequate channels of communication should exist, using all available and appropriate technology;
> that individuals and groups who wish to use those channels should have fair and equitable access to them, and opportunities for participation in them, without discrimination of any kind;
> that such channels of communication should be available to those who wish to take part in public affairs, or to exercise any other of those of their human rights and fundamental freedoms protected by international law, including the right to health, education, assembly, and association, and to take part in cultural life, enjoy the benefits of scientific progress and its applications, and of the freedom indispensable for scientific research and creative activity;
> that restriction on the exercise of the right to communicate should be strictly confined to those authorized by international law;
> that individuals and groups should be able to participate at all relevant levels and at all stages in communication, including the formulation, application, monitoring and review of communication policies.

The right to communicate seems like a logical next step in the evolution of human rights. It is surprising, then, "that in the 1980s this concept has been roundly denounced by the United States press and government officials as radical and subversive" (Roach, 1988, p. 18). As Roach points out, the American position completely ignores the fact that the concept arose in the West and was elaborated by Americans, Canadians, and the French.

A Vision

What changes would American media—both domestic and foreign—undergo if the United States obeyed international communication and information law (see National Lawyers Guild, 1989)? The answer is a vast list of modifications in media structure and content. Here are some points of departure that might spark further work.

On the domestic level, media have long perpetuated oppression of African-Americans. Black activists early on cited international human rights law and focused on media injustice. Such personalities as Patterson,

DuBois, and Robeson cited the genocide convention as prohibiting intentionally racist propaganda in the private media. The 1968 Kerner Commission Report, a report by the National Advisory Commission on Civil Disorders appointed by President Lyndon Johnson, confirmed these charges when it faulted media coverage of the riots as well as media perpetuation of racial stereotypes.

Were the United States truly in accordance with international law, minority coverage would be greatly increased. Instead of focusing on black youth crime, as was seen in the coverage of the Los Angeles rebellion of 1992, social and economic causes would be covered in more detail. Positive images would raise the self-esteem of young blacks. History books would redress the injustices done by historians who have ignored the contribution of Americans of color. On the positive side, prosocial obligations of the media would bring the principles of international law on racism into the curriculum and the workplace. Citizen initiatives and referenda would make the connection between international law and violations on the local level.

This is also true for Native American peoples, who have seen the worst kind of media distortions of their history. Hollywood cinema perpetuated their image as savages whom Europeans had the obligation to civilize. The Native American as enemy made it easier to commit genocide on an entire people. Such movie roles might today be questioned under international law.

One powerful tool is the 1948 *Convention on the Prevention and Punishment of the Crime of Genocide,* recently ratified and enacted into national law by the United States (18 USC 1091-1093). Not many Americans realize that it now is illegal under U.S. law for any group or individual to "directly and publicly incite another" to violate the 1948 Genocide Convention. This means that citizens groups may now have the legal means to force the Department of Justice and the Federal Communications Communication to close down Ku Klux Klan cable, white supremacist radio, and any other communications channels calling for the destruction of a national, ethnic, racial, or religious group.

Women too have suffered from the effects of the media. The 1979 *Convention on the Elimination of All Forms of Discrimination Against Women* calls on governments to abolish existing customs and practices that constitute discrimination against women, to abandon practices based on the idea of the women's inferiority, and to eliminate any stereotyped concept of roles of men and women. For example, the male-dominated media distorted the Equal Rights Campaign. Advertising portrays women in subordinate ways.

But interestingly, while international law explicitly prohibits racist or genocidal propaganda, the language of international law on women is not so explicit, perhaps because it was written largely by men. Nevertheless, some countries have enacted legislation prohibiting negative portrayals of women. In Nicaragua, women may not appear in commercial advertisements. Norway prohibits commercial speech showing women in a demeaning or subordinate fashion.

On the international level, U.S.-operated and -financed media would also be subject to changes if they were to obey international law. There would be no propounding of first strike nuclear philosophy. False reports would be subject to right to correction. Direct satellite broadcasts that flood third world countries with commercial programming would be a violation of cultural rights. Such programs as ABC's 14½-hour series *Amerika,* which presented a fictional account of a Soviet takeover of the United States, might also be questioned.

The Voice of America's Radio Martí service directed at the Cuban people is a direct violation of the *International Telecommunication Convention* which reserves AM broadcasting for domestic uses only. Radio Martí also violates the 1970 *Declaration on the Strengthening of International Security,* which prohibits states from "any attempt aimed at the partial or total disruption of the national unity." The 1981 *Declaration on the Inadmissibility of Intervention and Interference in the Internal Affairs of States* prohibits any "defamatory campaign, vilification or hostile propaganda for the purpose of intervening or interfering in the internal affairs of other States." The same was true of CIA-financed Contra radio directed against Nicaragua.

Indeed, Pentagon use of communication in low-intensity warfare violates international law. It seeks to isolate, divide and neutralize attentive publics who support revolutionary change. The purpose of low-intensity warfare is to undercut the insurgent movement, to destroy the hope of the people and to make them cease their struggle for a more just society. Communication channels are being used to disinform both the home population and the foreign population (see Frederick, 1987, 1989).

Conclusion

International communication and information law is one of the oldest bodies of continuously respected international law in the world today.

This law establishes widely accepted norms for media practice and governs the daily communication and information relations among states around the globe. Were it not this way, there would be chaos in the airwaves, incomprehensibility over the telephone lines, and anarchy in the geostationary orbit. There is clearly a built-in incentive for states to cooperate.

For the most part, nations respect and honor international communication and information law despite the fact that there is no enforcer. They do so because it yields short-term gains, for example, in avoiding radio interference with stations in neighboring countries. But when international media norms demand a more profound commitment, such as the prohibition on war propaganda, states may abandon international law when it no longer serves national interests.

The United States has yet to ratify and enact the important conventions with media provisions, especially the International Covenant on Civil and Political Rights; the International Covenant on Economic, Social and Cultural Rights; the American Convention on Human Rights; the Convention on the Elimination of All Forms of Racial Discrimination; and the Convention on the Elimination of All Forms of Discrimination Against Women. The Senate has rejected these and other human rights treaties on the grounds that they diminish basic rights guaranteed under the U.S. Constitution, violate the rights of U.S. states, promote world government, enhance Communist influence, subject citizens to trial abroad, threaten our form of government, infringe on domestic jurisdiction, and increase international entanglements (Kaufman & Whiteman, 1988). It is not surprising that the United States is seen as the chief laggard in international law because of its failure to ratify and enact international law (Korey, 1967).

As we enter the 1990s, there is a growing realization that communication and information are central to human rights. Communication media do not merely defend human rights by reporting violations and victories. There is a growing perception that the right to communicate should be added to the Universal Declaration among the basic human rights cherished by all peoples. This new right transcends the right to receive information, as guaranteed in the Universal Declaration. Today, communication among nations must be a two-way process in which partners—both individual and collective—carry on a democratic and balanced dialogue and the mass media operate in the service of peace and international understanding.

There is a huge gap between international law and international practice. Modern national states have been more than willing to use their military, economic, and propaganda power than to abide by international law. Yet Lacordaire's view—that between the strong and the weak it is freedom that oppresses and law that liberates—is gaining greater support around the world.

Just like their earthly counterparts, electronic highways require "rules of the road." Regulation is important and necessary for our highly congested communication thoroughfares. To carry this analogy one step further, rules prohibiting drunk drivers from our streets are not meant to limit freedom. They increase the freedom for the good drivers. In the same way, regulations against communication violating international norms are not meant to limit freedom to communicate. They are meant to strengthen the freedom for responsible communication. In our lifetimes, international law has grown immensely and is respected now more than ever. The evolutionary trend is apparent—and so is the work before us.

Notes

1. The instruments of international communication and information law cited in this chapter are *italicized* in the text at their first or primary reference. Information on U.S. adherence to a particular treaty is indicated by the following abbreviations: U.S. = SRE means that the United States has signed, ratified, and entered the declaration into force; U.S. = NS means that the United States has not signed that particular instrument; U. S. = S means that the United States has signed that treaty but not ratified it.

2. Many of the instruments cited in this chapter reach far beyond the areas of our interest. I only make reference to the communication and information aspects of them. Space limitations prevent me from examining the context in which these laws and treaties were adopted and the relative importance of communication and information in them compared with other areas of treatment.

3. For purposes of this discussion I will not treat the fourth instrument, the 1966 *International Covenant on Economic, Social and Cultural Rights* (U.S. = S) (Bowman & Harris, 1984, T497; Ploman, 1982, p. 21; Nordenstreng et al., p. 144), which deals tangentially with communication and information. Article 13 guarantees everyone the right to education, whereas Article 15 recognizes the right of everyone to take part in cultural life and to benefit from the "protection of the moral and material interests resulting from any scientific, literary or artistic production of which he is the author."

References

Anawalt, H. C. (1984). The right to communicate. *Denver Journal of International Law and Policy, 13*(2-3), 219-236.

Blanchard, M. (1986). *Exporting the first amendment: The press-government crusade of 1945-1952.* New York: Longman.

Bowman, M. J., & Harris, D. J. (Compilers). (1984). *Multilateral treaties: Index and current status.* London: Butterworths.

Bowman, M. J., & Harris, D. J. (Compilers). (1988). *Multilateral treaties: Fifth cumulative supplement.* London: Butterworths.

Canada. Department of Communications. Telecommission Directing Committee. (1971). *Instant World.* Ottawa: Information Canada.

Cathcart, D., & Cathcart, R. (1988). Japanese social experience and concept of groups. In L. A. Samovar & R. E. Porter (Eds.), *Intercultural communication: A reader.* Belmont, CA: Wadsworth.

Cocca, A. A. (1980). *The right to communicate: Some reflections on its legal foundation* (International Commission for the Study of Communication Problems, Document No. 38,3). Paris: UNESCO.

d'Arcy, J. (1969, November). Direct broadcast satellites and the right to communicate. *EBU Review,* (118), 14-18.

d'Arcy, J. (1980). *The right to communicate* (International Commission for the Study of Communication Problems, Document No. 36). Paris: UNESCO.

Downey, E. A. (1984). A historical survey of the international regulation of propaganda. In L. J. Anderson (Ed.), *Regulation of transnational communications: Michigan yearbook of international legal studies, 1984* (pp. 341-360). New York: Clark Boardman.

Editorial. (1991, December 7). *Editor and Publisher,* p. 6.

El-Oteifi, G. (1980). *Relation between the right to communicate and planning of communication* (International Commission for the Study of Communication Problems, Document No. 39bis). Paris: UNESCO.

Fisher, D. (1980). *The right to communicate: Towards a definition* (International Commission for the Study of Communication Problems, Document No. 37,2). Paris: UNESCO.

Fisher, D. (1982). *The right to communicate: A status report.* Paris: UNESCO.

Fisher, D., & Harms, L. S. (1983). *The right to communicate: A new human right.* Dublin: Boole.

Frederick, H. H. (1987). Electronic penetration in low intensity warfare: The case of Nicaragua. In T. W. Walker (Ed.), *Reagan versus the Sandinistas: The undeclared war on Nicaragua* (pp. 123-142). Boulder, CO: Westview.

Frederick, H. H. (1989). "Development communication" in low intensity warfare: Media strategies against democracy in Central America. In P. A. Bruck & M. Raboy, (Eds.), *Communication: For and against democracy* (pp. 19-35). Ottawa: Black Rose.

Frederick, H. H. (1993). *Global communications and international relations.* Belmont, CA: Wadsworth.

Ghandhi, P. R. (1986). The human rights committee and the right of individual communication. *British Year Book of International Law, 57,* 201-251.

Ginger, A. F. (1989a). The new U.S. criminal statute, the First Amendment, and the new international information order. *The National Lawyers Guild Practitioner, 46*(1), 16-27.

Ginger, A. F. (Ed.). (1989b). *Peace law almanac.* Berkeley, CA: Meiklejohn Civil Liberties Institute.

Harms, L. S. (1980). *The right to communicate: Concept* (International Commission for the Study of Communication Problems, Document No. 37,1). Paris: UNESCO.

Hindley, H. (1977). A right to communication? A Canadian approach. In L. S. Harms & J. Richstad (Eds.), *Evolving perspectives on the right to communicate* (pp. 119-127). Honolulu: East-West Center.

International Commission for the Study of Communication Problems. (1980). *Many voices, one world.* Paris: UNESCO.

International human rights instruments of the United Nations: 1948-1982. (1983). Pleasantville, NY: UNIFO Publishers.

Jankovic, B. M. (1984). *Public international law.* Dobbs Ferry, NY: Transnational.

Kaufman, M. M. (1968). The individual's duty under the law of Nurnberg: The effect of knowledge on justiciability. *The National Lawyers Guild Practitioner, 27*(1), 15-21.

Kaufman, N. H. & Whiteman, D. (1988). Opposition to human rights treaties in the United States Senate. *Human Rights Quarterly, 10*(3), 309-337.

Kiwanuka, R. N. (1988). The meaning of "people" in the African charter on human and peoples' rights. *American Journal of International Law, 82,* 80-101.

Korey, W. (1967). Human rights treaties: Why is the U.S. stalling? *Foreign Affairs, 45*(3), 414-424.

National Lawyers Guild & Union for Democratic Communication (Ed.). (1989). *Proceedings of the Symposium on Media Accountability Under International Law, June 14, 1989, Los Angeles.* Berkeley, CA: National Lawyers Guild.

Nordenstreng, K., Gonzales Manet, E., & Kleinwächter, W. (1986). *New international information and communication order: A sourcebook.* Prague: International Organization of Journalists.

Pastecka, J. (1980). *The right to communicate: A socialist approach* (International Commission for the Study of Communication Problems, Document No. 39). Paris: UNESCO.

Ploman, E. W. (Ed.). (1982). *International law governing communications and information: A collection of basic documents.* Westport, CT: Greenwood.

Richstad, J. (1980). *The right to communicate: Relationship with the mass media* (International Commission for the Study of Communication Problems, Document No. 38,4). Paris: UNESCO.

Roach, C. (1988). U.S. arguments on the right to communicate and people's rights. *Media Development, 35*(4), 18-21.

Sieghart, P. (1985). *The lawful rights of mankind: An introduction to the international legal code of human rights.* New York: Oxford.

Sohn, L. B. (1982). The new international law: Protection of the rights of individuals rather than states. *American University Law Review, 32*(1), 1-64.

Stover, J. (1984). *Information technology in the third world: Can I.T. lead to humane national development?* Boulder, CO: Westview.

UNESCO. (1982). *Right to communicate: Legal aspects. A consultation, Bucharest, February 9-12, 1982.* Paris: UNESCO.

Appendix I

Addresses of Organizations Cited in Text

United States

- Alternative Media Information Center
  39 West 14th Street
  Suite 403
  New York, NY 10011

- Center for War, Peace and the News Media
  New York University
  10 Washington Place
  New York, NY 10003

- Deep Dish TV
  339 Lafayette Street, No. 6
  New York, NY 10018

- Fairness and Accuracy in Reporting (FAIR)
  666 Broadway
  Suite 400
  New York, NY 10012

- Institute for Media Analysis (IMA)
  145 West Fourth Street
  New York, NY 10012

- Investigative Reporters & Editors (IRE)
  26A Walter Williams Hall
  University of Missouri
  School of Journalism
  Columbia, MO 65211

- National Alliance for Third World Journalists
  P.O. Box 43208
  Washington, D.C. 20010

- Paper Tiger Television
  339 Lafayette Street
  New York, NY 10012

- Peacenet
  18 De Boom Street
  San Francisco, CA 94107

- Telecommunications Research & Action Center
  901 Fifteenth Street NW
  Suite 230
  Washington, D.C. 20005-2301

- Union for Democratic Communication (UDC)
  Dept of Communication
  585 Manoogian Hall
   Wayne State University
   Detroit, MI 48202

- Women's Institute for Freedom of Press
  3306 Ross Place NW
  Washington, D.C. 20008

Canada

- ACT for Disarmament
  736 Bathurst Street
  Toronto, Ont. M5S 2R4

- Canadian Association of Journalists
  St. Patrick's Building
  School of Journalism,
  Carleton University
  Ottawa, Ont. K1S 5B6

- Friends of Canadian Broadcasting
  29 Prince Arthur Avenue
  Toronto, Ont. M5R 1B2

- Media Watch
  P.O. Box 823
  Vancouver, B.C. V6T 3B1

Index

About the Authors

Peter Bruck is Visiting Professor of Communication at the University of Salzburg, Austria and heads the International Comparative Research Program (Economy and the Future of the Print Media). His latest books include two works on the tabloid news: *Das österreichische Format* and *Die Mozart Krone*. He is on the faculty of the School of Journalism and Communication at Carleton University, Canada, and also teaches at the European Peace University Center in Schlaing, Austria.

Sheila Collins is Associate Professor of Political Science at William Paterson College in New Jersey. She is the author of *The Rainbow Challenge: The Jackson Campaign and the Future of U.S. Politics* and *A Different Heaven and Earth: A Feminist Perspective on Religion*. Her work on politics, culture, and education has appeared in the *Harvard Educational Review, Monthly Review,* and the *International Journal of Sociology and Social Policy.*

Riane Eisler is the author of the international best-seller *The Chalice and the Blade: Our History, Our Future* and coauthor of *The Partnership Way: New Tools for Living and Learning.* She has taught at the University of California at Los Angeles and Immaculate Heart College, is cofounder of the Center for Partnership Studies, and has published many other books and articles.

Howard Frederick is President of the International Communication Section of the International Association of Mass Communication Research (IAMCR). He also serves with the Center for Media and Values in Los Angeles and Radio for Peace International in Costa Rica. He is the author of *Cuban-American Radio Relations* and *Global Communication and International Relations.* His current teaching position is with the Department of Politics and Society at the University of California at Irvine.

Johan Galtung, widely recognized as one of the principal fathers of peace research has published innumerable books and articles in peace studies, communication, and international relations. He has taught and lectured at many universities around the world and is currently Professor of Peace Studies at the universities of Bern, Hawaii, and Saar and Witten-Herdecke.

Vincent Mosco is Professor of Journalism at Carleton University, Ottawa, Canada, and a researcher with the Harvard University Program on Information Resources Policy. One of his most recent books is *The Pay-Per Society: Computers and Communication in the Information Age.* He is also the coeditor of *Democratic Communication in the Information Age.*

Colleen Roach is Associate Professor at Queens College, City University of New York. She has taught at Fordham University, the New School for Social Research, New York, and Queens University in Canada. She worked for many years at UNESCO in Paris and is widely published both in the United States and abroad, particularly in the field of international communication. Her articles have appeared in journals such as *Media, Culture and Society; Journal of Communications;* and *Media Development.*

Herbert I. Schiller is Professor Emeritus of Communication at the University of California at San Diego and Visiting Professor at American University in Washington, D.C. He has lectured and taught at universities around the world. Among his books are *Culture Inc.: The Corporate Takeover of Public Expression; Communication and Cultural Domination;*and *Information in the Crisis Economy.* An updated edition of his *Mass Communications and American Empire* has recently been published.

Majid Tehranian is former Director of the Spark M. Matsunaga Institute for Peace and Professor of Communication at the University of Hawaii. He has worked with the United Nations; taught at Harvard, Stanford, and MIT; and currently edits the *Communication, Peace and Development* series of books published by Hampton Press. His many publications include *Technologies of Power: Information Machines and Democratic Prospects; Restructuring for Ethnic Peace; Socio-Economic and Communications Indicators in Development Planning: A Case Study of Iran,* and *Restructuring for World Peace: On the Threshold of the 21st Century.*

40 -461
DATE DUE